Vital

Vital Statistics on Congress
1999–2000

Norman J. Ornstein
American Enterprise Institute

Thomas E. Mann
Brookings Institution

Michael J. Malbin
State University of New York at Albany

The AEI Press

Publisher for the American Enterprise Institute
Washington, D.C.
2000

Available in the United States from the AEI Press, c/o Publisher Resources Inc., 1224 Heil Quaker Blvd., P.O. Box 7001, La Vergne, TN 37086-7001. To order, call toll free: 1-800-269-6267. Distributed outside the United States by arrangement with Eurospan, 3 Henrietta Street, London WC2E 8LU, England.

The AEI Press
Publisher for the American Enterprise Institute
1150 17th Street, N.W.
Washington, D.C. 20036

Printed in the United States of America

Contents

List of Tables and Figures

Tables

Figures

Preface

The contemporary Congress seems in constant tumult. Members themselves, often unsure of their status at any given moment, regularly shift their legislative focus. Just since 1994, Congress has considered legislation on divisive budgets under deficits and surpluses, massive welfare reform, tax cuts, and health care reform—to name only a few of the issues. At the international level, the members saw the country bombing Iraq and then conducting an even larger campaign in Bosnia. All of that came on top of angry partisan fighting that ultimately brought down a Speaker of the House and his presumed successor—during a year-long scandal that ultimately led to the second impeachment trial in our nation's history. In front of that backdrop of crises, the day-to-day business of Congress goes on. Exactly how different is the contemporary Congress from its predecessors in terms of its work product, its membership, its political orientation, or its performance? This tenth edition of *Vital Statistics on Congress, 1999–2000*, is your lens through which to observe and evaluate the changing shape of politics and the legislative branch of government.

Vital Statistics has been published and regularly updated for twenty years, beginning in the last year of the Carter administration. A glance at any table shows that a member who left in 1980 and won election again in 1998 would scarcely recognize the place, much less most of the members. Changes in the partisan balance, the characteristics of the members, the number of committees and subcommittees, and the staffs have all been considerable and not all linear.

One change has been in the size of Congress. After an explosive growth of government in the 1970s, we have witnessed a focus on downsizing the federal government—including the legislative branch—coupled with the resurgence of hotly contested budget politics. A member in the early 1980s needed a position on deficits as far as the eye could see; few anticipated that the average member in the late 1990s would need a position on surpluses extended into the far future. The characteristics of members have also changed. Retirements and more defeated incumbents have led to extraordinary turnover. Over two-thirds of the current members have been elected since 1990. With the dramatic 1994 elections, party control of the chambers has shifted, along with the makeup of those parties. The Southern-dominated GOP of today is a far cry from the party in 1980. Congress finds itself responding to an increasingly energized public that is demanding change as well as greater account-ability from all elected officials.

The hostility toward Congress that dominated the landscape before the 1994 elec-tion was replaced with more satisfaction and complacency by 1996. A public worried more about the economy than about Republican social concerns dealt the GOP a defeat in 1998 by handing the party the first midterm loss since 1934 for a party not holding the White House. But by and large the public returned Congress's members. And congressional approval ratings remain relatively high.

How Congress reacts to public views and moods and has reacted to them in the past can teach us a great deal about politics in America. This book is intended for all those who watch Congress for that reason or who observe the institution as journal-ists, political scientists, students, lobbyists, citizens, or even as congressional members and staff.

A good portion of the data here can be found in various congressional reports or publications. Our intention in *Vital Statistics on Congress* is to bring all the data together in one convenient volume. The book would not be possible without its many indirect contributors and those who helped us locate some pieces of data. Institutions such as Congressional Quarterly, the Congressional Research Service, the Federal Election Commission, and several committee staffs in both the House and the Senate were very helpful. Each is cited herein. Several people have worked on past editions, but we are particularly grateful this time to Elizabeth Fitton, Paul Rosen, Ben Lentz, and Barry Klein for helping acquire data. Paula Ramer and Brian Waterman helped with both data and the enormous task of checking page proofs. Jean-Marie Navetta helped typeset the manuscript. Most of all, we salute Jeremy Pope, who served as overseer for this edition from start to finish, worked doggedly on each table and each chapter, collaborated closely with all those mentioned above, and made sure that the three of us were on time and on board. Despite the fact that the basic structure and tables in *Vital Statistics* have remained intact for twenty years, the amount of work necessary to create a new edition, to review the many tricky decision rules, and to catch errors and inconsistencies is enormous. Jeremy did it with competence and good humor.

1

Members of Congress

C ongress, on the verge of the twenty-first century, has a very different complexion from only a decade ago. Members are still often described as white, male, and entrenched. But that description is more and more shaky. Today's Congress (particularly the House) has more women than ever, a relatively high proportion of African Americans and Hispanics, somewhat fewer members who can be described as "careerist," and a much more Southern and Western regional makeup than only ten years ago. Whether those differences make the body a better legislature is a difficult question to answer, but for better or worse Congress is indisputably beginning to look more like the country than it once did.

Migration to the South and West—particularly to sunbelt states like California, Texas, and Florida—has dramatically shifted the balance of power in the House of Representatives. (See table 1-1 and figure 1-1.) In 1910 California had only eleven representatives (just over 2 percent of the total). Today, California has fifty-two representatives, almost 12 percent of the body. The gain of the South, Rocky Mountain, and Pacific regions has come at the expense of New England, the Mid-Atlantic, the Midwest, and the Plains states. Since 1910 each of those regions has lost between one-half and one-third of its representatives in the House. In the 1940s the largest delegations came from New York, Pennsylvania, Illinois, and Ohio (California was fifth). Today, the largest delegation by far comes from California and is followed by New York, Texas, and Florida. Current population projections indicate that the trend is nowhere near subsiding. California may hold as much as 25 percent of the U.S. population—and a corresponding number of House seats—by the mid–twenty-first century.

Accompanying that regional shift has been a partisan regional realignment of immense proportions. In the 1920s the South was monolithically Democratic. Democrats held close to 100 percent of House and Senate seats in all the elections through the 1960s. Roosevelt's party held a substantial edge in most other regions of the country as well, although that edge diminished in the 1940s and 1950s. Republicans were only somewhat stronger in New England, the Midwest, and the Plains states. After the height of the civil rights battles, Republicans began to make inroads in the South by employing Nixon's "Southern Strategy." After the 1994 "Republican Revolution," things seem to have utterly changed. (See tables 1-2 and 1-3 and figure 1-2.) In 1998 the Democrats held only 43.2 percent of the Southern House seats and 20.8 percent of the Rocky Mountain seats. But in some respects those numbers show a rebound from the low of 1994. Democratic numbers have increased in the two elections since 1994.

Today, the Democrats are increasingly a bicoastal party. Strong on the Pacific Coast, where they hold 56.5 percent of the House seats, and in New England and the Mid-Atlantic, where they hold 81.8 and 54.5 percent, respectively, they are even with the GOP in the Midwest and at a substantial disadvantage in the other regions. Republicans are building on their strength in the Southern, Plains, and Rocky Mountain districts. From that base they hope to make advances in other parts of the country, particularly as redistricting looms. Republicans enjoy a redistricting advantage in several large states—with the notable exception of California—because they control the state legislature and the state house. The two parties possess large numbers of "safe" seats going into the next redistricting cycle. Relatively few seats are truly competitive (although that may change after redistricting), but competition for majority status in the House is intense.

As each party has built a base in different regions of the country, the regional composition of the parties in each house has changed. In the 1920s Southerners were a majority of the Democratic party. After World War II they were only a large plurality; today, they make up barely one-quarter of the Democratic Party in the House and just over one-third in the Senate. (See tables 1-3 and 1-4.) Now, over half of the Democratic party comes from the Pacific, Mid-Atlantic, and Midwestern regions, so it is the somewhat more regionally diverse party. In the 1940s, when the Republicans were at their lowest ebb, their strength was in the New England, Mid-Atlantic, and Midwestern regions. Today, almost one-third of the Republican Party comes from the South, with all the other regions' making up a much smaller proportion of the party. For example, less than 2 percent of House Republicans come from New England and less than 6 percent come from the Plains states.

The broad party trends are similar for the House and the Senate, but the different bases of election lead to significant differences in the regional makeup of the respective parties. (Compare tables 1-2 and 1-3 with tables 1-4 and 1-5.) Both Senate parties (particularly the GOP) show considerably more Plains, Rocky Mountain, and New England influence than their House counterparts do, because those three regions, although relatively sparsely populated, elect forty senators. Close to half the GOP senators come from the South and the West, while the Democrats have a much more balanced makeup across regions. All the regional differences within parties and across chambers have important implications for House-versus-Senate responses to future Sunbelt-Frostbelt or other regional tensions that may flare in the coming years: environmental regulation, economics, and budget politics.

While in recent years the turnover in Congress has been substantial, seniority remains an important factor for members of both houses. Democratic Congressman John Dingell, the most senior member of the House, has been serving Michigan since 1955. Throughout the 1960s, the proportion of very senior House members—"careerists"—increased steadily, while the proportion of the most junior House members suffered a sporadic but real decline. (See table 1-6.) Both trends peaked in the Ninety-second Congress (1971)—the twenty-year club reached 20 percent of the House membership, while the proportion that had served six years or less fell to 34 percent. In the 1970s a wave of post-Vietnam retirements and several large congressional classes reversed both those trends. By the middle of the Reagan administration, junior House members made up close to half of the body, while the "careerists" declined to around 10 percent. Those changes in the "maturity" of the body contributed to several reforms in the same period in areas such as campaign finance, war powers, and government access or "sunshine" laws. Those new classes shaped the House for more than a decade. By 1991 the cycle had come full circle. The ratio of junior members to senior members was down to 1.8 to 1—reflecting very low turnover. In 1992 near-record retirements and a substantial number of defeats produced a 110-member freshman House class (the largest since 1949). That trend continued in 1994. The proportion of members serving their second term leapt from 9 percent to 23 percent, and another eighty-six freshmen were added to the body, so that in the pivotal 104th Congress over half of the representatives were in their first, second, or third term. The past two elections have moderated that trend; by 1998 only 43 percent of the members were in their first three terms, a number that is historically above average but a significant decrease over the most recent years. But the total turnover means that 67.4 percent of the 106th House was elected for the first time in the 1990s.

The seniority patterns of the Senate have traveled a slightly different path. (See table 1-7.) The percentage of senior senators, those with three terms or more, generally increased from a low of around 10 percent in the 1950s to around 20 percent in the 1970s. The number of freshman senators also jumped markedly after Vietnam and reached an extraordinary high of fifty-five in 1981. In recent elections a large freshman class has balanced against an increasingly large set of senators in the twenty-year club. Consequently, despite the election of fifteen new senators in 1996, the mean for years of service was still at 11.2, near the all-time high of 11.6. Today, the distribution looks somewhat bipolar. The 106th Congress has forty-three members serving in their freshman term and twenty senators serving twenty years or more—many of them, like Strom Thurmond, much more.

Members of Congress are most often former lawyers, business executives, or bankers. Their background has grown more diverse over time, however. (See tables 1-8 through 1-13.) In 1953, 247 House members had a background in law, a group that has steadily declined to only 163 today. The Senate has a significantly higher percentage of lawyers, with fifty-five claiming that background. But that is also down from sixty-eight in 1973. In 1997 the number of businessmen and bankers eclipsed the number of lawyers in the House, but both declined in 1999, and the lawyers once again had the most common occupation. (For the first time, Congressional Quarterly differentiated real estate from business and banking, which probably depressed the number of businessmen. Together, the two categories make up 179 members in the House—more than the lawyers.)

In the 1950s around 12 percent of House members were farmers, and close to 20 percent held that job in the Senate. Today, that number has decreased to around 5 and 8 percent, respectively. The number of educators decreased in the 1980s but has rebounded significantly in the past few elections, reaching eighty-four in the House and thirteen in the Senate.

Party differences, though not startling ones, exist with respect to occupation. More House Republicans than House Democrats come from the world of business and banking. And the gap seems to be widening. Currently, more than 47 percent of the

House Republican members are business people and bankers, while only 25 percent of the Democratic members hold those occupations. More Democrats than Republicans in the House are lawyers and educators, although those disparities seem to be getting less extreme.

Religious patterns in Congress show relatively small but significant change. (See tables 1-14 and 1-15.) Since the 1960s both Jews and Catholics have increased in representation. In the 1980s Baptists gained slowly but steadily. The new Republican majority seems to comprise relatively more Baptists and Catholics than in years past—although both those denominations are more likely to send Democrats to Congress. The "other" category has grown in the Republican ranks. Before the 1994 House elections, typically forty to fifty members of each party belonged to less traditional denominations. In 1998 the GOP claimed sixty-two members of such denominations, and the number of Democrats declined slightly to forty.

In 1990 J. C. Watts was the first African American Republican elected to Congress in more than a half century. In the Ninety-first and Ninety-second Congresses, the number of African Americans elected to Congress increased suddenly. (See table 1-16.) A second surge—based in part on redistricting and the creation of controversial "majority minority" districts, some of which have since been redrawn to fit the Supreme Court's guidelines—occurred in the early 1990s. With the defeat of Carol Moseley-Braun, the Senate no longer has any African American members and has never had more than one African American member at one time.

In contrast, Hispanic gains have been far more steady—slowly trending upward. (See table 1-17.) The 106th Congress boasts more Hispanics than ever before at nineteen—most of them in the Democratic Party. The Senate has no Hispanic representation today.

Soon after women received the right to vote, they made quicker and earlier gains than those other groups. (See table 1-18.) At first, little partisan difference existed in the number of women serving in Congress, but by the 1970s Democrats outnumbered Republicans by more than two to one. Nineteen ninety-two was proclaimed the year of the woman as the total number of women in Congress jumped from thirty to fifty-four. In 1990 women made up only 6.4 percent of the House, while in 2000 women will make up almost 13 percent. Gains in the Senate have been similar in recent years.

Many other changes in Congress pale in comparison with those caused by the dramatic election of 1994, which produced GOP majorities in both the House and the Senate. Between 1932 and 1992 Republicans won control of the House only twice (1946 and 1952). (See table 1-19.) Democrats did well in the Senate over the same period, holding control between 1954 and 1980 and then again after 1986. The 1994 election brought in a period of distinct competition between the two parties. Both now look to the 2000 elections with hope and trepidation. This era of close electoral competition is virtually unprecedented. The current Congress was elected with the closest partisan division since 1952. The parties seem to dominate various regions and constituencies but without the possibility of achieving the kind of ascension congressional Democrats enjoyed in the 1960s through the 1980s. Although the country may be realigning along regional grounds, the nation seems to be more narrowly divided than at any point in living memory.

Table 1-1   Apportionment of House Seats, by Region and State, 1910–1990

Region and state	1910	1930	1940	1950	1960	1970	1980	1990
South	104	102	105	106	106	108	116	125
Alabama	10	9	9	9	8	7	7	7
Arkansas	7	7	7	6	4	4	4	4
Florida	4	5	6	8	12	15	19	23
Georgia	12	10	10	10	10	10	10	11
Louisiana	8	8	8	8	8	8	8	7
Mississippi	8	7	7	6	5	5	5	5
North Carolina	10	11	12	12	11	11	11	12
South Carolina	7	6	6	6	6	6	6	6
Tennessee	10	9	10	9	9	8	9	9
Texas	18	21	21	22	23	24	27	30
Virginia	10	9	9	10	10	10	10	11
Border	47	43	42	38	36	35	34	32
Kentucky	11	9	9	8	7	7	7	6
Maryland	6	6	6	7	8	8	8	8
Missouri	16	13	13	11	10	10	9	9
Oklahoma	8	9	8	6	6	6	6	6
West Virginia	6	6	6	6	5	4	4	3
New England	32	29	28	28	25	25	24	23
Connecticut	5	6	6	6	6	6	6	6
Maine	4	3	3	3	2	2	2	2
Massachusetts	16	15	14	14	12	12	11	10
New Hampshire	2	2	2	2	2	2	2	2
Rhode Island	3	2	2	2	2	2	2	2
Vermont	2	1	1	1	1	1	1	1
Mid-Atlantic	92	94	93	88	84	80	72	66
Delaware	1	1	1	1	1	1	1	1
New Jersey	12	14	14	14	15	15	14	13
New York	43	45	45	43	41	39	34	31
Pennsylvania	36	34	33	30	27	25	23	21
Midwest	86	90	87	87	88	86	80	74
Illinois	27	27	26	25	24	24	22	20
Indiana	13	12	11	11	11	11	10	10
Michigan	13	17	17	18	19	19	18	16
Ohio	22	24	23	23	24	23	21	19
Wisconsin	11	10	10	10	10	9	9	9
Plains	41	34	31	31	27	25	24	22
Iowa	11	9	8	8	7	6	6	5
Kansas	8	7	6	6	5	5	5	4
Minnesota	10	9	9	9	8	8	8	8
Nebraska	6	5	4	4	3	3	3	3
North Dakota	3	2	2	2	2	1	1	1
South Dakota	3	2	2	2	2	2	1	1

(table continues)

Table 1-1   *(continued)*

Region and state	1910	1930	1940	1950	1960	1970	1980	1990
Rocky Mountain	14	14	16	16	17	19	24	24
Arizona	1	1	2	2	3	4	5	6
Colorado	4	4	4	4	4	5	6	6
Idaho	2	2	2	2	2	2	2	2
Montana	2	2	2	2	2	2	2	1
Nevada	1	1	1	1	1	1	2	2
New Mexico	1[a]	1	2	2	2	2	3	3
Utah	2	2	2	2	2	2	3	3
Wyoming	1	1	1	1	1	1	1	1
Pacific Coast	19	29	33	43	52	57	61	69
Alaska	—	—	—	1[b]	1	1	1	1
California	11	20	23	30	38	43	45	52
Hawaii	—	—	—	1[b]	2	2	2	2
Oregon	3	3	4	4	4	4	5	5
Washington	5	6	6	7	7	7	8	9

a. New Mexico became a state in 1912; in 1910 it had a nonvoting delegate in Congress.
b. Alaska became a state on January 3, 1959, and Hawaii on August 21, 1959. In 1950 each had a nonvoting delegate in Congress, so that the total for that year was 437; subsequent reapportionment reduced the total to 435.

Sources: Congressional Quarterly's Guide to U.S. Elections (Washington, D.C.: Congressional Quarterly, 1975), 531; *Congressional Quarterly's Guide to U.S. Elections,* 2d ed. (Washington, D.C.: Congressional Quarterly, 1985), 1125; Richard E. Cohen, "House Headed for a Big Reshuffling," *National Journal,* January 7, 1989, 25; *Congressional Quarterly Weekly Report,* December 29, 1990, 4240.

Figure 1-1 Apportionment of House Seats by Region, 1910 and 1990

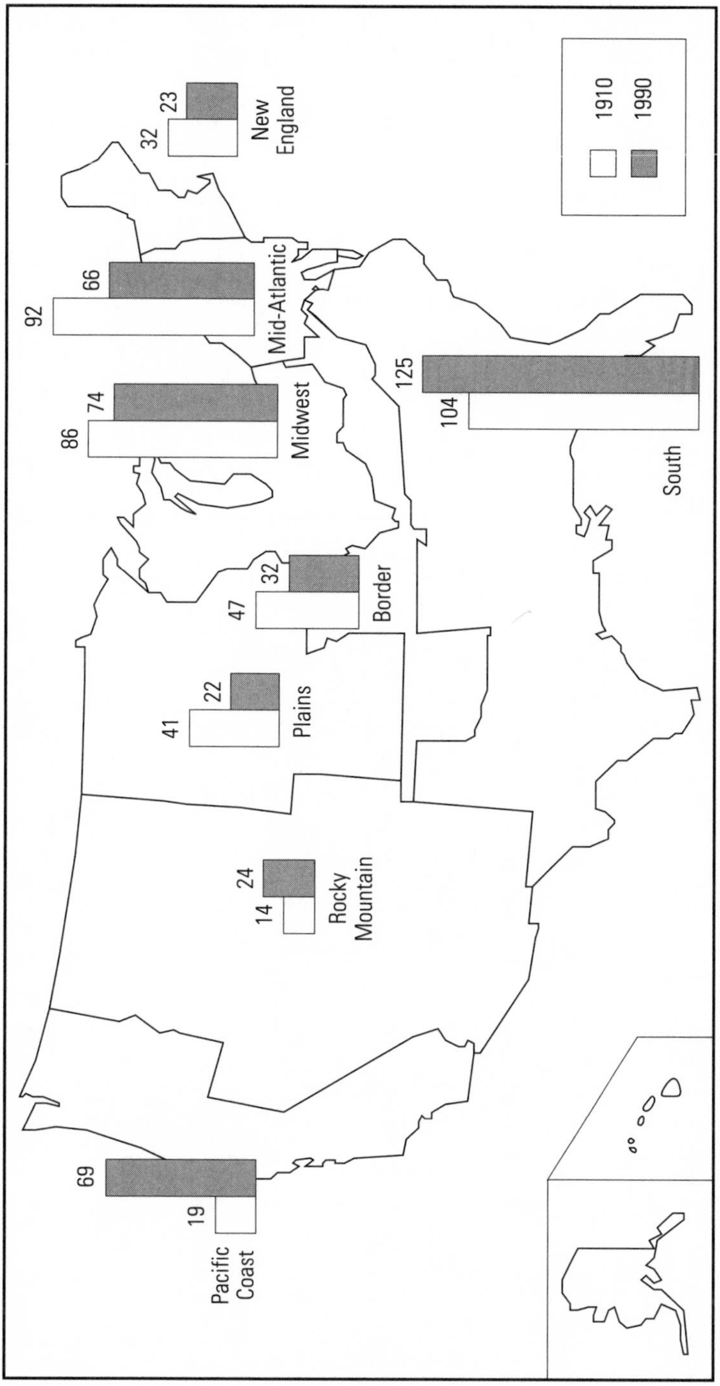

	1910	1990
New England	32	23
Mid-Atlantic	92	66
Midwest	86	74
South	104	125
Border	47	32
Plains	41	22
Rocky Mountain	14	24
Pacific Coast	19	69

Source: Table 1-1.

Table 1-2 Democratic Party Strength in the House, by Region, 1924–1998

Region	1924	1936	1948	1960	1972	1980	1982	1986	1988	1990	1992	1994	1996	1998
South														
Percent	97.1	98.0	98.1	94.2	68.2	64.5	71.2	66.4	66.4	66.4	61.6	48.8	43.2	43.2
Seats	104	101	105	104	107	107	116	116	116	116	125	125	125	125
Border														
Percent	58.7	95.2	88.1	84.2	77.1	67.6	76.4	67.6	67.6	67.6	65.6	50.0	40.6	40.6
Seats	46	42	42	38	35	34	34	34	34	34	32	32	32	32
New England														
Percent	12.5	44.8	39.3	50.0	64.0	64.0	66.6	62.5	58.3	69.6	63.6	63.6	81.8	81.8
Seats	32	29	28	28	25	25	24	24	24	23[a]	22[a]	22[a]	22[a]	22[a]
Mid-Atlantic														
Percent	26.7	68.0	48.9	49.4	53.8	53.8	58.3	56.9	58.3	56.9	54.5	50.0	53.0	54.5
Seats	90[b]	94	92[c]	87	80	80	72	72	72	72	66	66	66	66
Midwest														
Percent	16.9	78.3	43.7	40.7	38.4	51.2	55.0	57.5	58.8	61.2	58.1	43.2	50.0	50.0
Seats	83[d]	83[e]	87	86	86	84	80	80	80	80	74	74	74	74
Plains														
Percent	15.4	44.8	16.1	19.4	33.3	36.0	54.2	45.8	50.0	54.2	54.5	36.4	36.4	40.9
Seats	39[f]	29[g]	31	31	24	25	24	24	24	24	22	22	22	22

Rocky Mountain													
Percent	28.6	93.3	75.0	73.3	42.1	36.8	33.3	37.5	37.5	45.8	45.8	25.0	20.8	20.8
Seats	14	15	16	15	19	19	24	24	24	24	24	24	24	24
Pacific Coast													
Percent	19.0	80.0[h]	36.3	51.2	57.9	56.1	62.3	59.0	59.0	60.6	63.8	49.3	55.1	56.5
Seats	21	30[h]	33	43	57	57	61	61	61	61	69	69	69	69

Note: Numbers refer to the Congress that followed the election. Number of seats is total for all parties in the region (exceptions noted below). Does not include vacant seats. Discrepancy in the number of regional seats before and after 1980 is caused by post-1980 redistricting.

a. Excludes one seat held by an Independent from Vermont.
b. Excludes one seat held by a Socialist from New York.
c. Excludes one seat occupied by a representative from New York who was a member of the American Labor Party.
d. Excludes one seat held by a Socialist from Wisconsin.
e. Excludes seven seats held by Progressives from Wisconsin.
f. Excludes two seats occupied by representatives from Minnesota who were members of the Farmer Labor Party.
g. Excludes five seats occupied by representatives from Minnesota who were members of the Farmer Labor Party.
h. Excludes one seat held by a Progressive from California.

Sources: Congressional Directory (Washington, D.C.: Government Printing Office, 1925, 1937, 1949, 1961, 1973, 1981, 1983, 1985); *Congressional Quarterly Weekly Report,* November 8, 1986, 2843; November 22, 1986, 2958; November 12, 1988, 3269; November 10, 1990, 3802; November 7, 1992, 3571; November 12, 1994, 3236; November 9, 1996, 3226; November 7, 1998, 3027.

Table 1-3 Democratic and Republican Seats in the House, by Region, 1924–1998

Region	1924 D	1924 R	1936 D	1936 R	1948 D	1948 R	1960 D	1960 R	1972 D	1972 R	1980 D	1980 R	1988 D	1988 R	1990 D	1990 R	1992 D	1992 R	1994 D	1994 R	1996 D	1996 R	1998 D	1998 R
South																								
Percent	54.9	1.2	29.8	2.2	39.2	1.2	37.5	3.5	30.3	17.7	28.5	20.1	29.6	22.2	28.9	23.3	29.8	27.2	30.0	27.7	26.1	31.3	25.6	31.8
Seats	101	3	99	2	103	2	98	6	73	34	69	38	77	39	77	39	77	48	61	64	54	71	54	71
Border																								
Percent	14.7	7.8	12.0	2.2	14.1	2.9	12.3	3.5	11.2	4.2	9.5	5.8	8.8	6.2	8.6	6.6	8.1	6.2	7.9	6.9	6.3	8.3	6.2	8.5
Seats	27	19	40	2	37	5	32	6	27	8	23	11	23	11	23	11	21	11	16	16	13	19	13	19
New England																								
Percent	2.2	11.4	3.9	17.6	4.2	9.9	5.4	8.2	6.6	4.7	6.6	4.8	5.4	5.7	6.0	4.3	5.4	4.5	6.9	3.5	8.7	1.8	8.5	1.8
Seats	4	28	13	16	11	17	14	14	16	9	16	9	14	10	16	7	14	8	14	8	18	4	18	4
Mid-Atlantic																								
Percent	13.0	26.9	19.3	33.0	17.1	27.5	16.5	25.7	17.8	19.3	17.8	19.6	16.2	17.1	15.3	18.6	14.0	17.0	16.2	14.3	17.0	13.6	17.1	13.5
Seats	24	66	64	30	45	47	43	44	43	37	43	37	42	30	41	31	36	30	33	33	35	31	36	30
Midwest																								
Percent	7.6	28.2	19.6	19.8	14.4	28.7	13.4	29.8	13.7	27.6	17.8	21.7	18.1	18.9	18.4	18.6	16.7	17.6	15.8	18.2	18.0	16.2	17.5	16.6
Seats	14	69	65	18	38	49	35	51	33	53	43	41	47	33	49	31	43	31	32	42	37	37	37	37
Plains																								
Percent	3.3	13.5	4.0	17.6	1.9	15.2	2.3	14.6	3.3	8.3	3.7	8.5	4.6	6.9	4.9	6.6	4.6	5.7	3.9	6.1	3.4	6.1	4.3	5.8
Seats	6	33	13	16	5	26	6	25	8	16	9	16	12	12	13	11	12	10	8	14	8	14	9	13

Rocky Mountain																								
Percent	2.2	4.1	4.2	1.1	4.6	2.3	4.2	2.3	3.3	5.7	2.9	6.3	3.5	8.6	4.1	7.8	4.3	7.4	3.0	7.8	2.4	8.3	2.4	8.5
Seats	4	10	14	1	12	4	11	4	8	11	7	12	9	15	11	13	11	13	6	18	5	19	5	19
Pacific Coast																								
Percent	2.2	6.9	7.2	6.6	4.6	12.3	8.4	12.3	13.7	12.5	13.2	13.2	13.8	14.3	13.8	14.4	17.0	14.2	16.7	15.2	18.4	13.6	18.5	13.5
Seats	4	17	24	6	12	21	22	21	33	24	32	25	36	25	37	24	44	25	34	35	38	31	39	30
Total seats	184	245	332	91	263	171[a]	261	171	241	192	242	189	260	175	267	167[b]	258	176[b]	204	230[b]	207	227[b]	211	223[b]

Note: D indicates Democrats; R indicates Republicans. We have excluded third-party members and vacant seats. Percentages may not add to 100.0 because of rounding.

a. One Independent was elected in 1948.
b. Bernard Sanders was elected as an Independent from Vermont.

Sources: Congressional Directory, 1925, 1937, 1949, 1961, 1973, 1981, 1983, 1985; *Congressional Quarterly Weekly Report,* November 12, 1988, 3269; November 10, 1990, 3802; November 7, 1992, 3571; November 12, 1994, 3236; November 9, 1996, 3226; November 7, 1998, 3027.

Table 1-4 Democratic Party Strength in the Senate, by Region, 1924–1998

Region	1924	1936	1948	1960	1972	1980	1982	1984	1986	1988	1990	1992	1994	1996	1998
South															
Percent	100.0	100.0	100.0	100.0	68.2	54.4	50.0	54.5	72.7	68.2	68.2	59.1	40.9[a]	31.8	36.4
Seats	22	22	22	22	22	22	22	22	22	22	22	22	22	22	22
Border															
Percent	50.0	100.0	80.0	60.0	50.0	70.0	70.0	60.0	60.0	60.0	60.0	60.0	50.0	50.0	40.0
Seats	10	10	10	10	10	10	10	10	10	10	10	10	10	10	10
New England															
Percent	8.3	50.0	25.0	41.7	58.3	50.0	50.0	50.0	50.0	58.3	58.3	58.3	50.0	50.0	50.0
Seats	12	12	12	12	12	12	12	12	12	12	12	12	12	12	12
Mid-Atlantic															
Percent	37.5	75.0	37.5	25.0	25.0	50.0	50.0	50.0	50.0	50.0	50.0	62.5	50.0	50.0	62.5
Seats	8	8	8	8	8	8	8	8	8	8	8	8	8	8	8
Midwest															
Percent	10.0	88.9[b]	20.0	70.0	60.0	60.0	60.0	70.0	70.0	70.0	70.0	80.0	60.0	60.0	50.0
Seats	10	9[b]	10	10	10	10	10	10	10	10	10	10	10	10	10
Plains															
Percent	0.0	66.7[d]	16.7	25.0	58.3	25.0	25.0	33.3	50.0	50.0	58.3	58.3	58.3	58.3	58.3
Seats	11[c]	9[d]	12	12	12	12	12	12	12	12	12	12	12	12	12

Rocky Mountain														
Percent	50.0	93.8	75.0	75.0	56.2	31.3	31.3	31.3	37.5	37.5	37.5	37.5	31.2[e]	25.0	25.0
Seats	16	16	16	16	16	16	16	16	16	16	16	16	16	16	16
Pacific Coast														
Percent	16.7	50.0	33.3	80.0	60.0	40.0	40.0	30.0	40.0	40.0	40.0	50.0	50.0	60.0	60.0
Seats	6	6	6	10	10	10	10	10	10	10	10	10	10	10	10

Note: Number of seats is total for all parties in the region (exceptions noted below).

a. Includes Sen. Richard Shelby (Ala.), who switched from the Democratic to the Republican Party on the day following the election.
b. Excludes one Progressive from Wisconsin.
c. Excludes one senator from Minnesota who was a member of the Farmer Labor Party.
d. Excludes two senators from Minnesota and one senator from Nebraska who were members of the Farmer Labor Party.
e. Does not include Sen. Ben Nighthorse Campbell (Colo.), who switched from the Democratic to the Republican Party on March 3, 1995.

Sources: Congressional Directory, 1925, 1937, 1949, 1961, 1973, 1981, 1983, 1985; *Congressional Quarterly Weekly Report,* November 8, 1986, 2812, 2839; November 12, 1988, 3264; November 10, 1990, 3826; November 7, 1992, 3558; November 12, 1994, 3236; November 9, 1996, 3226; November 7, 1998, 3027.

Table 1-5 Democratic and Republican Seats in the Senate, by Region, 1924–1998

Region	1924 D	1924 R	1936 D	1936 R	1948 D	1948 R	1960 D	1960 R	1972 D	1972 R	1980 D	1980 R	1988 D	1988 R	1990 D	1990 R	1992 D	1992 R	1994 D	1994 R	1996 D	1996 R	1998 D	1998 R
South																								
Percent	53.7	0.0	28.9	0.0	40.7	0.0	33.8	0.0	26.3	16.3	25.5	18.9	27.3	15.6	26.8	15.9	22.8	20.9	19.1	24.5a	15.6	27.3	17.8	25.5
Seats	22	0	22	0	22	0	22	0	15	7	12	10	15	7	15	7	13	9	9	13	7	15	8	14
Border																								
Percent	12.2	9.3	13.2	0.0	14.8	4.8	9.2	11.4	8.8	11.6	14.9	5.7	10.6	8.9	10.7	9.1	10.5	7.3	10.6	9.4	11.1	9.1	8.9	10.9
Seats	5	5	10	0	8	2	6	4	5	5	7	3	6	4	6	4	6	4	5	5	5	5	4	6
New England																								
Percent	2.4	20.4	7.9	37.5	5.6	21.4	7.7	20.0	12.3	11.6	12.8	11.3	12.7	11.1	12.5	11.4	12.3	11.6	12.8	11.3	13.3	10.9	13.3	10.9
Seats	1	11	6	6	3	9	5	7	7	5	6	6	7	5	7	5	7	5	6	6	6	6	6	6
Mid-Atlantic																								
Percent	7.3	9.3	7.9	12.5	5.6	11.9	3.1	17.1	3.5	13.9	8.5	7.5	7.3	8.9	7.1	9.1	8.8	7.0	8.5	7.5	8.9	7.3	11.1	5.5
Seats	3	5	6	2	3	5	2	6	2	6	4	4	4	4	4	4	5	3	4	4	4	4	5	3
Midwest																								
Percent	2.4	16.7	10.5	6.3	3.7	19.0	10.8	8.6	10.5	9.3	12.8	7.5	12.7	6.7	12.5	6.8	14.0	4.6	12.8	7.5	13.3	7.3	11.1	9.1
Seats	1	9	8	1	2	8	7	3	6	4	6	4	7	3	7	3	8	2	6	4	6	4	5	5
Plains																								
Percent	0.0	20.4	7.9	18.8	3.7	23.8	4.6	25.7	12.3	11.6	6.4	17.0	10.9	13.3	12.5	11.4	12.3	11.6	14.9	9.4	15.6	9.1	15.6	9.1
Seats	0	11	6	3	2	10	3	9	7	5	3	9	6	6	7	5	7	5	7	5	7	5	7	5

Rocky Mountain																								
Percent	19.5	14.8	19.7	6.3	22.2	9.5	18.5	11.4	15.8	16.3	10.6	20.8	10.9	22.2	10.7	22.7	10.5	23.2	10.6	20.8[b]	8.8	21.8	8.8	21.8
Seats	8	8	15	1	12	4	12	4	9	7	5	11	6	10	6	10	6	10	5	11	4	12	4	12
Pacific Coast																								
Percent	2.4	9.3	3.9	18.8	3.7	9.5	12.3	5.7	10.5	9.3	8.5	11.3	7.3	13.3	7.1	13.6	8.8	11.6	10.6	9.4	13.3	7.3	13.3	7.3
Seats	1	5	3	2	4	4	8	2	6	4	4	6	4	6	4	6	5	5	5	5	6	4	6	4
Total seats	41	54	76	16	54	42	65	35	57	43	47	53	55	45	56	44	57	43	47	53	45	55	45	55

Note: D indicates Democrats; R indicates Republicans. We have excluded third-party members who did not caucus with either major party. Percentages may not add to 100.0 because of rounding.

a. This includes Sen. Richard Shelby (Ala.), who switched from the Democratic to the Republican Party on the day following the election.
b. This does not include Sen. Ben Nighthorse Campbell (Colo.), who switched from the Democratic to the Republican Party on March 3, 1995.

Sources: Congressional Directory, 1925, 1937, 1949, 1961, 1973, 1981, 1983, 1985; *Congressional Quarterly Weekly Report,* November 12, 1988, 3264; November 10, 1990, 3826; November 7, 1992, 3558; November 12, 1994, 3236; November 9, 1996, 3226; November 7, 1998, 3027.

Table 1-6 Seniority of Representatives, 83d–106th Congresses, 1953–1999

Congress	1 term	2 terms	3 terms	1–3 terms	4–6 terms	7–9 terms	10 + terms	Total	Mean term	Median term
83d (1953)										
Percent	19	17	15	50	27	13	9	100	4.5	3
Seats	81	73	64	218	117	58	40	433		
84th (1955)										
Percent	13	17	14	44	27	17	12	100	5.0	4
Seats	57	73	63	193	119	73	50	435		
85th (1957)										
Percent	11	12	15	38	33	15	15	100	5.4	4
Seats	46	50	66	162	142	66	63	433		
86th (1959)										
Percent	19	10	11	40	31	15	13	100	5.2	4
Seats	82	45	49	176	136	64	57	436[a]		
87th (1961)										
Percent	14	15	8	37	30	17	15	100	5.5	5
Seats	62	65	36	163	131	76	67	437[b]		
88th (1963)										
Percent	15	14	12	42	24	18	16	100	5.5	5
Seats	67	62	53	182	106	78	68	434		
89th (1965)										
Percent	21	13	11	46	22	17	15	100	5.1	4
Seats	91	58	49	198	97	73	67	435		
90th (1967)										
Percent	17	15	11	42	25	16	17	100	5.3	4
Seats	73	64	47	184	108	69	74	435		
91st (1969)										
Percent	9	17	13	39	29	15	17	100	5.6	5
Seats	40	75	56	171	126	65	73	435		
92d (1971)										
Percent	13	10	15	37	28	16	19	100	5.8	5
Seats	56	42	64	162	121	68	83	434		
93d (1973)										
Percent	16	13	9	38	29	15	17	100	5.5	5
Seats	69	55	38	162	128	66	76	432		
94th (1975)										
Percent	21	15	9	45	23	18	14	100	5.2	4
Seats	92	64	40	196	100	78	61	435		
95th (1977)										
Percent	15	22	13	50	20	16	14	100	4.9	3
Seats	67	94	58	219	87	70	59	435		

	Percentage of representatives serving									Me-dian
Congress	1 term	2 terms	3 terms	1–3 terms	4–6 terms	7–9 terms	10 + terms	Total	Mean term	dian term
96th (1979)										
Percent	18	15	18	51	22	15	12	100	4.8	3
Seats	77	64	78	219	95	65	54	433		
97th (1981)										
Percent	17	17	14	48	28	13	11	100	4.7	4
Seats	74	76	59	209	121	56	49	435		
98th (1983)										
Percent	18	15	15	48	29	10	12	100	4.7	4
Seats	80	64	66	210	125	45	54	434		
99th (1985)										
Percent	10	18	14	42	32	13	12	100	5.1	4
Seats	43	79	62	184	138	58	54	434		
100th (1987)										
Percent	11	9	17	37	33	15	16	100	5.5	5
Seats	50	38	75	163	143	64	65	435		
101st (1989)										
Percent	8	12	8	28	38	20	14	100	5.8	5
Seats	33	54	33	120	167	86	60	433		
102d (1991)										
Percent	10	9	11	32	31	21	17	100	6.1	5
Seats	44	41	48	133	137	91	74	435		
103d (1993)										
Percent	25	10	9	44	25	16	15	100	5.2	4
Seats	110	44	38	192	109	69	65	435		
104th (1995)										
Percent	20	22	9	51	16	18	14	100	4.9	3
Seats	86	97	37	220	78	78	59	435		
105th (1997)										
Percent	18	17	20	56	16	15	13	100	4.8	3
Seats	79	76	88	243	71	65	56	435		
106th (1999)										
Percent	9	17	16	43	29	13	15	100	4.8	3
Seats	41	75	69	185	127	58	65	435		

Note: Terms are consecutive. Percentages may not add to totals because of rounding.

a. Alaska was admitted as a state in 1958. The total figure includes the addition of Alaska's representative.

b. Alaska was admitted as a state in 1958 and Hawaii in 1959. The total figure includes the addition of Alaska's and Hawaii's representatives. In 1963 the other states absorbed the proportionate loss in representatives necessary to give Alaska and Hawaii permanent representation under the 435-member figure established in 1911.

Sources: Congressional Quarterly Almanac, 1953–1994; *Congressional Quarterly Weekly Report,* January 10, 1981; January 8, 1983; December 27, 1986; January 7, 1989; January 12, 1991; January 16, 1993; February 18, 1995; February 22, 1997; *Congressional Directory,* 1962–1999.

Figure 1-2 Democratic Party Strength in Congress, by Region, 1924–1998
(percentage of Democratic seats in regional delegation)

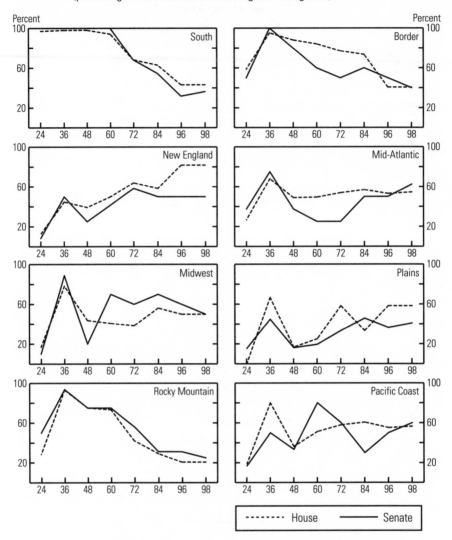

Note: The number of years between the labels on the horizontal axis differs over time.

Sources: Tables 1-2 and 1-4.

Table 1-7 Seniority of Senators, 83d–106th Congresses, 1953–1999

Congress		6 years or less	7–12 years	13–18 years	19 years or more	Total	Mean years service	Median years service
		Number of senators serving						
83d	(1953)	46 (16)	29	14	7	96	8.5	7
84th	(1955)	42 (14)	37	8	9	96	8.4	7
85th	(1957)	37 (10)	36	13	10	96	9.6	9
86th	(1959)	42 (20)	30	14	12	98	9.4	8
87th	(1961)	42 (7)	25	22	11	100	9.7	9
88th	(1963)	42 (12)	26	18	14	100	9.9	7
89th	(1965)	29 (8)	36	16	19	100	11.1	9
90th	(1967)	28 (7)	34	19	19	100	11.6	9
91st	(1969)	32 (14)	32	17	19	100	11.2	11
92d	(1971)	25 (10)	24	29	22	100	11.5	11
93d	(1973)	40 (13)	20	20	20	100	11.2	9
94th	(1975)	35 (11)	22	23	19	99	11.5	9
95th	(1977)	42 (17)	25	13	20	100	10.6	9
96th	(1979)	48 (20)	24	10	18	100	9.6	7
97th	(1981)	55 (18)	20	10	15	100	8.5	5
98th	(1983)	43 (5)	28	16	13	100	9.6	7
99th	(1985)	32 (7)	38	18	12	100	10.1	9
100th	(1987)	26 (13)	44	16	14	100	9.6	8
101st	(1989)	31 (10)	26	29	14	100	9.8	10
102d	(1991)	30 (5)	23	28	19	100	11.1	11
103d	(1993)	30 (13)	17	32	21	100	11.3	12
104th	(1995)	29 (11)	26	20	25	100	12.3	11
105th	(1997)	40 (15)	24	13	23	100	11.2	9
106th	(1999)	43 (8)	25	12	20	100	11.0	10

Note: Figures in parentheses are the number of freshman senators. Senators who are currently in their first full term are listed under the "6 years or less" column.

Sources: Congressional Directory, 1953 through 1985; *Congressional Quarterly Almanac* (Washington, D.C.: Congressional Quarterly, various years); *Congressional Quarterly Weekly Report,* October 11, 1986; November 8, 1986; November 12, 1988; November 19, 1988; November 10, 1990; *National Journal,* November 7, 1992, 2562; November 12, 1994, 2644; November 9, 1996; November 7, 1998; *Congressional Directory*, 1999.

Table 1-8 Prior Occupations or Occupational Fields of Representatives, 83d–106th Congresses, 1953–1999

Occupation	83d 1953	84th 1955	86th 1959	89th 1965	90th 1967	91st 1969	92d 1971	93d 1973	94th 1975
Acting/entertainer	—	—	—	—	—	—	—	—	—
Aeronautics	—	—	—	—	—	—	—	—	—
Agriculture	53	51	45	44	39	34	36	38	31
Business or banking	131	127	130	156	161	159	145	155	140
Clergy	—	—	—	3	3	2	2	4	5
Congressional aide	—	—	—	—	—	—	—	—	—
Education	46	47	41	68	57	59	61	59	64
Engineering	5	5	3	9	6	6	3	2	3
Journalism	36	33	35	43	39	39	30	23	24
Labor leader	—	—	—	3	2	3	3	3	3
Law	247	245	242	247	246	242	236	221	221
Law enforcement	—	—	—	—	—	2	1	2	2
Medicine	6	5	4	3	3	5	6	5	5
Military	—	—	—	—	—	—	—	—	—
Professional sports	—	—	—	—	—	—	—	—	—
Public service/politics	—	—	—	—	—	—	—	—	—
Real estate	—	—	—	—	—	—	—	—	—
Veteran	246	261	261	310	320	320	316	317	307

Note: Dashes indicate years and occupations or occupational fields for which Congressional Quarterly did not compile data.

a. Includes Bernard Sanders (I-Vt.).

Sources: Congressional Quarterly Almanac; Congressional Quarterly Weekly Report, November 8, 1986, 2862; November 12, 1988, 3295; November 10, 1990, 3837; November 7, 1992, Supplement, 9; November 12, 1994, Supplement, 11; January 4, 1997, 29; January 9, 1999, 63.

95th 1977	96th 1979	97th 1981	98th 1983	99th 1985	100th 1987	101st 1989	102d 1991	103d 1993	104th 1995	105th 1997	106th 1999
—	—	—	—	—	1	2	2	1	1	1	1
—	—	—	3	4	3	3	1	2	1	1	1
16	19	28	26	29	20	19	20	19	20	22	22
118	127	134	138	147	142	138	157	131	162	181	159
6	6	3	2	2	2	2	2	2	2	1	1
5	10	11	16	16	—	—	—	—	—	—	—
70	57	59	43	37	38	42	57[a]	66[a]	75[a]	74[a]	84[a]
2	2	5	5	6	4	4	7	5	6	8	9
27	11	21	22	20	20	17	25[a]	24[a]	15[a]	12[a]	9[a]
6	4	5	2	2	2	2	3	2	2	1	1
222	205	194	200	190	184	184	183	181	171	172	163
7	5	5	5	8	7	8	5	10	11	10	10
2	6	6	6	5	3	4	5	6	10	12	15
—	—	—	1	1	0	0	1	0	0	1	1
—	—	—	3	3	5	4	3	1	2	3	2
—	—	—	—	—	94	94	61	87	102	100	106
—	—	—	—	—	—	—	—	—	—	—	20
—	—	—	—	—	—	—	—	—	—	—	—

Table 1-9 Prior Occupations or Occupational Fields of Democratic Representatives, 83d–106th Congresses, 1953–1999

Occupation	83d 1953	84th 1955	86th 1959	89th 1965	90th 1967	91st 1969	92d 1971	93d 1973	94th 1975
Acting/entertainer	—	—	—	—	—	—	—	—	—
Aeronautics	—	—	—	—	—	—	—	—	—
Agriculture	21	22	28	26	17	14	19	14	13
Business or banking	55	59	71	98	82	76	70	72	84
Clergy	—	—	—	2	1	1	1	2	4
Congressional aide	—	—	—	—	—	—	—	—	—
Education	18	26	30	54	43	40	39	41	51
Engineering	3	3	2	6	4	3	2	1	1
Journalism	18	16	21	27	22	22	17	16	19
Labor leader	—	—	—	3	2	3	3	3	3
Law	130	136	168	171	150	150	150	137	158
Law enforcement	—	—	—	—	—	1	1	1	2
Medicine	2	2	2	1	1	2	4	3	3
Military	—	—	—	—	—	—	—	—	—
Professional sports	—	—	—	—	—	—	—	—	—
Public service/politics	—	—	—	—	—	—	—	—	—
Real estate	—	—	—	—	—	—	—	—	—
Veteran	118	131	175	210	183	181	185	175	198
Total number of Democratic members	213	232	283	295	248	243	255	243	291

Note: Dashes indicate years and occupations or occupational fields for which Congressional Quarterly did not compile data.

Sources: Congressional Quarterly Almanac, various years; *Congressional Quarterly Weekly Report,* November 8, 1986, 2862; November 12, 1988, 3295; November 10, 1990, 3837; November 7, 1992, Supplement, 9; November 12, 1994, Supplement, 11; January 4, 1997, 29; January 9, 1999, 63.

95th 1977	96th 1979	97th 1981	98th 1983	99th 1985	100th 1987	101st 1989	102d 1991	103d 1993	104th 1995	105th 1997	106th 1999
—	—	—	—	—	0	1	1	0	0	0	0
—	—	—	0	1	0	0	0	0	0	0	0
6	10	11	13	13	10	8	11	7	6	8	8
69	71	58	73	72	66	66	77	56	46	55	53
4	4	2	2	2	2	2	2	1	1	1	0
3	7	9	10	10	—	—	—	—	—	—	—
56	44	39	29	24	24	25	37	45	39	40	49
0	0	2	2	2	2	2	4	2	1	1	1
15	6	9	13	10	11	9	14	11	4	4	2
6	3	4	2	2	2	2	3	2	1	1	1
154	135	121	132	122	122	122	126	122	93	87	87
7	4	4	2	6	6	6	4	8	7	8	8
1	1	2	2	3	1	2	3	4	2	3	5
—	—	—	0	0	0	0	0	0	0	0	0
—	—	—	2	2	3	3	2	0	0	0	0
—	—	—	—	—	59	58	41	51	53	54	57
—	—	—	—	—	—	—	—	—	—	—	3
—	—	—	—	—	—	—	—	—	—	—	—
292	277	243	267	253	258	260	267	258	204	207	211

Table 1-10 Prior Occupations or Occupational Fields of Republican Representatives, 83d–106th Congresses, 1953–1999

Occupation	83d 1953	84th 1955	86th 1959	89th 1965	90th 1967	91st 1969	92d 1971	93d 1973	94th 1975
Acting/entertainer	—	—	—	—	—	—	—	—	—
Aeronautics	—	—	—	—	—	—	—	—	—
Agriculture	32	29	17	18	22	20	17	24	18
Business or banking	76	68	59	58	79	83	75	83	56
Clergy	—	—	—	1	2	1	1	2	1
Congressional aide	—	—	—	—	—	—	—	—	—
Education	28	21	11	14	14	19	22	18	13
Engineering	2	2	1	3	2	3	1	1	2
Journalism	18	17	14	16	17	17	13	7	5
Labor leader	—	—	—	0	0	0	0	0	0
Law	117	109	74	76	96	92	86	84	63
Law enforcement	—	—	—	—	—	1	0	1	0
Medicine	4	3	2	2	2	3	2	2	2
Military	—	—	—	—	—	—	—	—	—
Professional sports	—	—	—	—	—	—	—	—	—
Public service/politics	—	—	—	—	—	—	—	—	—
Real estate	—	—	—	—	—	—	—	—	—
Veteran	128	130	86	100	137	139	131	142	109
Total number of Republican members	221	203	153	140	187	192	180	192	144

Note: Dashes indicate years and occupations or occupational fields for which Congressional Quarterly did not compile data.

Sources: Congressional Quarterly Almanac, various years; *Congressional Quarterly Weekly Report,* November 8, 1986, 2862; November 12, 1988, 3295; November 10, 1990, 3837; November 7, 1992, Supplement, 9; November 12, 1994, Supplement, 11; January 4, 1997, 29; January 9, 1999, 63.

95th 1977	96th 1979	97th 1981	98th 1983	99th 1985	100th 1987	101st 1989	102d 1991	103d 1993	104th 1995	105th 1997	106th 1999
—	—	—	—	—	1	1	1	1	1	1	1
—	—	—	3	3	3	3	1	2	1	1	1
10	9	17	13	16	10	11	9	12	14	14	14
49	56	76	65	75	76	72	80	75	116	126	106
2	2	1	0	0	0	0	0	1	1	0	1
2	3	2	6	6	—	—	—	—	—	—	—
14	13	20	14	13	14	17	19	20	35	33	34
2	2	3	3	4	2	2	3	3	5	7	8
12	5	12	9	10	9	8	10	12	10	7	6
0	1	1	0	0	0	0	0	0	1	0	0
68	70	73	68	68	62	62	57	59	78	85	76
0	1	1	3	2	1	2	1	2	4	2	2
1	5	4	4	2	2	2	2	2	8	9	10
—	—	—	1	1	0	0	1	0	0	1	1
—	—	—	1	1	2	1	1	1	2	3	2
—	—	—	—	—	35	36	20	36	49	46	49
—	—	—	—	—	—	—	—	—	—	—	17
—	—	—	—	—	—	—	—	—	—	—	—
143	158	192	167	182	177	175	167	176	230	227	223

Table 1-11 Prior Occupations or Occupational Fields of Senators, 83d–106th Congresses, 1953–1999

Occupation	83d 1953	84th 1955	86th 1959	89th 1965	90th 1967	91st 1969	92d 1971	93d 1973	94th 1975
Acting/entertainer	—	—	—	—	—	—	—	—	—
Aeronautics	—	—	—	—	—	—	—	—	—
Agriculture	22	21	17	18	18	16	13	11	10
Business or banking	28	28	28	25	23	25	27	22	22
Clergy	—	—	—	0	0	0	0	0	0
Congressional aide	—	—	—	—	—	—	—	—	—
Education	17	17	16	16	15	14	11	10	8
Engineering	5	2	2	2	2	2	2	2	2
Journalism	10	10	13	10	10	8	7	5	5
Labor leader	—	—	—	1	0	0	0	0	0
Law	59	60	61	67	68	68	65	68	67
Law enforcement	—	—	—	—	—	0	0	0	0
Medicine	1	2	1	1	1	0	1	1	1
Military	—	—	—	—	—	—	—	—	—
Professional sports	—	—	—	—	—	—	—	—	—
Public service/politics	—	—	—	—	—	—	—	—	—
Real estate	—	—	—	—	—	—	—	—	—
Veteran	63	62	61	63	65	69	73	73	73

Note: Dashes indicate years and occupations or occupational fields for which Congressional Quarterly did not compile data.

Sources: Congressional Quarterly Almanac, various years; *Congressional Quarterly Weekly Report,* November 8, 1986, 2862; November 12, 1988, 3295; November 10, 1990, 3837; November 7, 1992, Supplement, 9; November 12, 1994, Supplement, 11; January 4, 1997, 29; January 9, 1999, 63.

95th 1977	96th 1979	97th 1981	98th 1983	99th 1985	100th 1987	101st 1989	102d 1991	103d 1993	104th 1995	105th 1997	106th 1999
—	—	—	—	—	0	0	0	0	1	1	1
—	—	—	2	2	2	2	1	1	1	1	0
9	6	9	9	10	5	4	8	8	9	8	6
24	29	28	29	31	28	28	32	24	24	33	24
1	1	1	1	1	1	1	1	1	0	1	1
0	0	0	0	0	—	—	—	—	—	—	—
13	7	10	12	12	12	11	10	11	10	13	13
0	0	2	0	1	1	0	0	0	0	0	0
6	2	7	7	8	8	8	10	9	8	9	8
0	0	0	0	0	0	0	0	0	0	0	0
68	65	59	61	61	62	63	61	58	54	53	55
0	0	0	0	0	0	0	0	0	0	0	0
1	1	1	1	1	1	0	0	0	1	2	2
—	—	—	1	1	1	1	1	1	1	1	1
—	—	—	1	1	1	1	1	1	1	0	1
—	—	—	—	—	20	20	5	10	12	26	18
—	—	—	—	—	—	—	—	—	—	—	4
—	—	—	—	—	—	—	—	—	—	—	—

Table 1-12 Prior Occupations or Occupational Fields of Democratic Senators, 83d–106th Congresses, 1953–1999

Occupation	83d 1953	84th 1955	86th 1959	89th 1965	90th 1967	91st 1969	92d 1971	93d 1973	94th 1975
Acting/entertainer	—	—	—	—	—	—	—	—	—
Aeronautics	—	—	—	—	—	—	—	—	—
Agriculture	8	7	7	10	9	7	5	4	5
Business or banking	11	10	14	14	12	12	15	12	12
Clergy	—	—	—	0	0	0	0	0	0
Congressional aide	—	—	—	—	—	—	—	—	—
Education	11	11	13	12	10	9	6	7	6
Engineering	2	0	2	2	2	2	2	2	2
Journalism	5	6	10	7	7	5	5	4	4
Labor leader	—	—	—	1	0	0	0	0	0
Law	34	27	43	48	48	42	41	42	45
Law enforcement	—	—	—	—	—	—	0	0	0
Medicine	1	2	1	1	1	0	1	1	1
Military	—	—	—	—	—	—	—	—	—
Professional sports	—	—	—	—	—	—	—	—	—
Public service/politics	—	—	—	—	—	—	—	—	—
Real estate	—	—	—	—	—	—	—	—	—
Veteran	31	32	40	44	43	41	41	42	45
Total number of Democratic members	46	48	64	68	64	58	54	56	60

Note: Dashes indicate years and occupations or occupational fields for which Congressional Quarterly did not compile data.

Sources: Congressional Quarterly Almanac, various years, *Congressional Quarterly Weekly Report,* November 8, 1986, 2862; November 12, 1988, 3295; November 10, 1990, 3837; November 7, 1992, Supplement, 9; November 12, 1994, Supplement, 11; January 4, 1997, 29; January 9, 1999, 63.

95th 1977	96th 1979	97th 1981	98th 1983	99th 1985	100th 1987	101st 1989	102d 1991	103d 1993	104th 1995	105th 1997	106th 1999
—	—	—	—	—	0	0	0	0	0	0	0
—	—	—	1	1	1	1	1	1	1	1	0
3	2	2	2	3	2	1	3	3	4	2	1
14	15	13	14	12	13	13	15	12	11	8	6
0	0	0	0	0	0	0	0	0	0	0	0
0	0	0	0	0	—	—	—	—	—	—	—
8	4	5	5	4	6	6	6	6	5	5	5
0	0	1	0	0	0	0	0	0	0	0	0
4	2	4	5	6	6	5	8	7	5	2	2
0	0	0	0	0	0	0	0	0	0	0	0
46	43	33	32	32	35	36	35	33	26	26	27
0	0	0	0	0	0	0	0	0	0	0	0
1	1	1	1	1	1	0	0	0	0	0	0
—	—	—	0	1	0	0	0	0	0	0	0
—	—	—	1	0	1	1	1	1	1	0	0
—	—	—	—	—	13	14	4	8	7	9	10
—	—	—	—	—	—	—	—	—	—	—	2
—	—	—	—	—	—	—	—	—	—	—	—
61	58	46	46	47	55	55	56	57	47	45	45

Table 1-13 Prior Occupations or Occupational Fields of Republican Senators, 83d–106th Congresses, 1953–1999

Occupation	83d 1953	84th 1955	86th 1959	89th 1965	90th 1967	91st 1969	92d 1971	93d 1973	94th 1975
Acting/entertainer	—	—	—	—	—	—	—	—	—
Aeronautics	—	—	—	—	—	—	—	—	—
Agriculture	14	14	10	8	9	9	8	7	5
Business or banking	17	18	14	11	11	13	12	10	10
Clergy	—	—	—	0	0	0	0	0	0
Congressional aide	—	—	—	—	—	—	—	—	—
Education	6	6	3	4	5	5	5	3	2
Engineering	3	2	0	0	0	0	0	0	0
Journalism	5	4	3	3	3	3	2	1	1
Labor leader	—	—	—	0	0	0	0	0	0
Law	25	33	18	19	20	26	24	26	22
Law enforcement	—	—	—	—	0	0	0	0	0
Medicine	0	0	0	0	0	0	0	0	0
Military	—	—	—	—	—	—	—	—	—
Professional sports	—	—	—	—	—	—	—	—	—
Public service/politics	—	—	—	—	—	—	—	—	—
Real estate	—	—	—	—	—	—	—	—	—
Veteran	32	30	21	19	22	28	32	31	28
Total number of Republican members	48	47	34	32	36	42	44	42	37

Note: Dashes indicate years and occupations or occupational fields for which Congressional Quarterly did not compile data.

Sources: Congressional Quarterly Almanac, various years; *Congressional Quarterly Weekly Report,* November 8, 1986, 2862; November 12, 1988, 3295; November 10, 1990, 3837; November 7, 1992, Supplement, 9; November 12, 1994, Supplement, 11; January 4, 1997, 29; January 9, 1999, 63.

95th 1977	96th 1979	97th 1981	98th 1983	99th 1985	100th 1987	101st 1989	102d 1991	103d 1993	104th 1995	105th 1997	106th 1999
—	—	—	—	—	0	0	0	0	1	1	1
—	—	—	1	1	1	1	0	0	0	0	0
6	4	7	7	7	3	3	5	5	5	6	5
10	14	15	15	19	15	15	17	12	13	25	18
1	1	1	1	1	1	1	1	1	0	1	1
0	0	0	0	0	—	—	—	—	—	—	—
5	3	5	7	8	6	5	4	5	5	8	8
0	0	1	0	1	1	0	0	0	0	0	0
2	0	3	2	2	2	3	2	2	3	7	6
0	0	0	0	0	0	0	0	0	0	0	0
22	22	26	29	29	27	27	26	25	28	27	28
0	0	0	0	0	0	0	0	0	0	0	0
0	0	0	0	0	0	0	0	0	1	2	2
—	—	—	1	1	1	1	1	1	1	1	1
—	—	—	0	0	0	0	0	0	0	0	1
—	—	—	—	—	7	6	1	2	5	17	8
—	—	—	—	—	—	—	—	—	—	—	2
—	—	—	—	—	—	—	—	—	—	—	—
38	41	53	54	53	45	45	44	43	53	55	55

Table 1-14 Religious Affiliations of Representatives, 89th–106th Congresses, 1965–1999

	89th (1965)			90th (1967)			91st (1969)			92d (1971)			93d (1973)			94th (1975)			95th (1977)			96th (1979)		
	D	R	Total	D	R	Total	D	R	Total	D	R	Total	D	R	Total	D	R	Total	D	R	Total	D	R	Total
Catholic	81	13	94	73	22	95	72	24	96	77	24	101	69	30	99	88	22	110	95	24	119	93	23	116
Jewish	14	1	15	14	2	16	15	2	17	10	2	12	10	2	12	17	3	20	20	3	23	18	5	23
Protestant																								
Baptist	33	9	42	30	12	42	30	13	43	32	10	42	33	12	45	37	10	47	36	10	46	33	10	43
Episcopalian	29	25	54	25	25	50	22	27	49	27	22	49	25	25	50	29	21	50	26	22	48	29	22	51
Methodist	46	23	69	37	32	69	34	32	66	33	32	65	30	33	63	40	23	63	36	24	60	32	26	58
Presbyterian	30	26	56	27	37	64	26	38	64	26	41	67	25	35	60	25	25	50	23	22	45	25	27	52
All other	62	43	105	43	54	97	44	56	100	49	49	98	50	55	105	55	40	95	56	38	94	47	45	92
Total	295	140	435	249	184	433	243	192	435	254	180	434	242	192	434	291	144	435	292	143	435	277	158	435

	97th (1981)			99th (1985)			101st (1989)			102d (1991)			103d (1993)			104th (1995)			105th (1997)			106th (1999)		
	D	R	Total	D	R	Total	D	R	Total	D	R	Total	D	R	Total	D	R	Total	D	R	Total	D	R	Total
Catholic	81	38	119	82	43	125	81	39	120	85	37	122	77	41	118	71	54	125	76	51	127	76	50	126
Jewish	21	6	27	24	6	30	26	5	31	26	6	33[a]	26	5	32[a]	20	4	25[a]	21	3	25[a]	21	1	23[a]
Protestant																								
Baptist	28	13	41	27	9	36	33	10	43	35	12	47	38	13	51	30	27	57	31	27	58	34	28	62
Episcopalian	25	27	52	22	22	44	22	21	43	24	17	41	18	17	35	13	21	34	10	21	31	9	21	30
Methodist	26	30	56	35	27	62	38	25	63	38	24	62	31	23	54	21	29	50	17	29	46	16	34	50
Presbyterian	18	28	46	22	25	47	16	26	42	15	27	42	20	26	46	17	30	47	15	28	43	15	26	41
All other	44	50	94	41	50	91	44	49	93	44	44	88	49	50	99	32	65	97	37	68	105	40	62	102
Total	243	192	435	253	182	435	260	175	435	267	167	435[a]	258	176	435[a]	204	230	435[a]	207	227	435[a]	211	222[b]	435[a]

Note: D indicates Democrats; R indicates Republicans.

a. Totals include Bernard Sanders (I-Vt.).

b. This does not include Johnny Isakson (Ga).

Sources: Congressional Quarterly Almanac, various years; *Congressional Quarterly Weekly Report,* November 10, 1984, 2922; November 12, 1988, 3295; November 10, 1990, 3837; November 7, 1992, Supplement, 9; November 12, 1994, Supplement, 11; January 4, 1997, 29; January 9, 1999, 63.

Table 1-15   Religious Affiliations of Senators, 89th–106th Congresses, 1965–1999

	89th (1965)			90th (1967)			91st (1969)			92d (1971)			93d (1973)			94th (1975)			95th (1977)			96th (1979)		
	D	R	Total	D	R	Total	D	R	Total	D	R	Total	D	R	Total	D	R	Total	D	R	Total	D	R	Total
Catholic	12	2	14	11	2	13	10	3	13	9	3	12	10	4	14	11	4	15	10	3	13	9	4	13
Jewish	1	1	2	1	1	2	1	1	2	1	1	2	1	1	2	2	1	3	4	1	5	5	2	7
Protestant																								
Baptist	9	3	12	7	4	11	6	3	9	5	3	8	5	3	8	6	3	9	6	3	9	6	5	11
Episcopalian	8	7	15	8	7	15	5	10	15	4	13	17	6	11	17	6	9	15	6	11	17	5	12	17
Methodist	15	7	22	15	8	23	14	8	22	13	7	20	13	5	18	11	5	16	13	7	20	13	6	19
Presbyterian	8	3	11	8	4	12	8	5	13	10	6	16	8	6	14	10	7	17	9	5	14	10	2	12
All other	15	9	24	14	10	24	14	12	26	13	12	25	15	12	27	15	9	24	14	8	22	11	10	21
Total	68	32	100	64	36	100	58	42	100	55	45	100	58	42	100	61	38	99	62	38	100	59	41	100

	97th (1981)			99th (1985)			101st (1989)			102d (1991)			103d (1993)			104th (1995)			105th (1997)			106th (1999)		
	D	R	Total	D	R	Total	D	R	Total	D	R	Total	D	R	Total	D	R	Total	D	R	Total	D	R	Total
Catholic	9	8	17	11	8	19	12	7	19	12	8	20	15	8	23	12	8	20	15	9	24	14	11	25
Jewish	3	3	6	4	4	8	5	3	8	6	2	8	9	1	10	8	1	9	9	1	10	10	1	11
Protestant																								
Baptist	3	6	9	4	7	11	4	8	12	4	8	12	4	7	11	3	7	10	2	7	9	1	7	8
Episcopalian	5	15	20	4	17	21	7	13	20	6	12	18	4	11	15	4	10	14	2	9	11	4	9	13
Methodist	9	9	18	9	7	16	9	4	13	9	4	13	7	5	12	5	6	11	5	8	13	5	7	12
Presbyterian	8	2	10	8	1	9	7	2	9	7	2	9	5	3	8	4	4	8	2	8	10	1	6	7
All other	10	10	20	7	9	16	11	8	19	11	9	20	13	8	21	11	17	28	10	13	23	10	14	24
Total	47	53	100	47	53	100	55	45	100	55	45	100	57	43	100	47	53	100	45	55	100	45	55	100

Note: D indicates Democrats; R indicates Republicans.

Sources: Congressional Quarterly Almanac, various years; *Congressional Quarterly Weekly Report*, November 10, 1984, 2922; November 12, 1988, 3295; November 10, 1990, 3837; November 7, 1992, Supplement, 9; November 12, 1994, Supplement, 11; January 4, 1997, 29; January 9, 1999, 63

Table 1-16 African Americans in Congress, 41st–106th Congresses, 1869–1999

Congress		House D	House R	Senate D	Senate R	Congress		House D	House R	Senate D	Senate R
41st	(1869)	—	2	—	1	81st	(1949)	2	—	—	—
42d	(1871)	—	5	—	—	82d	(1951)	2	—	—	—
43d	(1873)	—	7	—	—	83d	(1953)	2	—	—	—
44th	(1875)	—	7	—	1	84th	(1955)	3	—	—	—
45th	(1877)	—	3	—	1	85th	(1957)	3	—	—	—
46th	(1879)	—	—	—	1	86th	(1959)	3	—	—	—
47th	(1881)	—	2	—	—	87th	(1961)	3	—	—	—
48th	(1883)	—	2	—	—	88th	(1963)	4	—	—	—
49th	(1885)	—	2	—	—	89th	(1965)	5	—	—	—
50th	(1887)	—	—	—	—	90th	(1967)	5	—	—	1
51st	(1889)	—	3	—	—	91st	(1969)	9	—	—	1
52d	(1891)	—	1	—	—	92d	(1971)	13	—	—	1
53d	(1893)	—	1	—	—	93d	(1973)	16	—	—	1
54th	(1895)	—	1	—	—	94th	(1975)	16	—	—	1
55th	(1897)	—	1	—	—	95th	(1977)	15	—	—	1
56th	(1899)[a]	—	1	—	—	96th	(1979)	15	—	—	—
71st	(1929)	—	1	—	—	97th	(1981)	17	—	—	—
72d	(1931)	—	1	—	—	98th	(1983)	20	—	—	—
73d	(1933)	—	1	—	—	99th	(1985)	20	—	—	—
74th	(1935)	1	—	—	—	100th	(1987)	22	—	—	—
75th	(1937)	1	—	—	—	101st	(1989)	23	—	—	—
76th	(1939)	1	—	—	—	102d	(1991)	25	1	—	—
77th	(1941)	1	—	—	—	103d	(1993)	38	1	1	—
78th	(1943)	1	—	—	—	104th	(1995)	37	2	1	—
79th	(1945)	2	—	—	—	105th	(1997)	36	1	1	—
80th	(1947)	2	—	—	—	106th	(1999)	36	1	—	—

Note: The data do not include Eleanor Holmes Norton, a nonvoting delegate who represents Washington, D.C.

a. After the Fifty-sixth Congress, there were no African American members in either the House or Senate until the Seventy-first Congress.

Sources: Black Americans in Congress, 1870–1977, H. Doc. 95-258, 95th Cong., 1st sess., 1977; *Congressional Quarterly Almanac,* various years; *Congressional Quarterly Weekly Report,* November 10, 1984, 2921; November 8, 1986, 2863; November 12, 1988, 3294; November 10, 1990, 3836; November 7, 1992, Supplement, 8; November 12, 1994, Supplement, 10; January 4, 1997, 28; January 9, 1999, 62.

Table 1-17 Hispanic Americans in Congress, 45th–106th Congresses, 1877–1999

Congress		House D	House R	Senate D	Senate R	Congress		House D	House R	Senate D	Senate R
45th	(1877)	—	1	—	—	76th	(1939)	1	—	1	—
46th	(1879)	—	1	—	—	77th	(1941)	—	—	1	—
47th	(1881)	—	1	—	—	78th	(1943)	1	—	1	—
48th	(1883)	—	—	—	—	79th	(1945)	1	—	1	—
49th	(1885)	—	—	—	—	80th	(1947)	1	—	1	—
50th	(1887)	—	—	—	—	81st	(1949)	1	—	1	—
51st	(1889)	—	—	—	—	82d	(1951)	1	—	1	—
52d	(1891)	—	—	—	—	83d	(1953)	1	—	1	—
53d	(1893)	—	—	—	—	84th	(1955)	1	—	1	—
54th	(1895)	—	—	—	—	85th	(1957)	1	—	1	—
55th	(1897)	—	—	—	—	86th	(1959)	1	—	1	—
56th	(1899)	—	—	—	—	87th	(1961)	2	—	1	—
57th	(1901)	—	—	—	—	88th	(1963)	3	—	1	—
58th	(1903)	—	—	—	—	89th	(1965)	3	—	1	—
59th	(1905)	—	—	—	—	90th	(1967)	3	—	1	—
60th	(1907)	—	—	—	—	91st	(1969)	3	1	1	—
61st	(1909)	—	—	—	—	92d	(1971)	4	1	1	—
62d	(1911)	—	—	—	—	93d	(1973)	4	1	1	—
63d	(1913)	1	—	—	—	94th	(1975)	4	1	1	—
64th	(1915)	1	1	—	—	95th	(1977)	4	1	—	—
65th	(1917)	1	—	—	—	96th	(1979)	5	1	—	—
66th	(1919)	1	1	—	—	97th	(1981)	6	1	—	—
67th	(1921)	1	1	—	—	98th	(1983)	9	1	—	—
68th	(1923)	1	—	—	—	99th	(1985)	10	1	—	—
69th	(1925)	1	—	—	—	100th	(1987)	10	1	—	—
70th	(1927)	1	—	—	1	101st	(1989)	9	1	—	—
71st	(1929)	—	—	—	—	102d	(1991)	10	1	—	—
72d	(1931)	2	—	—	—	103d	(1993)	14	3	—	—
73d	(1933)	2	—	—	—	104th	(1995)	14	3	—	—
74th	(1935)	1	—	1	—	105th	(1997)	14	3	—	—
75th	(1937)	1	—	1	—	106th	(1999)	16	3	—	—

Note: Statistics do not include delegates or commissioners. Since the Seventeenth Congress, three Democrats and five Republicans have served in the House of Representatives as delegates for territories that would later become states. In addition, Joseph Marion Hernandez (W-Fla.) served as a delegate to the U.S. House of Representatives during the Seventeenth Congress. Since 1901, nineteen Hispanic Americans, representing the territories of Puerto Rico, Guam, and the Virgin Islands, have also served as delegates to the House of Representatives.

Sources: Biographical Directory of the United States Congress 1774–1989; Congressional Quarterly Almanac, various years; *Congressional Quarterly Weekly Report,* January 9, 1999, 62.

Table 1-18 Women in Congress, 65th–106th Congresses, 1917–1999

	House		Senate			House		Senate	
Congress	D	R	D	R	Congress	D	R	D	R
65th (1917)	—	1	—	—	86th (1959)	9	8	—	1
66th (1919)	—	—	—	—	87th (1961)	11	7	1	1
67th (1921)	—	2	—	1	88th (1963)	6	6	1	1
68th (1923)	—	1	—	—	89th (1965)	7	4	1	1
69th (1925)	1	2	—	—	90th (1967)	5	5	—	1
70th (1927)	2	3	—	—	91st (1969)	6	4	—	1
71st (1929)	4	5	—	—	92d (1971)	10	3	—	1
72d (1931)	4	3	1	—	93d (1973)	14	2	1	—
73d (1933)	4	3	1	—	94th (1975)	14	5	—	—
74th (1935)	4	2	2	—	95th (1977)	13	5	—	—
75th (1937)	4	1	2	—	96th (1979)	11	5	1	1
76th (1939)	4	4	1	—	97th (1981)	10	9	—	2
77th (1941)	4	5	1	—	98th (1983)	13	9	—	2
78th (1943)	2	6	1	—	99th (1985)	13	9	—	2
79th (1945)	6	5	—	—	100th (1987)	12[a]	11	1	1
80th (1947)	3	4	—	1	101st (1989)	14	11	1	1
81st (1949)	5	4	—	1	102d (1991)	19	9	1	1
82d (1951)	4	6	—	1	103d (1993)	36	12	5	1
83d (1953)	5	7	—	1	104th (1995)	31	17	5	3[b]
84th (1955)	10	7	—	1	105th (1997)	35	16	6	3
85th (1957)	9	6	—	1	106th (1999)	40	16	6	3

Note: The data include only women who were sworn in as members and served more than one day.

a. The number includes the late Sala Burton, who died after being sworn into the 100th Congress and who was replaced by another Democratic woman, Nancy Pelosi.

b. Sheila Frahm (R-Kan.) was appointed to fill the vacancy left by Sen. Robert Dole (R-Kan.) and brought the total to four Republican woman senators. Frahm ran for the open Senate seat but lost in the Kansas Republican primary.

Sources: Women in Congress, H. Rept. 94-1732, 94th Cong., 2d sess., 1976; *Congressional Quarterly Almanac,* various years; *Congressional Quarterly Weekly Report,* November 10, 1984, 2921; November 8, 1986, 2863; November 12, 1988, 3294; November 10, 1990, 3836; November 7, 1992, Supplement, 8; November 12, 1994, Supplement, 10; January 4, 1997, 28; January 9, 1999, 62.

Table 1-19 Political Parties of Senators and Representatives, 34th–106th Congresses, 1855–1999

		Senate				House of Representatives				
Congress	Number of senators	Demo-crats	Repub-licans	Other parties	Vacant	Number of repre-sentatives	Demo-crats	Repub-licans	Other parties	Vacant
34th (1855–1857)	62	42	15	5	—	234	83	108	43	—
35th (1857–1859)	64	39	20	5	—	237	131	92	14	—
36th (1859–1861)	66	38	26	2	—	237	101	113	23	—
37th (1861–1863)	50	11	31	7	1	178	42	106	28	2
38th (1863–1865)	51	12	39	—	—	183	80	103	—	—
39th (1865–1867)	52	10	42	—	—	191	46	145	—	—
40th (1867–1869)	53	11	42	—	—	193	49	143	—	1
41st (1869–1871)	74	11	61	—	2	243	73	170	—	—
42d (1871–1873)	74	17	57	—	—	243	104	139	—	—
43d (1873–1875)	74	19	54	—	1	293	88	203	—	2
44th (1875–1877)	76	29	46	—	1	293	181	107	3	2
45th (1877–1879)	76	36	39	1	—	293	156	137	1	—
46th (1879–1881)	76	43	33	—	—	293	150	128	14	1
47th (1881–1883)	76	37	37	2	—	293	130	152	11	—
48th (1883–1885)	76	36	40	—	—	325	200	119	6	—
49th (1885–1887)	76	34	41	—	1	325	182	140	2	1
50th (1887–1889)	76	37	39	—	—	325	170	151	4	—
51st (1889–1891)	84	37	47	—	—	330	156	173	1	—
52d (1891–1893)	88	39	47	2	—	333	231	88	14	—
53d (1893–1895)	88	44	38	3	3	356	220	126	10	—
54th (1895–1897)	88	39	44	5	—	357	104	246	7	—
55th (1897–1899)	90	34	46	10	—	357	134	206	16	1
56th (1899–1901)	90	26	53	11	—	357	163	185	9	—

(table continues)

Table 1-19 (continued)

Congress		Senate					House of Representatives				
		Number of senators	Demo-crats	Repub-licans	Other parties	Vacant	Number of repre-sentatives	Demo-crats	Repub-licans	Other parties	Vacant
58th	(1903–1905)	90	32	58	—	—	386	178	207	—	—
59th	(1905–1907)	90	32	58	—	—	386	136	250	—	—
60th	(1907–1909)	92	29	61	—	2	386	164	222	—	—
61st	(1909–1911)	92	32	59	—	1	391	172	219	1	—
62d	(1911–1913)	92	42	49	—	1	391	228	162	1	—
63d	(1913–1915)	96	51	44	1	—	435	290	127	18	—
64th	(1915–1917)	96	56	39	1	—	435	231	193	8	3
65th	(1917–1919)	96	53	42	1	—	435	210[a]	216	9	—
66th	(1919–1921)	96	47	48	1	—	435	191	237	7	—
67th	(1921–1923)	96	37	59	—	—	435	132	300	1	2
68th	(1923–1925)	96	43	51	2	—	435	207	225	3	—
69th	(1925–1927)	96	40	54	1	1	435	183	247	5	—
70th	(1927–1929)	96	47	48	1	—	435	195	237	3	—
71st	(1929–1931)	96	39	56	1	—	435	163[b]	267	1	4
72d	(1931–1933)	96	47	48	1	—	435	216	218	1	—
73d	(1933–1935)	96	59	36	1	—	435	313	117	5	—
74th	(1935–1937)	96	69	25	2	—	435	322	103	10	—
75th	(1937–1939)	96	75	17	4	—	435	333	89	13	—
76th	(1939–1941)	96	69	23	4	—	435	262	169	4	—
77th	(1941–1943)	96	66	28	2	—	435	267	162	6	—
78th	(1943–1945)	96	57	38	1	—	435	222	209	4	—
79th	(1945–1947)	96	57	38	1	—	435	243	190	2	—
80th	(1947–1949)	96	45	51	—	—	435	188	246	1	—
81st	(1949–1951)	96	54	42	—	—	435	263	171	1	—
82d	(1951–1953)	96	48	47	1	—	435	234	199	1	—
83d	(1953–1955)	96	46	48	2	—	435	213	221	2	—
84th	(1955–1957)	96	48	47	1	—	435	232	203	—	—

Congress	Years	Senate					House				
		N	D	R	Other	Vac.	N	D	R	Other	Vac.
85th	(1957–1959)	96	49	47	—	—	435	234	201	—	—
86th	(1959–1961)	98	64	34	—	—	436[c]	283	153	—	—
87th	(1961–1963)	100	64	36	—	—	437[d]	262	175	—	1
88th	(1963–1965)	100	67	33	—	—	435	258	176	—	—
89th	(1965–1967)	100	68	32	—	—	435	295	140	—	—
90th	(1967–1969)	100	64	36	—	—	435	248	187	—	—
91st	(1969–1971)	100	58	42	2	—	435	243	192	—	—
92d	(1971–1973)	100	54	44	2	—	435	255	180	—	—
93d	(1973–1975)	100	56	42	2	—	435	242	192	—	—
94th	(1975–1977)	100	61	37	1	—	435	291	144	—	—
95th	(1977–1979)	100	61	38	1	—	435	292	143	—	—
96th	(1979–1981)	100	58	41	1	—	435	277	158	—	—
97th	(1981–1983)	100	46	53	—	—	435	243	192	—	—
98th	(1983–1985)	100	46	54	—	—	435	268	167	—	—
99th	(1985–1987)	100	47	53	—	—	435	253	182	—	—
100th	(1987–1989)	100	55[e]	45	—	—	435	258	177	—	—
101st	(1989–1991)	100	55	45	—	—	435	260	175	—	—
102d	(1991–1993)	100	56	44	—	—	435	267	167	—	—
103d	(1993–1995)	100	57	43	—	—	435	258	176	1	—
104th	(1995–1997)	100	47[f]	53	—	—	435	204	230	1	—
105th	(1997–1999)	100	45	55	—	—	435	207	227[h]	1	—
106th	(1999–2000)	100	45	55[g]	—	—	435	211	223[h]	1	—

Note: All figures reflect immediate election results.

a. Democrats organized the House with the help of other parties.

b. Democrats organized the House because of Republican deaths.

c. The proclamation declaring Alaska a state was issued on January 3, 1959.

d. The proclamation declaring Hawaii a state was issued on August 21, 1959.

e. The number includes the late Sen. Edward Zorinsky (D-Neb.), who was replaced by Sen. David Karnes, a Republican, thus changing the numbers when he was sworn in on March 11, 1987, to fifty-four Democrats and forty-six Republicans.

f. Sen. Ben Nighthorse Campbell (Colo.) switched from the Democratic to the Republican Party on March 3, 1995, thus changing the numbers to forty-six Democrats and fifty-four Republicans.

g. The number includes New Hampshire Sen. Robert Smith, who left the Republican Party on July 12, 1999.

h. The number includes New York Rep. Michael Forbes, who became a Democrat on July 17, 1999.

Sources: Statistics of the Presidential and Congressional Elections of November 4, 1980, compiled from official sources by Thomas E. Ladd, under direction of Edmund L. Henshaw, Jr., clerk of the House of Representatives (Washington, D.C., 1981); *Congressional Directory* (1983, 1985); *Congressional Quarterly Weekly Report,* November 8, 1986, 2812, 2839, 2843, 2856–57; November 22, 1986; March 14, 1987, 483; November 12, 1988; November 10, 1990; November 7, 1992; November 12, 1994; January 4, 1997, 3; November 7, 1998, 2990.

2

Elections

For the members of the House and Senate, the most vital statistics are those on congressional elections. Whatever their personal goals within Congress, members must first win reelection. Yet, as the dramatic change in party control of the Senate in the 1980 elections and both chambers in the 1994 elections made clear, individual electoral success is not enough—the fate of party colleagues is extraordinarily important in shaping the internal character of Congress and consequently the ability of individual members to accomplish their legislative and political goals.

The two chambers are very closely divided between the parties. The Republicans, apparently ascendant after the 1994 elections, have slipped in 1996 and 1998, though not badly enough to lose their majority. Since the Civil War, a president's party failed to lose seats in a midterm election in only two elections: 1934 and 1998. The surprising Democratic victory in 1998 left the Democrats only six seats shy of regaining control of the House in 2000. They need another six (or five seats and the presidency) to regain control of the Senate.

Turnout in national elections has been on a downward path, albeit fitfully, over the past forty years. (See table 2-1.) Fewer people voted in each subsequent presidential election after 1960 until 1992, when a three-candidate field increased turnout. In 1996 the downward trend returned—less than half of the public voted in the presidential contest, and only 47 percent voted in local House races. In recent midterm elections turnout has been well under 40 percent.

In 1994 the Democrats had controlled the House of Representatives for forty consecutive years, since the 1954 elections in Eisenhower's first term. (See table 2-2.) Throughout most of that period, Republicans did not come close to a majority, although in parts of the mid-1960s and early 1980s they were within striking distance. In 1980 Republicans received 48 percent of the vote, but only 44.1 percent of the seats in the House. That imbalance, in which the majority party enjoys seat margins much more favorable than its vote margins, is common to systems with single-member districts. A gain of a certain percentage of votes in a party's popular vote usually allows it to pick up two or three times that percentage in seats. The 1980 Republican gains cut the Democratic seat bonus to half of what it had been only four years earlier. Unable to translate President Ronald Reagan's popularity into congressional majorities, the GOP in 1988 managed to increase its percentage of the popular vote while simultaneously losing seats.

President Bill Clinton rode into office in 1992 on a note of optimism for the Democratic Party, but that year Democrats received their lowest national percentage in congressional vote totals since 1980. In 1994 the Republicans made the most sizable increase in votes and seats by either party since 1948. The GOP almost eliminated the seat bonus, ended the forty-year Democratic dominance over the chamber, and ushered in the current era of striking competition. In 1996 and 1998 the seat bonus saved the GOP when its vote percentages slid back down. In 1998 with only 48 percent of the vote, the GOP controlled 51.3 percent of the seats.

The long-term Democratic dominance and Republican resurgence depended on several crucial electoral victories. In 1958 the Democrats gained a net of forty-nine House seats and fifteen Senate seats. (See table 2-3.) That gain became part of the bedrock of strength that protected the Democrats' enduring majority until the Republicans picked up twelve Senate seats in 1980 to regain control of the Senate for a brief six-year period. In the House the pattern was different over the same period. The Democratic majority eroded in most years until 1974, when another gain of forty-nine House seats reestablished the Democrats' strong majority, which held and expanded up to the late 1980s, when each party enjoyed only small gains. In 1994 the Republicans shocked the political world by gaining fifty-two House and eight Senate seats, the largest single gain since 1948, when Democrats beat the Do-Nothing Congress, berated by Harry Truman, and gained seventy-five House seats. Republicans now face the pattern the Democrats faced in the 1960s and 1970s. The GOP majority has eroded by a net thirteen seats over the past two elections (counting five party switchers), and now the loss of only six seats separates the GOP from the minority.

The president's party has almost invariably lost House seats in midterm elections. (See table 2-4.) The one notable exception before 1998 occurred during the last major realignment of the party system in 1934. In the early and mid–twentieth century, those midterm elections produced enormous gains for the party out of power. The Senate pattern is different because only one-third of the members stands for election in any given cycle. The president's party has gained Senate seats ten times in midterm elections since the Civil War. In the latter third of the twentieth century, the magnitude of House seat losses diminished. In the five midterm elections before 1994, the average seat loss was only thirteen. But in 1994 the Democrats suffered the greatest midterm loss in more than five decades. That was particularly surprising to observers of Congress because the magnitude of the loss is partially determined by the previous presidential election: larger numbers of candidates elected on the coattails of the president increase the number of midterm losses and vice versa. But in 1992 the Democrats had actually suffered a loss of ten seats—making the huge loss in 1994 a larger shock.

The 1998 elections provided a surprise of a different sort. Whether from anger over Independent Counsel Kenneth Starr's investigation, frustration with the muddled Republican agenda, or contentment with a robust economy, the voters actually handed Clinton the second midterm seat gain for a president's party of the century—approximately one month before he became only the second president in history to be impeached by the House and tried in the Senate.

It is tempting to look at particular dramatic elections and discuss the striking contests and wide swings between the parties, but the stability of Congress may be its most important feature. In no election in the twentieth century has more than 14 percent of the 435 seats actually changed party hands. In 1988 a paltry nine seats changed parties—less than any previous election in American history. But in the early 1990s Congress saw greater turnover and instability: in 1994 sixty seats or 13.8 percent of the body switched party control in the largest shift recorded in table 2-5. By the end of the decade, the pattern of party stability within the districts had returned. (See table 2-5 and figure 2-1.) In addition, despite the impressive advantages of incumbency, parties have in most cases picked up more of their gains not in open seats but in races against incumbents.

In contrast to the small percentage of party change in the House, as many as one-third of the Senate seats up for election in any one year has changed party control. Change is not always the rule, however; in 1990 only one seat changed hands. (See table 2-6 and figure 2-2.) In recent years fewer Senate seats have changed hands and correspondingly fewer incumbents were defeated. The importance of particular elections for long-term party control stands out in table 2-6 as well. Republicans hoped that 1994 would turn out to be a year like both 1958 and 1974 were for the Democrats. The GOP gained Senate seats again in 1996 (while losing House seats) but stalled in the 1998 elections. It remains to be seen whether 1994 was an aberration or the beginning of enduring GOP majorities.

The bulk of House and Senate incumbents who seek reelection usually succeed. (See tables 2-7 and 2-8.) Even landslides in the general election ordinarily lead to the defeat of only 10 percent of the incumbents seeking reelection. A substantial increase in retirements in the 1970s was largely responsible for the relatively high turnover during that period, which was immediately followed by a decade with very low turnover: only twelve House incumbents were defeated in 1986 and 1988. That "permanent Congress" generated outcries from various groups that believed campaign and election rules unfairly favored incumbents. The trend reversed in the early 1990s, however, when relatively high numbers of incumbents lost elections. Election year 1992 saw the largest number of voluntary retirements (sixty-five) from the House in the postwar era. And another forty-three incumbents were defeated (nineteen in primaries, the highest number in years), so that the 1992 elections produced the most turnover in a single election since 1948. The 1998 elections fit the earlier pattern well: only six incumbents were defeated in the general election. And 98.3 percent of those seeking reelection won.

Senate incumbents have never fared quite so well as their House counterparts because the level of competition in statewide races is usually much higher. For instance, in the high-turnover year of 1992, 82.1 percent of senators seeking reelection succeeded, compared with 88.3 percent of House members. In 1986 voters actually defeated more senators than House members for reelection. The only break in that pattern occurred in 1994, when 92.3 percent of the senators seeking reelection won. In recent years the Senate has seen more retirements, particularly on the Democratic side. (See table 2-9.) A record thirteen senators retired in 1996.

Freshman members of the House and Senate worry about their next election, because they know that it is more likely that an incumbent will lose early in his term—although the threat never completely disappears. (See tables 2-10 and 2-11.) In the mid–twentieth century most defeated House incumbents were in their first term: 54

percent of those defeated in 1946 were freshmen; 55 percent lost in 1948; and 60 percent lost in 1966. In the 1970s and 1980s that pattern shifted, and the number of years members served until a defeat was spread much more evenly across the first four terms. In 1992 the largest number of defeated incumbents were in their fifth term. But in 1994 voters ousted thirty-eight members, seventeen of them in their first term. Republicans lost a number of freshmen in 1996, so that the average term of defeated incumbents fell to 2.1, the lowest total since 1986. When seven relatively new incumbents lost in 1998, the average number of terms fell even further—into a tie with the 1986 mark of 1.6.

The Senate pattern is similar in that defeated members are almost always in their first or second term, although the number of defeats has varied much over time. The 1980 election, when seven of the thirteen defeated incumbents were in their third, fourth, or sixth terms, was the only real deviation from that trend.

The proportion of House incumbents who won reelection with at least 60 percent of the major party vote increased from about three-fifths in the 1950s and early 1960s to three-fourths in the 1970s and to almost nine-tenths in the late 1980s. (See table 2-12.) Those occupying the so-called safe seats grew more nervous in the 1990s when more incumbents began to face tougher battles. In 1994 only 64.5 percent reached the 60 percent threshold, fewer than at any time since 1964. By 1998 things had improved for incumbents—75.6 percent of them were reelected with 60 percent or more of the major party vote.

Senators have far less safety than House members, although between 1944 and 1954 Southern senators were elected 100 percent of the time with a "safe" margin. By the close of the 1970s only 57.1 percent of Southern senators were so safe. (See table 2-13.) Ironically, margins for the rest of the country increased approximately fifteen points over the same period. The 1980s and 1990s have seen fewer and fewer senators win by wide margins. In 1996 not a single Northern senator won with 60 percent of the major party vote.

Viewed from the perspective of congressional careers, elections still pose a significant challenge to incumbents. More than 75 percent of the senators and almost 60 percent of the representatives serving in the 106th Congress received less than 55 percent of the vote, and even more of them less than 60 percent, in at least one election. (See table 2-14.) Moreover, when we examine the conditions of initial election to Congress, we find that many representatives and a majority of senators have either defeated incumbents or replaced retiring incumbents of the other party. (See table 2-15.)

Since 1956, when the Democrats in the House and Senate withstood Dwight D. Eisenhower's sweeping victory in the presidential election, more than one-fourth of all congressional districts have supported a presidential candidate of one party and a House candidate of the other. (See table 2-16.) The proportion of districts with split results reached a peak in 1972, when Richard Nixon received 60.8 percent of the presidential vote while his party's candidates won only 46.4 percent of the congressional vote so that the Democrats had a solid majority in the House. In 1992 the percentage of districts with split-ticket results fell to its lowest level since 1952 and rebounded slightly in 1996.

A president's ability to claim long coattails depends on both the size of his victory and the number of seats his party gains in Congress. Presidents John F. Kennedy and Jimmy Carter lost on both counts: the Republicans actually gained twenty-two House seats in 1960 and held their ground in 1976, while both victorious Democratic presidents ran ahead of Democratic representatives in only twenty-two districts. (See table 2-17.) In 1972 Richard Nixon ran ahead of a majority of the Republicans elected to the House, but that was small consolation in view of his failure to pull a sizable bloc of new Republicans into the House. In contrast, Lyndon Johnson could claim credit for dramatically increasing his party's margin in Congress. His reward was the Great Society legislation of 1965 and 1966.

In 1980 Ronald Reagan's presidential victory was accompanied by impressive Republican gains in the House but fell short of the number needed to take control. Moreover, Reagan ran behind most of his party colleagues in the House. The more important manifestation of a Reagan tide was thought to be in the Senate, where a total of 50,000 votes accounted for seven Republican victories and, as a consequence, majority status. Reagan's 1984 landslide in the presidential sweepstakes, however, left barely a trace in the Senate and House, a result that underscored the absence of presidential coattails. The Democrats suffered a similar fate in 1992 by losing seats in the House while winning back the presidency after twelve years of Republican rule. President Clinton fared somewhat better in 1996, although Democrats failed to win enough seats to reclaim a House majority.

Since the 1950s we have witnessed a substantial increase in the impact of local forces in congressional elections. Although the United States has never had a uniform swing across constituencies as Britain has, it is still extremely difficult to make national interpretations of the results of U.S. congressional elections. (See table 2-18.) Election returns at the district level have often diverged from the national returns. Those figures suggest an electoral base for the increasingly individualized behavior in the House of Representatives. The range in the swing across districts increased markedly in the 1960s and 1970s, and the variance, which measures the extent to which changes in local returns differ from the change in national returns, more than doubled in that period. After a plateau in the 1980s the variance seems to have diminished somewhat in the 1990s. The 1994 elections were widely seen as a partisan contest of ideologies, but the range of variation across districts was still wide. The highly partisan nature of the two most recent elections has driven the variance back down to its lowest levels since the 1950s.

The decline in the proportion of party-line voters in House elections during the late 1960s and 1970s is consistent with the view that voting became increasingly candidate-centered. (See table 2-19.) Yet the resurgence of party-line voting in the past three elections suggests that the electorate retains the capacity to respond in highly partisan ways to national political events, like the Contract with America and the Clinton scandals.

Table 2-1 Turnout in Presidential and House Elections, 1930–1998 (percentage of voting age population)

Year	Presidential elections	House elections
1930	—	33.7
1932	52.4	49.7
1934	—	41.4
1936	56.9	53.5
1938	—	44.0
1940	58.9	55.4
1942	—	32.5
1944	56.0	52.7
1946	—	37.1
1948	51.1	48.1
1950	—	41.1
1952	61.6	57.6
1954	—	41.7
1956	59.3	55.9
1958	—	43.0
1960	62.8	58.8
1962	—	47.6
1964	61.9	58.2
1966	—	48.6
1968	60.9	55.3
1970	—	46.8
1972	55.2	50.1
1974	—	38.8
1976	53.5	48.9
1978	—	37.8
1980	52.6	47.4
1982	—	40.1
1984	53.1	47.6
1986	—	36.4
1988	50.1	45.0
1990	—	36.5
1992	55.2	50.8
1994	—	38.8
1996	49.0	45.9
1998	—	36.1

Sources: U.S. Bureau of the Census, *Statistical Abstract of the United States* (Washington, D.C.: Government Printing Office, 1930–1958); for 1960–1998 numbers were compiled by Curtis Gans of the Committee for the Study of the American Electorate.

Figure 2-1 House Seats That Changed Party, 1954–1998

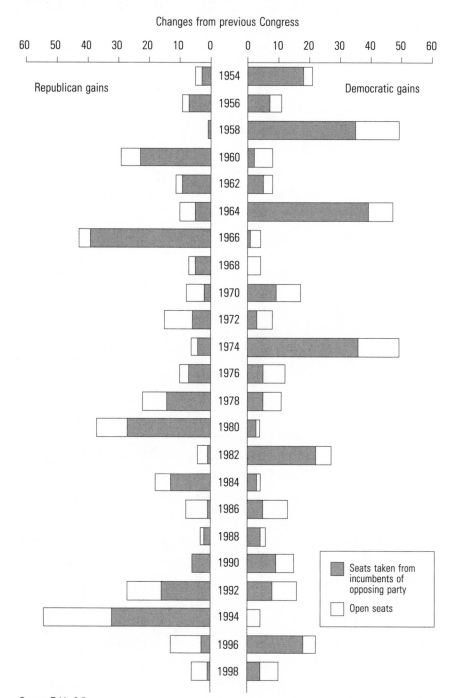

Changes from previous Congress

Republican gains

Democratic gains

Seats taken from incumbents of opposing party

Open seats

Source: Table 2-5.

Table 2-2 Popular Vote and House Seats Won by Party, 1946–1998

| Year | Democratic candidates | | Republican candidates | | Change from last election[a] | | Difference between Democratic percentage of seats and votes won |
	Percentage of all votes[b]	Percentage of seats won	Percentage of all votes[b]	Percentage of seats won	Percentage of major party votes	Percentage of seats won	
1946	44.3	43.3	53.5	56.7	6.4R	12.8R	-1.0
1948	51.6	60.6	45.4	39.4	7.9D	17.3D	9.0
1950	48.9	54.0	48.9	46.0	3.2R	6.6R	5.1
1952	49.2	49.1	49.3	50.9	0.1R	4.9R	-0.1
1954	52.1	53.3	47.0	46.7	2.6D	4.2D	1.2
1956	50.7	53.8	48.7	46.2	1.5R	0.5D	3.1
1958	55.5	64.9	43.6	35.1	5.0D	11.1D	9.4
1960	54.4	60.0	44.8	40.0	1.2R	4.9R	5.6
1962	52.1	59.4	47.1	40.6	2.3R	0.6R	7.3
1964	56.9	67.8	42.4	32.2	4.8D	8.4D	10.9
1966	50.5	57.0	48.0	43.0	6.0R	10.8R	6.5
1968	50.0	55.9	48.2	44.1	0.3R	1.1R	5.9
1970	53.0	58.6	44.5	41.4	3.4D	2.7D	5.6
1972	51.7	55.8	46.4	44.2	1.7R	2.8R	4.1
1974	57.1	66.9	40.5	33.1	5.8D	11.1D	9.8
1976	56.2	67.1	42.1	32.9	1.3R	0.2D	10.9
1978	53.4	63.7	44.7	36.3	2.8R	3.4R	10.3
1980	50.4	55.9	48.0	44.1	3.2R	7.8R	5.5
1982	55.2	61.8	43.3	38.2	5.2D	5.9D	6.6
1984	52.1	58.2	47.0	41.8	4.1R	3.6R	6.1

1986	54.5	59.3	44.6	40.7	2.4D	1.2D	4.8
1988	53.3	59.8	45.5	40.2	1.1R	0.5D	6.5
1990	52.9	61.4	45.0	38.4[c]	0.1D	1.6D	8.5
1992	50.8	59.3	45.6	40.5[c]	1.4R	2.1R	8.5
1994	45.4	46.9	52.4	52.9[c]	6.3R	12.4R	-1.5
1996	48.5	47.6	48.9	52.2[c]	3.4D	0.7D	-0.9
1998	47.1	48.5	48.0	51.3[c]	0.7R	1.0D	0.6

a. The data show the percentage-point increase over the previous election in votes or seats won by Republicans (R) or Democrats (D).

b. Republican and Democratic percentages of all votes exclude districts in which candidates ran unopposed and no vote was recorded: for 1978, eight districts from Arkansas, Florida, and Oklahoma; for 1980, twelve districts from Arkansas, Florida, Louisiana, and Oklahoma; for 1982, eleven districts from Florida and Louisiana; for 1984, sixteen districts from Arkansas, Florida, and Louisiana; for 1986, fourteen districts from Florida, Louisiana, and Oklahoma; for 1988, sixteen districts from Florida and Louisiana; for 1990, twelve districts from Florida and Louisiana; for 1994, thirteen districts from Florida and Louisiana; for 1996, twelve districts from Florida, Louisiana, Kentucky, West Virginia, and Georgia; for 1998, twenty-one districts from Arkansas, Florida, and Louisiana.

c. For 1990–1998, the total percentage of seats won—Democratic and Republican—does not equal one hundred owing to the election of Bernard Sanders (I-Vt.).

Sources: Congressional Quarterly Weekly Report, June 11, 1977, 1141; March 31, 1979, 571; April 25, 1981, 713; November 11, 1982, 2817–25; February 19, 1983, 387; April 15, 1985, 687; March 14, 1987, 484; May 6, 1989, 1063; February 23, 1991, 487; April 17, 1993, 965–68; April 15, 1995, 1076–79; February 15, 1997, 444; Thomas E. Mann and Norman J. Ornstein, eds., *The American Elections of 1982* (Washington, D.C.: American Enterprise Institute, 1983). For 1998, the data were computed from official election returns.

Table 2-3 Net Party Gains in House and Senate Seats, General and Special Elections, 1946–1998

Year	General elections[a] House	General elections[a] Senate	Special elections[b] House	Special elections[b] Senate
			2R (13)	3R (8)
1946	56R	13R		
			0 (16)	0 (3)
1948	75D	9D		
			0 (10)	2R (6)
1950	28R	5R		
			3R (13)	2R (4)
1952	22R	1R		
			2D (8)	0 (9)
1954	19D	2D		
			0 (2)	2R (3)
1956	2D	1D		
			0 (10)	1D (4)
1958	49D	15D		
			1R (7)	1D (3)
1960	22R	2R		
			0 (12)	0 (6)
1962	1R	3D		
			2R (9)	0 (2)
1964	37D	1D		
			0 (8)	1R (3)
1966	47R	4R		
			1R (5)	0 (0)
1968	5R	6R		
			3D (9)	0 (2)
1970	12D	2R		
			0 (9)	0 (2)
1972	12R	2D		
			4D (10)	0 (0)
1974	49D	4D		
			0 (6)	1D (1)
1976	1D	0		
			4R (6)	1R (2)
1978	15R	3R		
			1R (6)	0 (0)
1980	34R	12R		
			1D (8)	0 (0)
1982	26D	1R		
			1R (7)	1R (1)
1984	14R	2D		
			0 (4)	1D (1)
1986	5D	8D		
			1R (6)	0 (0)

	General elections[a]		Special elections[b]	
Year	House	Senate	House	Senate
1988	2D	0		
			1D (11)	0 (1)
1990	9D	1D		
			1D (6)	2D (3)[c]
1992	10R	0		
			2R (7)	1R (2)
1994	52R	8R[d]		
			1R (5)	1D (1)
1996	3D[e]	2R		
			0 (8)	0
1998	4D	0		

Note: D indicates Democrats; R indicates Republicans.

a. The general-election figure is the difference between the number of seats won by the party gaining seats in that election and the number of seats won by that party in the preceding general election.

b. The special-election figure is the net shift in seats held by the major parties as a result of special elections held between the two general elections. The figure does not include special elections held on the day of the general election. The number of special elections appears in parentheses.

c. The total number of special elections (3) includes the special election of Dianne Feinstein (D-Calif.) to fill the seat to which John Seymour was temporarily appointed. The special election was held at the same time as the general election (November 3, 1992).

d. Sen. Richard Shelby (Ala.) switched from the Democratic to the Republican Party the day after the election and brought the total Republican gain to nine.

e. Between the two elections, Reps. Greg Laughlin (Tex.), Nathan Deal (Ga.), W. J. Tauzin (La.), Mike Parker (Miss.), and Jimmy Hayes (La.) switched parties. When we consider those switches and special-election Republican gains, the total 1996 Democratic gain was nine seats.

Sources: Statistics of the Congressional Election of November 7, 1978 (Washington, D.C.: Government Printing Office, 1979), 45; *Congressional Quarterly Almanac,* vols. 2–50 (Washington, D.C.: Congressional Quarterly, 1946–1994); *Congressional Quarterly's Guide to U.S. Elections* (Washington, D.C.: Congressional Quarterly, 1975); *Congressional Quarterly Weekly Report,* November 8, 1986; November 12, 1988; and conversations with the Federal Election Commission. For 1992: *National Journal,* November 7, 1992, 2555; *Congressional Quarterly Almanac 1991.* For 1993–1994: *Congressional Quarterly Almanac 1993; Congressional Quarterly Weekly Report,* various issues, 1994; Congressional Quarterly Research Service. For 1995–1998: *Congressional Quarterly Weekly Report,* various issues.

Table 2-4 Losses by the President's Party in Midterm Elections, 1862–1998

Year	Party holding presidency	President's party gain/loss of seats in House	President's party gain/loss of seats in Senate
1862	R	−3	8
1866	R	−2	0
1870	R	−31	−4
1874	R	−96	−8
1878	R	−9	−6
1882	R	−33	3
1886	D	−12	3
1890	R	−85	0
1894	D	−116	−5
1898	R	−21	7
1902	R	9[a]	2
1906	R	−28	3
1910	R	−57	−10
1914	D	−59	5
1918	D	−19	−6
1922	R	−75	−8
1926	R	−10	−6
1930	R	−49	−8
1934	D	9	10
1938	D	−71	−6
1942	D	−55	−9
1946	D	−45	−12
1950	D	−29	−6
1954	R	−18	−1
1958	R	−48	−13
1962	D	−4	3
1966	D	−47	−4
1970	R	−12	2
1974	R	−48	−5
1978	D	−15	−3
1982	R	−26	1
1986	R	−5	−8
1990	R	−8	−1
1994	D	−52	−8[b]
1998	D	5	0

Note: Each entry is the difference between the number of seats won by the president's party in that midterm election and the number of seats won by that party in the preceding general election. Because of changes in the overall number of seats in the Senate and House, in the number of seats won by third parties, and in the number of vacancies, a Republican loss does not always precisely match a Democratic gain, or vice versa.

a. Although the Republicans gained nine seats in the 1902 elections, they actually lost ground to the Democrats, who gained twenty-five seats after the increase in the total number of representatives after the 1900 census.

b. Sen. Richard Shelby (Ala.) switched from the Democratic to the Republican Party the day following the election, so that the total loss was nine seats.

Sources: Statistics of the Congressional Election of November 7, 1978, 44–45; Thomas E. Mann and Norman J. Ornstein, "The 1982 Election: What Will It Mean?" *Public Opinion,* June/July 1981, 49; *Congressional Quarterly Almanac,* vols. 10–40; *Congressional Quarterly Weekly Report,* November 8, 1986; November 10, 1990; November 7, 1998, 2990; *National Journal,* November 12, 1994.

Table 2-5   House Seats That Changed Party, 1954–1998

Year	Total changes	Incumbent defeated		Open seat	
		D→R	R→D	D→R	R→D
1954	26	3	18	2	3
1956	20	7	7	2	4
1958	50	1	35	0	14
1960	37	23	2	6	6
1962	19	9	5	2	3
1964	57	5	39	5	8
1966	47	39	1	4	3
1968	11	5	0	2	4
1970	25	2	9	6	8
1972	23	6	3	9	5
1974	55	4	36	2	13
1976	22	7	5	3	7
1978	33	14	5	8	6
1980	41	27	3	10	1
1982	31	1	22	3	5
1984	22	13	3	5	1
1986	21	1	5	7	8
1988	9	2	4	1	2
1990	21	6	9	0	6
1992	43	16	8	11	8
1994	60	34	0	22	4
1996	35	3	18	10	4
1998	17	1	5	5	6

Note: D indicates Democrat; R indicates Republican. This table reflects shifts in party control of seats from immediately before to immediately after the November elections. It does not include party gains resulting from the creation of new districts and does not account for situations in which two districts were reduced to one, thus forcing incumbents to run against each other.

Sources: Congressional Quarterly Almanac, vols. 10–40; *Congressional Quarterly Weekly Report,* November 10, 1984, 2900; November 8, 1986, 2844; November 12, 1988, 3270; November 10, 1990, 3801; *National Journal,* November 7, 1992, 2555; November 12, 1994, 2652; November 9, 1996; November 7, 1998, 2604.

Table 2-6 Senate Seats That Changed Party, 1954–1998

Year	Total changes	Incumbent defeated		Open seat	
		D→R	R→D	D→R	R→D
1954	8	2	4	1	1
1956	8	1	3	3	1
1958	13	0	11	0	2
1960	2	1	0	1	0
1962	8	2	3	0	3
1964	4	1	3	0	0
1966	3	1	0	2	0
1968	9	4	0	3	2
1970	6	3	2	1	0
1972	10	1	4	3	2
1974	6	0	2	1	3
1976	14	5	4	2	3
1978	13	5	2	3	3
1980	12	9	0	3	0
1982	4	1	1	1	1
1984	4	1	2	0	1
1986	10	0	7	1	2
1988	7	1	3	2	1
1990	1	0	1	0	0
1992	4	2	2	0	0
1994	8[a]	2	0	6	0
1996	4	0	1	3	0
1998	6	1	2	2	1

Note: D indicates Democrat; R indicates Republican. This table reflects shifts in party control of seats from immediately before to immediately after the November election.

a. Sen. Richard Shelby (Ala.) switched from the Democratic to the Republican Party the day after the election and brought the total change to nine.

Sources: Congressional Quarterly Almanac, vols. 10–40; *National Journal,* November 10, 1984, 2137, 2147; *Congressional Quarterly Weekly Report,* November 8, 1986, 2813; November 12, 1988, 3264; November 10, 1990, 3825; *National Journal,* November 7, 1992, 2555; November 12, 1994, 2635; November 9, 1996; November 7, 1998, 2609.

Table 2-7 House Incumbents Retired, Defeated, or Reelected, 1946–1998

Year	Retired[a]	Total seeking reelection	Defeated in primaries	Defeated in general election	Total reelected	Percentage of those seeking reelection	Reelected as percentage of House membership
1946	32	398	18	52	328	82.4	75.4
1948	29	400	15	68	317	79.3	72.9
1950	29	400	6	32	362	90.5	83.2
1952	42	389	9	26	354	91.0	81.4
1954	24	407	6	22	379	93.1	87.1
1956	21	411	6	16	389	94.6	89.4
1958	33	396	3	37	356	89.9	81.8
1960	26	405	5	25	375	92.6	86.2
1962	24	402	12	22	368	91.5	84.6
1964	33	397	8	45	344	86.6	79.1
1966	22	411	8	41	362	88.1	83.2
1968	23	409	4	9	396	96.8	91.0
1970	29	401	10	12	379	94.5	87.1
1972	40	393	11	13	365	93.6	83.9
1974	43	391	8	40	343	87.7	78.9
1976	47	384	3	13	368	95.8	84.6
1978	49	382	5	19	358	93.7	82.3
1980	34	398	6	31	361	90.7	83.0
1982	40	393	10	29	354	90.1	81.4
1984	22	411	3	16	392	95.4	90.1
1986	40	394	3	6	385	97.7	88.5
1988	23	409	1	6	402	98.3	92.4
1990	27	406	1	15	390	96.0	89.7
1992	65	368	19	24	325	88.3	74.7
1994	48	387	4	34	349	90.2	80.0
1996	49	384	2	21	361	94.0	83.0
1998	33	402	1	6	395	98.3	90.1

a. This entry does not include persons who died or resigned before the election.

Sources: Congressional Quarterly Weekly Report, January 12, 1980, 81; April 5, 1980, 908; November 8, 1980, 3320–21; November 10, 1984, 2900; October 11, 1986, 2398; November 8, 1986, 2844; November 12, 1988, 3270; November 7, 1992, 3579; *National Journal*, November 6, 1982, 1881; November 10, 1984, 2147; November 10, 1990, 2719; November 12, 1994, 2650–51; November 9, 1997; November 7, 1998.

Table 2-8   Senate Incumbents Retired, Defeated, or Reelected, 1946–1998

Year	Retired[a]	Total seeking reelection	Defeated in primaries	Defeated in general election	Total reelected	Reelected as percentage of those seeking reelection
1946	9	30	6	7	17	56.7
1948	8	25	2	8	15	60.0
1950	4	32	5	5	22	68.8
1952	4	31	2	9	20	64.5
1954	6	32	2	6	24	75.0
1956	6	29	0	4	25	86.2
1958	6	28	0	10	18	64.3
1960	5	29	0	1	28	96.6
1962	4	35	1	5	29	82.9
1964	2	33	1	4	28	84.8
1966	3	32	3	1	28	87.5
1968	6	28	4	4	20	71.4
1970	4	31	1	6	24	77.4
1972	6	27	2	5	20	74.1
1974	7	27	2	2	23	85.2
1976	8	25	0	9	16	64.0
1978	10	25	3	7	15	60.0
1980	5	29	4	9	16	55.2
1982	3	30	0	2	28	93.3
1984	4	29	0	3	26	89.6
1986	6	28	0	7	21	75.0
1988	6	27	0	4	23	85.2
1990	3	32	0	1	31	96.9
1992	7	28	1	4	23	82.1
1994	9	26	0	2	24	92.3
1996	13	21	1[b]	1	19	90.5
1998	5	29	0	3	26	89.7

a. This entry does not include persons who died or resigned before the election.
b. Sheila Frahm, appointed to fill Robert Dole's term, is counted as an incumbent in Kansas's "B" seat.

Sources: Congressional Quarterly Weekly Report, January 12, 1980, 81; April 5, 1980, 908; November 8, 1980, 3302; November 6, 1982, 2791; November 10, 1984, 2905; October 11, 1986, 2398; November 8, 1986, 2813; November 12, 1988; November 10, 1990; November 7, 1992, 3557; November 7, 1998; *National Journal,* November 12, 1994; November 9, 1996.

Table 2-9   House and Senate Retirements by Party, 1930–1998

	House		Senate	
Year	D	R	D	R
1930	8	15	2	5
1932	16	23	1	1
1934	29	9	3	1
1936	29	3	4	2
1938	21	5	3	1
1940	16	6	1	2
1942	20	12	0	0
1944	17	5	3	2
1946	17	15	4	3
1948	17	12	3	4
1950	12	17	3	1
1952	25	17	2	1
1954	11	13	1	1
1956	7	13	4	1
1958	6	27	0	6
1960	11	15	3	1
1962	10	14	2	2
1964	17	16	1	1
1966	14	8	1	2
1968	13	10	4	3
1970	11	19	3	1
1972	20	20	3	3
1974	23	21	3	4
1976	31	16	4	4
1978	31	18	4	5
1980	21	13	2	3
1982	19	21	1	2
1984	9	13	2	2
1986	20	20	3	3
1988	10	13	3	3
1990	10	17	0	3
1992	41	24	4	3
1994	28	20	6	3
1996	28	21	8	5
1998	17	16	3	2

Note: These figures include members who did not run again for the office they held and members who sought other offices; the figures do not include members who died or resigned before the end of the particular Congress.

Sources: Mildred L. Amer, "Information on the Number of House Retirees, 1930–1992," Congressional Research Service, Staff Report, Washington, D.C., May 19, 1992; *Congressional Quarterly Weekly Report,* November 8, 1980, 3320–21; October 11, 1986, 2398; November 12, 1988; November 10, 1990; November 7, 1998, 2984; *National Journal,* November 6, 1982, 1881; November 11, 1984, 2147; November 10, 1990; November 7, 1992; November 12, 1994; November 9, 1996.

Table 2-10 Defeated House Incumbents, 1946–1998

Election	Party	Incumbents lost	Average terms	Consecutive terms served						
				1	2	3	1–3	4–6	7–9	10+
1946	Democrat	62	2.7	35	5	4	44	11	5	2
	Republican	7	3.6	2	0	1	3	3	1	0
	Total	69	2.8	37	5	5	47	14	6	2
1948	Democrat[a]	9	2.7	4	1	1	6	3	0	0
	Republican	73	2.2	41	3	12	56	14	2	1
	Total	82	2.2	45	4	13	62	17	2	1
1958	Democrat[b]	6	5.0	1	1	0	2	2	1	1
	Republican	34	4.3	9	0	4	13	14	6	1
	Total	40	4.4	10	1	4	15	16	7	2
1966	Democrat	43	3.3	26	6	0	32	4	1	6
	Republican	2	11.0	1	0	0	1	0	0	1
	Total	45	3.7	27	6	0	33	4	1	7
1974	Democrat	9	4.7	1	1	1	3	3	2	1
	Republican	39	3.8	11	2	6	19	15	2	3
	Total	48	3.9	12	3	7	22	18	4	4
1978	Democrat	19	4.0	3	8	2	13	2	1	3
	Republican	5	5.4	2	0	0	2	2	0	1
	Total	24	4.2	5	8	2	15	4	1	4
1980	Democrat	32	5.2	5	2	10	17	5	4	6
	Republican	5	5.3	1	0	1	2	1	1	1
	Total	37	5.2	6	2	11	19	6	5	7
1982	Democrat	4	2.9	1	0	1	2	2	0	0
	Republican[c]	23	3.0	12	3	2	17	2	2	2
	Total	27	3.0	13	3	3	19	4	2	2
1984	Democrat	16	4.1	6	1	2	9	4	1	2
	Republican	3	3.7	0	0	2	2	1	0	0
	Total	19	4.1	6	1	4	11	5	1	2

Year	Party									
1986	Democrat	3	1.8	2	0	0	2	1	0	0
	Republican	6	1.5	4	1	1	6	0	0	0
	Total	9	1.6	6	1	1	8	1	0	0
1988	Democrat	2	12.0	0	0	0	0	0	0	2
	Republican	5	1.6	2	3	0	5	0	0	0
	Total	7	4.6	2	3	0	5	0	0	2
1990	Democrat	6	6.3	0	1	0	1	3	1	1
	Republican[d]	10	3.6	2	3	0	5	4	1	0
	Total	16	4.6	2	4	0	6	7	2	1
1992	Democrat	30	5.6	2	1	4	7	12	10	1
	Republican	13	6.8	2	0	2	4	1	6	2
	Total	43	6.0	4	1	6	11	13	16	3
1994	Democrat	37	4.2	16	3	5	24	7	2	4
	Republican	1	1.0	1	0	0	1	0	0	0
	Total	38	4.1	17	3	5	25	7	2	4
1996	Democrat[e]	3	4.7	1	0	1	2	0	0	1
	Republican	18	1.8	12	4	1	17	0	1	0
	Total	21	2.1	13	4	2	19	0	1	1
1998	Democrat	1	1.0	1	0	0	1	0	0	0
	Republican	6	1.7	3	2	1	6	0	0	0
	Total	7	1.6	4	2	1	7	0	0	0

Note: The 1966 and 1982 numbers do not include races where incumbents ran against incumbents owing to redistricting. We counted incumbents who lost in the primary as their party's incumbent but then ran in the general election as a write-in or third-party candidate as an incumbent loss.

a. This includes Leo Isacson (N.Y.), who was a member of the American Labor Party.

b. This includes Vincent Delley (N.J.), who was elected as a Republican but switched to a Democrat. He ran for reelection as an Independent.

c. This includes Eugene Atkinson (Pa.), who began his House service on January 3, 1979, as a Democrat. He became a Republican on October 14, 1981.

d. This includes Donald Lukens (Ohio), who was defeated in the primary and then resigned on October 24, 1990, and Bill Grant (Fla.), who began his House service on January 6, 1987, as a Democrat but later switched parties. The Republican Conference let his seniority count from 1987.

e. One Democratic incumbent, who served more than ten terms in office, was defeated.

Sources: 1946, 1948, 1958, 1966, 1974, 1977–1993, *Congressional Quarterly Almanac; National Journal*, November 12, 1994; November 9, 1996; and November 7, 1998; *Biographical Directory of the United States Congress 1774–1989*.

Table 2-11 Defeated Senate Incumbents, 1946–1998

Election	Party	Incumbents lost	Average terms	Consecutive terms served					
				1	2	3	4	5	6+
1946	Democrat	11	1.6	7	2	1	1	0	0
	Republican	2	4.0	0	0	0	2	0	0
	Total	13	2.0	7	2	1	3	0	0
1948	Democrat	2	1.5	1	1	0	0	0	0
	Republican	8	1.0	8	0	0	0	0	0
	Total	10	1.1	9	1	0	0	0	0
1958	Republican	10	1.4	6	4	0	0	0	0
	Total	10	1.4	6	4	0	0	0	0
1966	Democrat	4	2.0	2	0	2	0	0	0
	Total	4	2.0	2	0	2	0	0	0
1974	Democrat	2	3.0	1	0	0	0	1	0
	Republican	2	1.5	1	1	0	0	0	0
	Total	4	2.2	2	1	0	0	1	0
1978	Democrat	7	0.9	6	0	1	0	0	0
	Republican	3	2.7	0	2	0	1	0	0
	Total	10	1.4	6	2	1	1	0	0
1980	Democrat	12	2.4	5	1	3	2	0	1
	Republican	1	4.0	0	0	0	1	0	0
	Total	13	2.6	5	1	3	3	0	1
1982	Democrat	1	4.0	0	0	0	1	0	0
	Republican	1	1.0	1	0	0	0	0	0
	Total	2	2.5	1	0	0	1	0	0

Year	Party											
1984	Democrat	1	2.0	0	0	0	0	0	0	0	0	0
	Republican	2	2.0	1	1	1	0	0	0	0	0	0
	Total	3	2.0	1	1	1	0	0	0	0	0	0
1986	Republican[a]	7	0.9	7	0	0	0	0	0	0	0	0
	Total	7	0.9	7	0	0	0	0	0	0	0	0
1988	Democrat	1	2.0	0	1	0	0	0	0	0	0	0
	Republican	3	1.4	2	0	1	0	0	0	0	0	0
	Total	4	1.6	2	1	1	0	0	0	0	0	0
1990	Republican	1	2.0	0	1	0	0	0	0	0	0	0
	Total	1	2.0	0	1	0	0	0	0	0	0	0
1992	Democrat	3	1.3	2	1	0	0	0	0	0	0	0
	Republican	2	1.2	1	1	0	0	0	0	0	0	0
	Total	5	1.3	3	2	0	0	0	0	0	0	0
1994	Democrat	2	1.8	1	1	1	0	0	0	0	0	0
	Total	2	1.8	1	1	1	0	0	0	0	0	0
1996	Republican	2	2.0	1	1	1	0	0	0	0	0	0
	Total	2	2.0	1	1	1	0	0	0	0	0	0
1998	Democrat	1	1.0	1	0	0	0	0	0	0	0	0
	Republican	2	2.0	1	1	0	0	0	0	0	0	0
	Total	3	1.7	2	1	0	0	0	0	0	0	0

a. This includes James Broyhill (N.C.), who was appointed on July 14, 1986, until November 4, 1986. He lost to Terry Sanford, who took over the seat on November 5, 1986.

Sources: 1946, 1948, 1958, 1966, 1974, 1977–1993, *Congressional Quarterly Almanac; National Journal,* November 12, 1994; November 9, 1996; November 7, 1998; *Biographical Directory of the United States Congress 1774–1989.*

Table 2-12   House Elections Won with 60 Percent or More of the Major Party Vote, 1956–1998

Year	Number of incumbents running in general election	Percentage of incumbents reelected with at least 60 percent of the major party vote
1956	403	59.1
1958	390	63.1
1960	400	58.9
1962	376	63.6
1964	388	58.5
1966	401	67.7
1968	397	72.2
1970	389	77.3
1972	373	77.8
1974	383	66.4
1976	381	71.9
1978	377	78.0
1980	392	72.9
1982	383	68.9
1984	406	74.6
1986	391	86.4
1988	407	88.5
1990	406	76.4
1992	349	65.6
1994	383	64.5
1996	383	73.6
1998	401	75.6

Sources: Albert D. Cover and David R. Mayhew, "Congressional Dynamics and the Decline of Competitive Congressional Elections," in *Congress Reconsidered,* 2d ed., ed. Lawrence C. Dodd and Bruce I. Oppenheimer (Washington, D.C.: CQ Press, 1981); *Congressional Quarterly Weekly Report,* April 25, 1981, 717–25; February 19, 1983, 386–94; April 13, 1985, 689–95; March 14, 1987, 486–93; November 12, 1988; February 23, 1991, 493–500; Thomas E. Mann and Norman J. Ornstein, eds., *The American Elections of 1982* (Washington, D.C.: American Enterprise Institute, 1983); *Congressional Quarterly Weekly Report,* April 17, 1993, 973–80; April 15, 1995, 1090–97; February 15, 1997, 447–55; November 7, 1998.

Table 2-13   Senate Elections Won with 60 Percent or More of the Major
Party Vote, 1944–1998

Election period	Number of incumbents running in general election	Percentage of incumbents reelected with at least 60 percent of the major party vote[a]		
		South	North	Total U.S.
1944–1948	61	100.0	22.9	39.3
1950–1954	76	100.0	18.3	35.5
1956–1960	84	95.5	24.2	42.9
1962–1966	86	70.0	36.4	44.2
1968–1972	74	71.4	38.3	44.6
1974–1978	70	57.1	37.5	41.4
1980–1984[b]	84	63.3	51.9	54.1
1986–1990	87	68.2	53.9	57.5
1992–1996	72	50.0	32.1	36.6
1998	34	50.0	60.0	58.1

a. For the purposes of this table, senators appointed to the Senate are not considered incumbents in the elections just after appointment.
b. Includes two Democratic incumbents from Louisiana, who, by winning more than 50 percent of the vote in that state's all-party primary, avoided a general-election contest. In 1980 Russell Long won 59.8 percent of the vote, and in 1984 J. Bennett Johnston won 86 percent of the vote.

Sources: Cover and Mayhew, "Congressional Dynamics"; *Congressional Quarterly Weekly Report,* April 25, 1981, 717–25; February 19, 1983, 386–94; April 13, 1985, 689–95; March 14, 1987, 484–93; November 12, 1988; February 23, 1991, 493–500; April 17, 1993, 973–80; April 15, 1995, 1090–97; *National Journal*, November 9, 1996; November 7, 1998.

Table 2-14   Marginal Races among Members of the 106th Congress, 1998

Chamber	Members who ever won a congressional election by 60 percent or less		Members who ever won a congressional election by 55 percent or less	
	Number	Percentage	Number	Percentage
House	338	77.7	257	59.1
Senate	94	94.0	78	78.0

Sources: The Almanac of American Politics, various issues, and *Politics in America,* various issues.

Table 2-15 Conditions of Initial Election for Members of the 106th Congress, 1998

Condition	House				Senate		
	Democrats	Republicans	Total	Percentage of entire house	Democrats	Republicans	Total
Defeated incumbent							
In primary	12	4	16	3.7	2	1	3
In general election	40	49	89	20.5	17	11	28
Succeeded retiring incumbent							
Of same party	103	90	193	44.4	19	23	42
Of other party	29	56	85	19.5	7	19	26
Succeeded deceased incumbent							
Of same party	5	6	11	2.5	0	0	0
Of other party	1	5	6	1.4	0	1	1
Defeated candidate in general election who had earlier defeated incumbent in primary	1	3	4	0.9	0	0	0
New districts	20	10	30	6.9	0	0	0
Total	211	223	434[a]	100.0	45	55	100

Note: Percentages do not add to 100.0 because of rounding.

a. The total does not include Bernard Sanders (I-Vt.).

Sources: Congressional Quarterly Almanac, vols. 11–39; *Congressional Directory* (Washington, D.C.: Government Printing Office, 1981, 1983, 1985); Alan Ehrenhalt, ed., *Politics in America* (Washington, D.C.: Congressional Quarterly, various years); Michael Barone and Grant Ujifusa, *The Almanac of American Politics* (Washington, D.C.: National Journal, various years); *Congressional Quarterly Weekly Report,* various issues.

Table 2-16 Ticket Splitting between Presidential and House Candidates, 1900–1996

Year	Districts[a]	Districts with split results[b]	
		Number	Percentage
1900	295	10	3.4
1904	310	5	1.6
1908	314	21	6.7
1912	333	84	25.2
1916	333	35	10.5
1920	344	11	3.2
1924	356	42	11.8
1928	359	68	18.9
1932	355	50	14.1
1936	361	51	14.1
1940	362	53	14.6
1944	367	41	11.2
1948	422	90	21.3
1952	435	84	19.3
1956	435	130	29.9
1960	437	114	26.1
1964	435	145	33.3
1968	435	139	32.0
1972	435	192	44.1
1976	435	124	28.5
1980	435	143	32.8
1984	435	190	43.7
1988	435	148	34.0
1992	435	100	23.0
1996	435	110	25.5

a. Before 1952 complete data are not available on every congressional district.
b. These are congressional districts carried by a presidential candidate of one party and a House candidate of another party.

Sources: Congressional Quarterly Weekly Report, April 22, 1978, 972; April 12, 1997, 862; Walter Dean Burnham, *Critical Elections* (New York: Norton, 1970), 109; Michael Barone and Grant Ujifusa, *The Almanac of American Politics 1982* (Washington, D.C.: Barone and Co., 1981); Michael Barone and Grant Ujifusa, *The Almanac of American Politics 1985* (Washington, D.C.: National Journal, 1984); *National Journal,* April 29, 1989, 1048–54; May 29, 1993, 1285–91.

Table 2-17   District Voting for President and Representative, 1952–1996

Year	Number of districts carried by president[a]	President's vote compared with vote for his party's successful House candidates	
		President ran ahead	President ran behind
1952	297	n.a.	n.a.
1956	329	155	43
1960	204	22	243
1964	375	134[b]	158[b]
1972	377	104	88
1976	220	22	270
1980	309	38[c]	150[c]
1984	372	59	123
1988	299	26	149
1992	257	4[b,d]	247[b,d]
1996	280	27[e]	174[e]

Note: n.a. = not available.

a. This refers to the winning presidential candidate in each election.

b. This does not include districts where the percentage of the total district vote won by House members equaled the percentage of the total district vote won by the president.

c. We computed this on the basis of the actual presidential vote with John Anderson and others included. If it is recomputed on the basis of Reagan's percentage of the major party vote, the president ran ahead in 59 districts and behind in 129 districts.

d. We computed this on the basis of the actual presidential vote with Ross Perot included. If we recomputed this on the basis of Clinton's percentage of the major party vote, the president ran ahead in 72 districts and behind in 179 districts.

e. We computed this on the basis of the actual presidential vote with Ross Perot included. If we recomputed this on the basis of Clinton's percentage of the major party vote, the president ran ahead in ninety-eight districts and behind in ninety-seven districts.

Sources: Compiled from information in the *Congressional Quarterly Weekly Report,* April 22, 1978, 972; April 12, 1997, 860; *Congressional Quarterly Almanac,* vol. 22; *Almanac of American Politics 1982* and *Almanac of American Politics 1986; National Journal,* April 29, 1989, 1048–54; May 29, 1993, 1285–91.

Table 2-18 Shifts in Democratic Major Party Vote in Congressional
Districts, 1956–1998

Period	Change in democratic percentage nationally	Change in Democratic percentage in congressional districts		
		Greatest loss	Greatest gain	Variance[a]
1956–1958	5.0	–9.5	27.3	30.3
1958–1960	–1.2	–22.1	14.4	31.4
1972–1974	5.8	–18.8	36.2	92.2
1974–1976	–1.3	–30.7	31.6	81.0
1976–1978	–2.8	–37.6	39.6	106.1
1978–1980	–3.2	–27.8	37.0	85.0
1982–1984	–4.1	–40.6	16.5	68.8
1984–1986	2.4	–46.1	22.5	63.6
1986–1988	–1.1	–23.5	36.1	65.9
1988–1990	0.1	–29.1	36.4	92.6
1992–1994	–6.3	–38.0	28.0	67.2
1994–1996	3.4	–31.2	21.5	51.1
1996–1998	–0.7	–16.3	21.0	46.0

Note: We include only those districts in which two major party candidates competed in both elections and in which the boundaries remained unchanged for both elections. Because of massive redrawing of district lines after each decennial census, no figures were computed for 1970–1972, 1980–1982, and 1990–1992.

a. Variance, the square of the standard deviation, measures the extent to which the changes in local returns differ from the change in national returns.

Sources: Information for 1956–1976 is from Thomas E. Mann, *Unsafe at Any Margin* (Washington, D.C.: American Enterprise Institute, 1978); for 1978–1980, the data were computed by Larry Bartels, University of California, Berkeley; for 1982–1998, the data were computed from official election returns.

Table 2-19 Party-Line Voting in Presidential and Congressional Elections, 1956–1998 (as a percentage of all voters)

Year	Presidential election			Senate elections			House elections		
	Party-line voters[a]	Defectors[b]	Pure independents[c]	Party-line voters[a]	Defectors[b]	Pure independents[c]	Party-line voters[a]	Defectors[b]	Pure independents[c]
1956	76	15	9	79	12	9	82	9	9
1958				85	9	5	84	11	5
1960	79	13	8	77	15	8	80	12	8
1962				n.a.	n.a.	n.a.	83	12	6
1964	79	15	5	78	16	6	79	15	5
1966				n.a.	n.a.	n.a.	76	16	8
1968	69	23	9	74	19	7	74	19	7
1970				78	12	10	76	16	8
1972	67	25	8	69	22	9	75	17	8
1974				73	19	8	74	18	8
1976	74	15	11	70	19	11	72	19	9
1978				71	20	9	69	22	9
1980	70	22	8	71	21	8	69	23	8
1982				77	17	6	76	17	6
1984	81	12	7	72	19	8	70	23	7

Year									
1986				76	20	4	72	22	6
1988	81	12	7	72	20	7	74	20	7
1990				75	20	5	72	22	5
1992	68	24	9	73	20	7	70	22	8
1994				76	18	5	77	17	6
1996	80	15	5	77	16	7	77	17	6
1998				77	15	8	74	20	6

Notes: n.a. = not available.
Percentages may not add to 100 because of rounding.

a. These are party identifiers who vote for the candidate of their party.
b. These are party identifiers who vote for the candidate of the other party.
c. The SRC/CPS National Election Surveys use a seven-point scale to define party identification, including three categories of Independents—those who "lean" to one or the other party and those who are "pure" Independents. The "leaners" are included here among the party-line voters. Party identification here means self-identification as determined by surveys.

Sources: SRC/CPS *National Election Studies, 1956–1996.* Calculations for 1956–1978 from Thomas E. Mann and Raymond E. Wolfinger, "Candidates and Parties in Congressional Elections," *American Political Science Review* (September 1980). Calculations for 1980 by Gary C. Jacobson, *The Politics of Congressional Elections* (Boston: Little, Brown, 1982). Calculations for 1982–1986 by Peverill Squire and Michael Hagen, University of California State Data Program. Calculations for 1988 by Jon Krasno, Brookings Institution. Calculations for 1990 by Benjamin Highton, University of California State Data Program. Calculations for 1992 by Herb Asher, Ohio State University. Calculations for 1994, 1996, and 1998 by Thomas Mann, Brookings Institution.

Figure 2-2 Senate Seats That Changed Party, 1954–1998

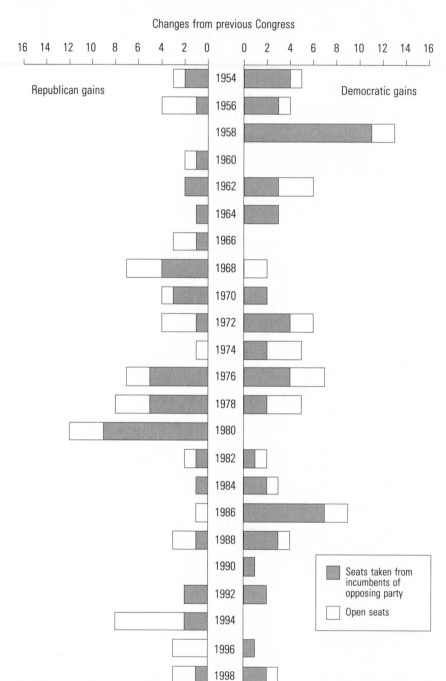

Source: Table 2-6.

3

Campaign Finance

The statistics for campaign spending during the 1998 election may seem confusing at first blush. Major party general-election candidates spent slightly *less* money on the 1998 congressional campaigns than on the 1996 campaigns: about $642 million in 1998 as opposed to $655 million in 1996. It cost the average winning House candidate about $675,000 to get elected in 1998 versus $688,000 in 1996. Adjusting for inflation, that means that it cost about 4 percent less to win in 1998 than it did in 1996. (See table 3-1.)

In light of the major cost increases of the past twenty years, that is puzzling. It is less so when we take account of some important nonfinancial facts about the election. The major national political headlines before the election were about whether (or how much) President Clinton's impending impeachment might affect congressional election results. But the unwritten story—as is often the case—turned out to be about incumbents and challengers. Four hundred incumbent members of the House ran in the 1998 general-election campaign. One hundred forty-nine of them (or 37 percent of the total) did not even have to face a major party opponent who filed financial reports with the Federal Election Commission. That 149 was the largest number of effectively unopposed incumbents since we began tracking FEC reports in 1976. In all respects, and despite impeachment, 1998 was a very good year for incumbents. Only 1.5 percent of the incumbents lost in the general election—the second lowest such total in American history.

That fact helps give meaning to the slight decline in election spending over the course of two years. If we compare like and like, spending in fact stayed fairly even for most kinds of races. Fewer races were competitive, however, and resources were concentrated on the close races that could have determined party control of the chamber.

None of that is meant to deny the obvious. House races have become more expensive. House winners may have spent a bit less in 1998 than in 1996, but they spent about 15 percent more in inflation-controlled dollars than in 1994 and 30 percent more than in 1986 or 1990. Senate election campaign spending by contrast has been more steady. To see that, one should look at costs every six years, when the same seats are up for renewal. Controlling for inflation, we find a basic stability in the spending of the Senate winners of 1986 compared with 1992 and 1998, 1988 compared with 1994, or 1990 compared with 1996. (See table 3-1.)

We can see two different patterns in the spending figures over time: a long-term upward trend and shorter-term variations within the basic long-term trend. Changes in campaign techniques, communications options, and communications costs have brought about the long-term increase in the cost of campaigning. That is evident in the numbers for both chambers. For Senate races, the long-term shift produced the steepest rate of increase from the mid-1970s to the early 1980s. Since then, Senate costs have generally tracked the cost of living. House costs have gone up more quickly, but in uneven steps. Since 1976, the two election cycles with the steepest jumps were those of 1982 and 1992. Further increases occurred during the rest of both decades, but nothing like the jumps (or step-level increases) of those two years. The fact that the House numbers show those steps, but the Senate numbers do not, is the clue to the second or shorter-term source of the cost fluctuations.

The elections of 1982 and 1992 were the first in their respective decades after redistricting, which affects the House but not the Senate. Those elections were unsettling for House members because most had to run in districts that were at least partially new to them. Because the incumbents in effect were not incumbents in parts of their districts, the elections also drew larger numbers of politically experienced challengers into the contest. In other words, the step-level increases in costs were associated with uncertainty and competition. Those same factors—uncertainty and competition—underlie many of the other variations we see in the numbers as well.

For example, we noted that Senate election costs went up quickly during the late 1970s and early 1980s. It turns out that Senate incumbents were at significant risk during those years. About one-third of the senators who sought reelection in 1978 and 1980 were defeated. Since 1988, however, Senate incumbents seem to have become stronger (perhaps because the Senate class of 1980 contained an unusually large number of political "amateurs"). At roughly the same time, the House became a more competitive institution—if not on a district-by-district basis, then for control of the chamber. In financial terms, Senate challengers were relatively well funded in the early 1980s, and the rate of growth of the 1990s began from a comparatively high base. In contrast, most House challengers of the middle to late 1980s were not credible political professionals, most were underfunded, and most had almost no chance of winning. When the political climate for the House became unsettled—with the anti-incumbent mood of 1990, the redistricting of 1992, the GOP victory of 1994, and the threat to the Republican majority in 1996—better challengers began looking seriously at running, the candidates on both sides raised more money, and more districts became competitive.

The 1998 election also took place in an unsettled climate, but not one that favored risk-taking by potential challengers. As a result, the total amount of spending by House candidates leveled off, but not the level of spending by competitive candidates. (See table 3-2.) The parties concentrated resources on fewer districts, where control of the chamber might be decided. Thus, the spending by incumbents and challengers, when we control for party and level of competition, was just about the same in 1996 and 1998 across all kinds of candidates and races. (See table 3-3.) Whatever differences show up in the summary numbers for incumbents and challengers come almost entirely from the numbers of people in each competitive category and not from how much each kind of person spent. By contrast, the spending by candidates for the open seats was up, across all categories. (See table 3-4 and figure 3-1.) Those were the districts that party leaders thought might determine whether Republicans or Democrats elected the next Speaker—the ones in which leaders tried to persuade good candidates to run and where money was channeled.

As for competitive incumbent-challenger races, for the second election in a row, incumbents who won with less than 60 percent of the vote spent an average of more than $1 million. So did incumbents who lost. In other words, the amount raised *by the incumbent* did not make for a decisive difference between success and failure. The story was different for challengers. The average successful challenger of 1998, for the second election in a row, spent more than $1 million to win. That was similar to the amount spent by incumbents in close races, but it was substantially more than the $618,000 spent by the strong challengers (40 percent or more) who lost. Moreover, challengers with under 40 percent of the vote raised less than one-fourth as much as the strong challengers. In other words, as has always been true, the single most important financial fact predicting whether a race would be competitive was *not* the amount raised or spent by the incumbent—most incumbents can raise money at will— but the amount raised by the challenger. (See table 3-3.)

Table 3-5 shows Senate campaign expenditures from 1980 through 1998, table 3-6 shows the expenditures of Senate incumbents and challengers by election outcome for the same period, and table 3-7 shows expenditures for open Senate seats by election outcome.

From table 3-8 to the end of this chapter, we turn our attention away from candidates' spending and margins of victory, toward candidates' sources of funds, including interest groups and political parties. In table 3-8 and figure 3-2, we see that despite all the publicity given to political action committees, House Republicans, Senate Republicans, and Senate Democrats continue to raise most of their money from individual contributors. Only House Democrats raised less than half their money from individuals, with House Democratic incumbents' raising almost the same amount from PACs (46 percent of their money) as from individuals (47 percent).

Table 3-9 shows how the number of political action committees grew since 1974, and table 3-10 shows their contributions to congressional candidates. In table 3-11 and figure 3-3 we see a significant, although perhaps temporary, increase in 1998 PAC support for House Democrats from 1996, which in turn was a substantial decline from 1994. During the 1970s and early 1980s, corporate and trade association PACs gave about one-fourth of their contributions each to House Democratic and House Republican incumbents. Then, from 1984 through 1994, business shifted money toward the Democrats. In 1994 corporate PACs gave 34 percent of their contributions to House Democratic incumbents and 22 percent to House Republican incumbents. When the Republicans won majority control after 1994, business funds reversed track: corporate funds in 1996 and 1998 went by almost a two to one margin to Republican rather than Democratic incumbents. Labor's contributions remained overwhelmingly Democratic (93 percent in 1998), while the Democrats picked up slightly in all other PAC categories.

Political party money was the big story of 1996 and 1998. Parties help their House and Senate candidates with direct support in two ways under the Federal Election Campaign Act: contributions and coordinated campaign expenditures. Those activities are paid with what some people refer to as "hard money"—money raised under the campaign law's contribution limits to influence federal elections. Such contributions and coordinated expenditures amounted to $34 million in 1998, which is about 14 percent *less* than in 1996 and 28 percent less than in 1994. (See table 3-12 and figure 3-4.) On the face of it, political parties might appear to be in decline. But the face of it is not all there is.

Disbursements for "nonfederal" activity from the parties' "soft money" accounts—money the parties can raise for accounts not covered by election law contribution limits—take up an increasing part of the whole picture. Those accounts for all national Democratic and Republican party committees combined amounted to $79 million in 1992, $98 million in 1994, $271 million in 1996, and $221 million in 1998. As a percentage of all spending by the national party committees, the accounts have grown from being less than 20 percent of all spending in 1992 to more than 50 percent in 1998. The House and Senate campaign committees alone (excluding the large accounts most relevant for presidential elections) grew at an even more dramatic rate: from $18 million in 1992 and $17 million in 1994 to $84 million in 1996 and $104 million in 1998. (See table 3-13.)

Political parties use "soft money" for a wide range of purposes. Through most of the 1980s, the parties used it primarily to pay for building and other operational overhead costs. By 1996, however, both parties were using "soft money" to pay for what is called "issue advertising." In classic form, issue advertising is literally advertising about issues. It does not advocate a candidate's or party's victory or defeat in an election. Generic political party advertising of the early 1980s was not "issue advocacy" under that definition because it usually ended by urging the audience to vote for the sponsoring political party. In 1996, however, President Clinton and, later, Republican candidate Robert Dole were featured prominently in advertising that omitted explicit requests for the viewer's vote. The parties claimed that under the law, those spots were not "election advocacy" but "issue ads." So far, the courts have sustained that position. As that interpretation remains law, it will be hard to know how much of the soft money reported by the House and Senate campaign committees was spent for advertising aimed at the general public, as opposed to internal organizational support.

A similar point applies to the millions of soft money dollars being raised and then spent on issue advocacy by private organizations or, beginning in 1999–2000, by issue-advocacy committees formed by congressional leaders. One important difference exists between all of that money on the one hand and the funds raised by the national party committees on the other. As imperfect as the reports about party spending might be, the party committees are required to report the sources for all their receipts. No similar reporting requirement exists for issue-advocacy funds raised by private or leadership-controlled, issue-advocacy organizations.

Our concluding table and figure showing independent expenditures thus mask an irony. (See table 3-14 and figure 3-5.) All money raised and then used for independent expenditures has to meet FECA guidelines: the receipts are covered by contribution limits; independent spenders and candidates may not coordinate their activities; and all spending is fully reported. Independent spending on congressional elections, under those guidelines, by everyone *other than* the political parties went up from $4.6 million in 1994 to $20.6 million in 1996 and $11.6 million in 1998. The problem here, as with our earlier statements about political parties, is that we simply cannot know from official records how that compares with the apparently larger pool of electorally relevant communication, paid for by private organizations and individuals, that does not meet the current legal tests for "election advocacy" and that, therefore, need not be disclosed. As a result, an increasing portion of the financial activity relevant for congressional elections may not be covered by the material presented in this chapter's tables.

Note on the Sources for Chapter 3

Except where specifically indicated, the data in this chapter come from the Federal Election Commission. The entries for the recent years in several tables (3-1 through 3-7) are based on computer data downloaded from the FEC's Direct Access Program. The numbers in tables 3-8 through 3-14 are either available in, or can be calculated from, the FEC's published press releases, available at the FEC's website (www.fec.gov). Final data for any given election normally are not available for more than a year after election day. For the most recent cycle, therefore, we have relied on year-end reports, which are still subject to correction.

Finally, we need to clarify a difference between our definitions of *challenger* and *open-seat candidate* and the FEC's. If an incumbent runs and is defeated in a primary election, the FEC will treat all the nonincumbent candidates in the congressional district as challengers. Because our own candidate-centered tables (3-1 through 3-7) include only candidates who run in the general election, we have defined a candidate as a challenger only if that person is running against an incumbent in the general election. If the incumbent was defeated in a primary, the general-election candidates are treated as if they are running for an open seat. For the tables we calculated directly from computer data, our definitions apply. The FEC calculated and used its own definitions for tables 3-8 and 3-11.

Table 3-1   The Cost of Winning an Election, 1986–1998
(in nominal and 1998 dollars)

	House Winners		*Senate Winners*	
	Nominal Dollars	1998 Dollars	Nominal Dollars	1998 Dollars
1986	359,577	526,012	3,067,559	4,487,416
1988	404,665	543,254	3,776,524	5,069,897
1990	428,477	517,183	3,308,182	3,993,060
1992	560,245	637,180	3,642,182	4,142,341
1994	542,078	584,807	4,503,440	4,858,421
1996	688,763	701,357	3,934,774	4,006,721
1998	675,478	675,478	4,660,847	4,660,847

Figure 3-1 Mean Expenditures of House Challengers Who Beat Incumbents, 1984–1998

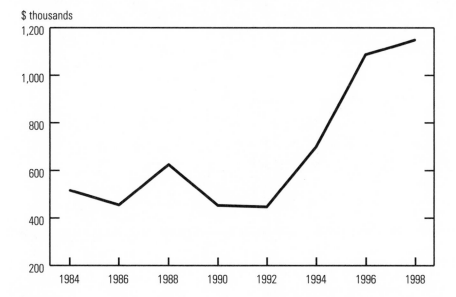

Source: Table 3-4.

Table 3-2 House Campaign Expenditures, 1980–1998 (net dollars)

	1980	1982	1984	1986	1988	1990	1992	1994	1996	1998
All candidates										
Total expenditures	115,222,222	174,921,844	176,882,849	217,562,967	222,258,024	237,680,795[a]	331,899,054	347,364,273	424,011,349	393,201,952
Mean expenditure	153,221 (N = 752)	228,060 (N = 767)	241,313 (N = 733)	295,602 (N = 736)	273,380 (N = 813)	325,145[a] (N = 731)	408,240[a] (N = 813)	441,378[a] (N = 787)[a]	517,718[a] (N = 819)[a]	547,635 (N = 718)
Mean, Democrats	143,277 (N = 396)	213,369 (N = 411)	237,732 (N = 399)	301,955 (N = 397)	286,851 (N = 429)	355,862 (N = 381)	462,897 (N = 409)	487,493 (N = 386)	472,251 (N = 413)	498,551 (N = 357)
Mean, Republicans	164,282 (N = 356)	245,020 (N = 356)	245,591 (N = 334)	290,092 (N = 340)	258,330 (N = 384)	290,910 (N = 349)	352,351 (N = 403)	396,411 (N = 400)	563,010 (N = 405)	596,361 (N = 360)
Incumbents										
Mean, all incumbents	165,081 (N = 391)	265,001 (N = 383)	279,044 (N = 408)	362,103 (N = 389)	378,544 (N = 412)	422,124 (N = 405)	594,699[a] (N = 349)	561,441 (N = 382)[a]	678,623 (N = 382)[a]	652,121 (N = 400)[a]
Mean, Democrats	158,010 (N = 248)	247,573 (N = 216)	279,203 (N = 254)	349,918 (N = 231)	358,260 (N = 248)	427,178 (N = 247)	621,890 (N = 211)	622,937 (N = 225)	589,449 (N = 168)	588,418 (N = 189)
Mean, Republicans	177,345 (N = 143)	287,543 (N = 167)	278,781 (N = 154)	379,917 (N = 158)	409,217 (N = 164)	414,222 (N = 158)	552,952 (N = 137)	473,281 (N = 157)	747,671 (N = 213)	710,038 (N = 210)

Challengers

Mean, all challengers	121,751 (N = 277)	151,717 (N = 270)	161,994 (N = 273)	155,607 (N = 262)	119,621 (N = 348)	134,465[a] (N = 270)	167,411 (N = 290)	240,188 (N = 302)	289,513 (N = 332)	321,973 (N = 251)
Mean, Democrats	93,313 (N = 105)	141,390 (N = 137)	124,508 (N = 119)	170,562 (N = 123)	143,785 (N = 154)	131,194 (N = 104)	143,935 (N = 110)	177,136 (N = 110)	321,097 (N = 192)	313,160 (N = 134)
Mean, Republicans	139,111 (N = 172)	162,354 (N = 133)	190,960 (N = 154)	141,356 (N = 139)	100,440 (N = 194)	133,889 (N = 165)	181,757 (N = 180)	276,312 (N = 192)	246,197 (N = 140)	332,066 (N = 117)

Open seats

Mean, all open-seat candidates	201,790 (N = 84)	284,476 (N = 114)	361,696 (N = 52)	430,484 (N = 86)	465,466 (N = 53)	543,129 (N = 56)	435,631 (N = 174)	585,991 (N = 103)	653,896 (N = 105)	769,227 (N = 67)
Mean, Democrats	180,312 (N = 43)	256,004 (N = 58)	350,804 (N = 26)	420,138 (N = 43)	446,959 (N = 27)	547,541 (N = 30)	480,375 (N = 88)	561,569 (N = 52)	648,334 (N = 53)	729,651 (N = 34)
Mean, Republicans	224,116 (N = 41)	314,547 (N = 56)	372,589 (N = 26)	440,830 (N = 43)	484,684 (N = 26)	538,037 (N = 26)	389,847 (N = 86)	611,911 (N = 51)	659,566 (N = 52)	810,002 (N = 33)

Note: The data include primary and general-election expenditures for general-election candidates who filed reports with the Federal Election Commission. The 1979 amendments to the Federal Election Campaign Act exempted low-budget (under $5,000) campaigns from reporting requirements. The table includes data for low-budget candidates who did file reports.

a. The entry includes Bernard Sanders (I-Vt.).

Table 3-3 Expenditures of House Incumbents and Challengers, by Election Outcome, 1980–1998 (mean net dollars)

	1980	1982	1984	1986	1988	1990	1992	1994	1996	1998
Incumbent won with 60% or more[a]										
Incumbents	125,912 (N=284)	200,170 (N=264)	232,853 (N=318)	291,876 (N=330)	349,380 (N=359)	362,563 (N=313)	491,345 (N=234)	454,126 (N=263)	518,913 (N=262)	563,298 (N=309)
Democrats	117,773 (N=170)	206,670 (N=178)	219,506 (N=183)	293,484 (N=209)	342,862 (N=220)	374,552 (N=197)	496,288 (N=138)	454,317 (N=120)	471,772 (N=124)	447,601 (N=144)
Republicans	138,050 (N=114)	186,717 (N=86)	250,945 (N=135)	289,099 (N=121)	359,697 (N=139)	342,200 (N=116)	483,265 (N=95)	453,965 (N=143)	558,414 (N=137)	614,219 (N=164)
Challengers	47,525 (N=170)	82,373 (N=163)	71,922 (N=184)	92,436 (N=202)	78,774 (N=235)	60,352 (N=180)	87,728 (N=187)	114,198 (N=183)	97,127 (N=212)	133,560 (N=160)
Democrats	44,120 (N=75)	36,628 (N=62)	73,835 (N=99)	72,769 (N=85)	87,597 (N=102)	43,088 (N=65)	76,024 (N=74)	133,025 (N=96)	94,240 (N=115)	113,294 (N=88)
Republicans	50,213 (N=95)	110,454 (N=101)	69,693 (N=85)	106,724 (N=117)	72,007 (N=133)	70,109 (N=115)	94,055 (N=111)	93,423 (N=87)	100,586 (N=96)	158,330 (N=72)
Incumbent won with <60%										
Incumbents	261,901 (N=76)	394,447 (N=90)	437,752 (N=74)	785,493 (N=52)	701,406 (N=44)	614,856 (N=77)	782,328 (N=91)	721,252 (N=85)	1,010,895 (N=99)	1,024,336 (N=85)
Democrats	223,345 (N=50)	446,542 (N=35)	421,834 (N=58)	938,374 (N=20)	691,035 (N=23)	640,623 (N=44)	833,388 (N=57)	732,729 (N=70)	936,497 (N=41)	1,043,315 (N=44)
Republicans	336,046 (N=26)	361,295[b] (N=55)	495,455 (N=16)	689,943 (N=32)	712,765 (N=21)	580,499 (N=33)	696,727 (N=34)	670,582 (N=14)	1,063,487 (N=58)	1,003,969 (N=41)

Challengers	197,499 (N = 76)	234,790 (N = 84)	307,938 (N = 72)	334,946 (N = 46)	391,549 (N = 44)	248,714 (N = 75)	281,211 (N = 84)	329,073 (N = 84)	532,866 (N = 99)	618,256 (N = 85)
Democrats	195,135 (N = 26)	182,232[b] (N = 53)	386,819 (N = 16)	353,939 (N = 28)	445,871 (N = 21)	213,907 (N = 31)	274,047 (N = 29)	479,611 (N = 14)	545,470 (N = 58)	632,863 (N = 41)
Republicans	198,728 (N = 50)	324,647 (N = 31)	285,401 (N = 56)	305,401 (N = 18)	341,951 (N = 23)	273,237 (N = 44)	283,801 (N = 56)	298,966 (N = 70)	515,035 (N = 41)	604,644 (N = 44)
Incumbent was defeated										
Incumbents	286,559 (N = 31)	453,459 (N = 29)	463,070 (N = 16)	582,647 (N = 6)	956,081 (N = 5)	675,605 (N = 15)	890,975 (N = 24)	992,023 (N = 34)	1,104,774 (N = 21)	1,343,995 (N = 6)
Democrats	285,636 (N = 28)	353,201[b] (N = 3)	483,204 (N = 13)	528,101 (N = 1)	935,494 (N = 2)	589,795 (N = 6)	951,743 (N = 16)	992,023 (N = 34)	710,406 (N = 3)	850,577 (N = 1)
Republicans	295,170 (N = 3)	465,027 (N = 26)	375,824 (N = 3)	593,556 (N = 5)	969,806 (N = 3)	732,812[c] (N = 9)	796,437 (N = 8)	0	1,170,502 (N = 18)	1,442,678 (N = 5)
Challengers	343,093 (N = 31)	296,273 (N = 23)	515,622 (N = 16)	455,071 (N = 11)	625,120 (N = 5)	452,582 (N = 15)	447,076 (N = 19)	698,668 (N = 34)	1,088,675 (N = 21)	1,148,979 (N = 6)
Democrats	353,855 (N = 4)	292,781 (N = 22)	249,462[d] (N = 3)	504,673 (N = 9)	808,908 (N = 3)	526,537 (N = 8)	351,847 (N = 6)	0	1,064,852 (N = 18)	1,209,237 (N = 5)
Republicans	341,499 (N = 27)	373,093 (N = 1)	577,044 (N = 13)	231,864 (N = 2)	349,438 (N = 2)	334,444 (N = 6)	491,028 (N = 13)	698,668 (N = 34)	1,231,615 (N = 3)	847,692 (N = 1)

Note: The data include primary and general-election expenditures for general-election candidates only.

a. This is the percentage of the vote the two leading candidates received.
b. The number of challengers does not equal that of incumbents because of six incumbent-incumbent races in 1982 resulting from redistricting. The mean expenditure for Democrats in those races was $585,205; for Republicans it was $592,080. The mean expenditure for winners (four Democrats, two Republicans) was $600,337; for losers it was $583,824.
c. One Republican incumbent was defeated by Bernard Sanders (I-Vt.), who spent $569,772.
d. This entry includes the expenditures of Albert G. Bustamante, who defeated Democratic incumbent Abraham Kazen, Jr, in a Texas primary.

Table 3-4 Expenditures for Open House Seats, by Election Outcome, 1984–1998 (mean net dollars)

	1984	1986	1988	1990	1992	1994	1996	1998
All winners	440,912 (N=26)	523,759 (N=46)	615,339 (N=27)	625,760 (N=30)	538,959 (N=91)	602,073 (N=52)	768,226 (N=53)	975,673 (N=35)
Democrats	428,416 (N=8)	515,570 (N=22)	554,500 (N=13)	593,699 (N=18)	508,167 (N=57)	676,437 (N=14)	749,392 (N=24)	936,974 (N=18)
Republicans	446,467 (N=18)	531,266 (N=24)	671,832 (N=14)	673,851 (N=12)	590,581 (N=34)	574,676 (N=38)	783,813 (N=29)	1,016,648 (N=17)
Winners with 60% or more	372,989 (N=8)	543,382 (N=19)	555,759 (N=11)	632,189 (N=14)	517,909 (N=44)	618,153 (N=21)	651,420 (N=18)	752,460 (N=11)
Democrats	290,693 (N=3)	537,552 (N=7)	397,458 (N=7)	534,671 (N=9)	397,636 (N=33)	587,314 (N=3)	593,859 (N=8)	655,755 (N=8)
Republicans	422,366 (N=5)	546,783 (N=12)	832,787 (N=4)	807,721 (N=5)	878,725 (N=11)	623,293 (N=18)	697,469 (N=10)	1,014,005 (N=3)
Winners with <60%	471,100 (N=18)	509,950 (N=27)	656,299 (N=16)	620,135 (N=16)	558,666 (N=47)	591,180 (N=31)	828,298 (N=35)	1,077,520 (N=24)
Democrats	511,049 (N=5)	505,312 (N=15)	737,714 (N=6)	652,727 (N=9)	660,147 (N=24)	700,743 (N=11)	827,158 (N=16)	1,161,949 (N=10)
Republicans	455,736 (N=13)	515,749 (N=12)	607,450 (N=10)	578,230 (N=7)	452,773 (N=23)	530,921 (N=20)	829,258 (N=19)	1,017,214 (N=14)

All losers	282,480 (N = 26)	323,718 (N = 40)	439,980 (N = 24)	447,785 (N = 26)	322,344 (N = 83)	569,593 (N = 51)	537,368 (N = 52)	543,207 (N = 32)
Democrats	316,309 (N = 18)	320,161 (N = 21)	436,127 (N = 13)	290,911 (N = 12)	429,273 (N = 31)	517,881 (N = 38)	564,701 (N = 29)	496,412 (N = 16)
Republicans	206,363 (N = 8)	326,596 (N = 19)	455,860 (N = 10)	421,625 (N = 14)	258,597 (N = 52)	720,753 (N = 13)	502,905 (N = 23)	590,441 (N = 16)
Losers with >40%	352,961 (N = 18)	360,978 (N = 23)	565,561 (N = 16)	472,178 (N = 16)	451,892 (N = 47)	683,257 (N = 31)	652,323 (N = 35)	728,974 (N = 23)
Democrats	393,262 (N = 13)	294,362 (N = 10)	506,283 (N = 9)	436,366 (N = 8)	476,578 (N = 23)	596,359 (N = 20)	657,299 (N = 19)	579,822 (N = 13)
Republicans	248,180 (N = 5)	412,220 (N = 13)	693,525 (N = 6)	507,989 (N = 8)	428,234 (N = 24)	841,253 (N = 11)	646,414 (N = 16)	923,131 (N = 10)
Losers with 40% or less	123,896 (N = 8)	193,794 (N = 15)	188,819 (N = 8)	408,756 (N = 10)	153,212 (N = 36)	393,415 (N = 20)	300,696 (N = 17)	69,250 (N = 9)
Democrats	116,232 (N = 5)	228,939 (N = 9)	278,276 (N = 4)	562,183 (N = 4)	293,272 (N = 8)	430,683 (N = 18)	388,764 (N = 10)	135,833 (N = 3)
Republicans	136,668 (N = 3)	141,077 (N = 6)	99,363 (N = 4)	306,472 (N = 6)	113,194 (N = 28)	58,005 (N = 2)	174,885 (N = 7)	35,959 (N = 6)

Table 3-5 Senate Campaign Expenditures, 1980–1998 (net dollars)

	1980	1982	1984	1986	1988	1990	1992	1994	1996	1998
All candidates										
Total expenditures	74,163,669	114,036,379	141,962,276	183,432,489	184,977,565	173,674,925	198,487,310	280,019,203	227,946,571	248,627,748
Mean expenditure	1,106,920 (N = 67)	1,781,815 (N = 64)	2,327,250 (N = 61)	2,737,798 (N = 67)	2,802,690 (N = 66)	2,592,163 (N = 67)	2,876,627 (N = 69)	4,000,274 (N = 70)	3,618,200 (N = 63)	3,767,087 (N = 66)
Mean, Democrats	1,170,580 (N = 34)	1,881,379 (N = 32)	2,160,637 (N = 31)	2,260,415 (N = 33)	2,938,533 (N = 33)	2,468,527 (N = 34)	2,815,826 (N = 35)	3,395,629 (N = 35)	3,474,231 (N = 31)	3,457,730 (N = 34)
Mean, Republicans	1,041,332 (N = 33)	1,682,252 (N = 32)	2,499,417 (N = 30)	3,201,141 (N = 34)	2,666,848 (N = 33)	2,719,546 (N = 33)	2,939,218 (N = 34)	4,604,919 (N = 35)	3,757,669 (N = 32)	4,095,779 (N = 32)
Incumbents										
Mean, all incumbents	1,301,692 (N = 25)	1,858,140 (N = 29)	2,539,929 (N = 28)	3,374,602 (N = 28)	3,748,126 (N = 27)	3,582,136 (N = 32)	3,852,428 (N = 27)	4,691,617 (N = 26)	4,238,654 (N = 20)	4,737,372 (N = 29)
Mean, Democrats	1,355,660 (N = 19)	1,696,226 (N = 18)	1,755,004 (N = 12)	2,712,796 (N = 9)	3,457,145 (N = 15)	3,618,244 (N = 17)	2,851,102 (N = 15)	5,154,744 (N = 16)	5,209,423 (N = 7)	4,562,158 (N = 15)
Mean, Republicans	1,130,792 (N = 6)	2,123,089 (N = 11)	3,128,622 (N = 16)	3,688,089 (N = 19)	4,111,852 (N = 12)	3,541,212 (N = 15)	5,104,086 (N = 12)	3,950,616 (N = 10)	3,715,932 (N = 13)	4,925,101 (N = 14)

Challengers									
Mean, all challengers	842,547 (N = 24)	1,217,034 (N = 29)	1,899,417 (N = 27)	1,820,058 (N = 17)	1,705,098 (N = 29)	1,824,993 (N = 26)	3,997,104 (N = 26)	3,114,529 (N = 17)	3,114,238 (N = 27)
Mean, Democrats	557,006 (N = 6)	1,516,015 (N = 11)	1,911,693 (N = 18)	2,160,770 (N = 12)	1,401,259 (N = 14)	2,551,654 (N = 12)	1,266,445 (N = 10)	2,920,075 (N = 11)	2,555,269 (N = 14)
Mean, Republicans	937,727 (N = 18)	1,034,324 (N = 18)	1,874,864 (N = 9)	1,547,489 (N = 15)	1,988,680 (N = 15)	1,202,141 (N = 14)	5,703,766 (N = 16)	3,471,029 (N = 6)	3,716,205 (N = 13)
Open seats									
Mean, all open-seat candidates	1,132,560 (N = 18)	4,142,687 (N = 6)	3,138,282 (N = 12)	2,886,383 (N = 12)	1,599,792 (N = 6)	2,938,871 (N = 16)	3,006,247 (N = 18)	3,470,250 (N = 26)	2,715,954 (N = 10)
Mean, Democrats	1,188,903 (N = 9)	4,331,959 (N = 3)	2,628,009 (N = 6)	3,197,528 (N = 6)	934,046 (N = 3)	3,145,940 (N = 8)	2,634,075 (N = 9)	3,008,799 (N = 13)	2,671,336 (N = 5)
Mean, Republicans	1,076,218 (N = 9)	3,953,415 (N = 3)	3,648,555 (N = 6)	2,575,237 (N = 6)	2,265,538 (N = 3)	2,731,801 (N = 8)	3,378,419 (N = 9)	3,931,701 (N = 13)	2,760,571 (N = 5)

Note: The data include primary and general-election expenditures for general-election candidates only.

Table 3-6 Expenditures of Senate Incumbents and Challengers, by Election Outcome, 1980–1998 (mean net dollars)

	1980	1982	1984	1986	1988	1990	1992	1994	1996	1998
Incumbent won with 60% or more[a]										
Incumbents	1,162,385 (N=10)	1,494,578 (N=13)	1,612,152 (N=18)	1,963,140 (N=14)	2,777,202 (N=15)	2,318,076 (N=19)	2,698,728 (N=13)	3,657,063 (N=10)	2,432,408 (N=6)	2,653,895 (N=19)
Democrats	1,220,616 (N=6)	1,401,794 (N=12)	1,620,869 (N=7)	1,672,182 (N=8)	2,355,863 (N=10)	2,441,681 (N=10)	2,661,953 (N=9)	1,736,702 (N=3)	2,266,951 (N=2)	3,134,448 (N=9)
Republicans	1,075,038 (N=4)	2,607,983 (N=1)	1,606,604 (N=11)	2,351,083 (N=6)	3,619,881 (N=5)	2,180,738 (N=9)	2,781,472 (N=4)	4,480,074 (N=7)	2,515,137 (N=4)	2,221,396 (N=10)
Challengers	302,812 (N=9)	777,830 (N=13)	384,263 (N=15)	451,671 (N=13)	591,566 (N=15)	853,376 (N=16)	701,442 (N=12)	1,002,523 (N=10)	762,003 (N=3)	447,769 (N=17)
Democrats	265,822 (N=4)	424,507 (N=1)	322,263 (N=10)	155,853 (N=5)	835,294 (N=5)	449,666 (N=8)	595,192 (N=4)	1,365,961 (N=7)	479,791 (N=2)	292,621 (N=10)
Republicans	332,404 (N=5)	807,276 (N=12)	508,264 (N=5)	636,557 (N=8)	469,702 (N=10)	1,253,086 (N=8)	754,568 (N=8)	54,500 (N=3)	1,326,427 (N=1)	669,410 (N=7)
Incumbent won with <60%										
Incumbents	945,423 (N=6)	2,224,235 (N=14)	4,505,574 (N=7)	5,213,789 (N=7)	6,235,410 (N=8)	5,279,645 (N=12)	4,922,413 (N=10)	5,313,837 (N=14)	5,054,630 (N=13)	6,608,446 (N=7)
Democrats	796,984 (N=4)	2,417,100 (N=5)	1,833,432 (N=4)	11,037,707 (N=1)	6,829,055 (N=4)	5,299,049 (N=7)	2,844,490 (N=4)	6,022,553 (N=11)	6,386,412 (N=5)	6,618,545 (N=5)
Republicans	1,242,300 (N=2)	2,117,088 (N=9)	8,068,429 (N=3)	4,243,136 (N=6)	5,641,766 (N=4)	5,252,478 (N=5)	6,307,696 (N=6)	2,715,212 (N=3)	4,222,266 (N=8)	6,583,197 (N=2)

Challengers	864,870 (N=6)	1,615,338 (N=14)	2,296,194 (N=7)	3,389,477 (N=7)	3,784,772 (N=8)	2,870,438 (N=12)	2,283,708 (N=10)	5,546,361 (N=14)	3,666,957 (N=13)	4,827,270 (N=7)
Democrats	1,139,376 (N=2)	1,629,490 (N=9)	4,028,715 (N=3)	1,990,836 (N=6)	3,209,075 (N=4)	2,927,948 (N=5)	3,032,533 (N=6)	1,034,241 (N=3)	3,521,336 (N=8)	3,922,146 (N=2)
Republicans	727,617 (N=4)	1,589,864 (N=5)	996,804 (N=4)	11,781,316 (N=1)	4,360,469 (N=4)	2,829,360 (N=7)	1,160,471 (N=4)	6,776,953 (N=11)	3,899,949 (N=5)	5,189,319 (N=5)
Incumbent was defeated										
Incumbents	1,693,991 (N=9)	1,658,623 (N=2)	3,520,088 (N=3)	4,358,340 (N=7)	2,579,437 (N=4)	7,229,154 (N=1)	4,926,992 (N=4)	5,508,854 (N=2)	4,468,434 (N=1)	13,566,890 (N=3)
Democrats	1,693,991 (N=9)	1,625,042 (N=1)	2,380,239 (N=1)	0	1,338,622 (N=1)	0	3,751,500 (N=2)	5,508,854 (N=2)	0	7,129,612 (N=1)
Republicans	0	1,692,204 (N=1)	4,090,013 (N=2)	4,358,340 (N=7)	2,993,042 (N=3)	7,229,154 (N=1)	6,138,484 (N=2)	0	4,468,434 (N=1)	16,785,529 (N=2)
Challengers	1,367,400 (N=9)	793,123 (N=2)	3,066,175 (N=3)	3,098,027 (N=7)	2,516,337 (N=4)	1,380,560 (N=1)	4,048,857 (N=4)	8,125,137 (N=2)	2,990,554 (N=1)	14,227,152 (N=3)
Democrats	0	1,586,245 (N=1)	3,711,199 (N=2)	3,098,027 (N=7)	2,996,572 (N=3)	1,380,560 (N=1)	5,021,938 (N=2)	0	2,990,554 (N=1)	12,501,630 (N=2)
Republicans	1,367,400 (N=9)	981,197 (N=1)	1,776,128 (N=1)	0	1,075,631 (N=1)	0	3,075,776 (N=2)	8,125,137 (N=2)	0	17,678,798 (N=1)

Note: The Federal Election Commission included the following disclaimer along with its 1986 data, and *Vital Statistics* considers it appropriate for all years: "The small *N*'s and unique nature of some Senate campaigns make all measures of central tendency like averages or medians problematic and, as a result, the Commission would not include tables such as these in its regular release of information."

a. This is the percentage of the vote the two leading candidates received.

Table 3-7 Expenditures for Open Senate Seats, by Election Outcome, 1986–1998 (mean net dollars)

	1986	1988	1990	1992	1994	1996	1998
All winners	3,827,158 (N = 7)	3,781,436 (N = 6)	2,265,538 (N = 3)	3,371,677 (N = 8)	3,378,419 (N = 9)	3,706,170 (N = 14)	3,820,843 (N = 5)
Democrats	2,714,673 (N = 4)	5,186,633 (N = 2)	0	4,186,216 (N = 5)	0	4,539,955 (N = 5)	3,518,576 (N = 2)
Republicans	5,310,471 (N = 3)	3,078,837 (N = 4)	2,265,538 (N = 3)	2,014,111 (N = 3)	3,378,419 (N = 9)	3,087,370 (N = 9)	4,022,354 (N = 3)
Winners with 60% or more	2,216,412 (N = 2)	1,879,272 (N = 2)	1,536,352 (N = 2)	1,191,005 (N = 1)	2,754,664 (N = 4)	2,518,955 (N = 2)	2,739,093 (N = 2)
Democrats	2,057,422 (N = 1)	2,881,666 (N = 1)	0	1,191,005 (N = 1)	0	2,732,011 (N = 1)	3,914,375 (N = 1)
Republicans	2,375,402 (N = 1)	876,877 (N = 1)	1,536,352 (N = 2)	0	2,754,664 (N = 4)	2,305,898 (N = 1)	1,563,811 (N = 1)
Winners with <60%	4,471,457 (N = 5)	4,732,518 (N = 4)	3,723,911 (N = 1)	3,683,201 (N = 7)	3,877,423 (N = 5)	3,787,350 (N = 12)	4,542,009 (N = 3)
Democrats	2,933,757 (N = 3)	7,491,600 (N = 1)	0	4,935,019 (N = 4)	0	4,991,941 (N = 4)	3,122,776 (N = 1)
Republicans	6,778,006 (N = 2)	3,812,824 (N = 3)	3,723,911 (N = 1)	2,014,111 (N = 3)	3,877,423 (N = 5)	3,185,054 (N = 8)	5,251,626 (N = 2)

All losers	2,952,009 (N=7)	2,000,372 (N=6)	934,046 (N=3)	2,506,064 (N=8)	2,634,075 (N=9)	3,052,384 (N=14)	1,611,064 (N=5)
Democrats	2,181,463 (N=3)	2,202,976 (N=4)	934,046 (N=3)	1,412,146 (N=3)	2,634,075 (N=9)	1,901,122 (N=9)	2,106,510 (N=3)
Republicans	3,529,919 (N=4)	1,595,165 (N=2)	0	3,162,415 (N=5)	0	5,126,336 (N=5)	867,896 (N=2)
Losers with >40%	3,686,638 (N=5)	2,792,524 (N=4)	1,936,914 (N=1)	2,792,915 (N=7)	2,802,500 (N=5)	3,439,376 (N=12)	2,390,365 (N=3)
Democrats	3,006,346 (N=2)	2,753,999 (N=3)	1,936,914 (N=1)	1,412,146 (N=3)	2,802,500 (N=5)	2,051,827 (N=8)	3,039,044 (N=2)
Republicans	4,140,166 (N=3)	2,908,101 (N=1)	0	3,828,492 (N=4)	0	6,214,473 (N=4)	1,093,007 (N=1)
Losers with 40% or less	1,115,437 (N=2)	416,069 (N=2)	432,613 (N=2)	498,107 (N=1)	2,423,544 (N=4)	734,636 (N=2)	442,114 (N=2)
Democrats	531,698 (N=1)	549,908 (N=1)	432,613 (N=2)	0	2,423,544 (N=4)	695,482 (N=1)	241,443 (N=1)
Republicans	1,699,175 (N=1)	282,229 (N=1)	0	498,107 (N=1)	0	773,789 (N=1)	642,784 (N=1)

Note: The Federal Election Commission included the following disclaimer along with its 1986 data, and *Vital Statistics* considers it appropriate for all years: "The small *N*'s and unique nature of some Senate campaigns make all measures of central tendency like averages or medians problematic and, as a result, the Commission would not include tables such as these in its regular release of information."

Figure 3-2 Percentage of Incumbents' Campaign Funds That Came from PACs, House and Senate, 1984–1998

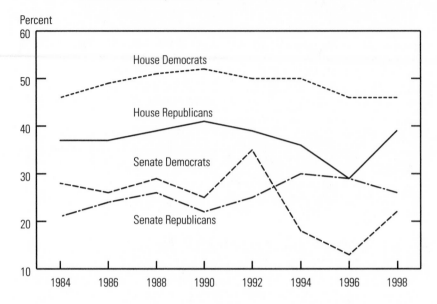

Source: Table 3-10.

Figure 3-3 Percentage of PAC Support for Nonincumbents, 1978–1998

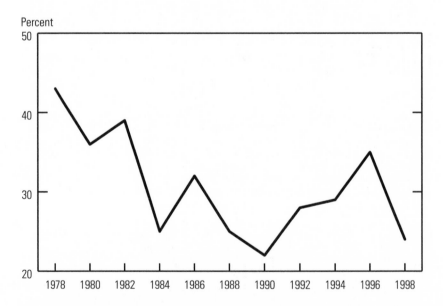

Note: Nonincumbents are challengers and open-seat candidates.
Source: Table 3-11.

Table 3-8 Campaign Funding Sources for House and Senate Candidates, 1984–1998

Party and candidate status	Number of candidates	Contributions plus party expenditures on behalf of candidates ($ millions)	Percentage coming from:				
			Individuals	PACs	Party (contributions plus expenditures)	Candidate to self (contributions plus loans)	Other
House, 1984							
All candidates[a]	816	203.8	47	36	7	6	5
Democrats	434	107.2	44	41	3	6	6
Incumbents	258	81.8	39	46	2	2	11
Challengers	152	16.3	43	29	6	18	5
Open seats	24	9.1	45	22	6	24	3
Republicans	382	96.6	49	30	11	6	5
Incumbents	154	52.1	51	37	6	1	5
Challengers	204	33.8	48	18	17	13	4
Open seats	24	10.7	47	31	13	7	2
Senate, 1984							
All candidates[a]	68	157.7	61	18	6	10	4
Democrats	33	73.1	56	18	6	16	4
Incumbents	12	22.8	61	28	3	<1	8
Challengers	17	25.5	69	17	9	2	3
Open seats	4	24.8	39	9	6	44	2

(table continues)

Table 3-8 (continued)

Party and candidate status	Number of candidates	Contributions plus party expenditures on behalf of candidates ($ millions)	Percentage coming from:				
			Individuals	PACs	Party (contributions plus expenditures)	Candidate to self (contributions plus loans)	Other
Republicans	35	84.6	65	18	6	5	4
Incumbents	17	55.7	68	21	6	1	5
Challengers	13	10.0	55	15	20	8	2
Open seats	5	19.0	60	10	9	17	8
House, 1986							
All candidates[a]	810	234.2	48	36	4	6	6
Democrats	427	125.7	44	42	2	6	6
Incumbents	235	84.1	42	49	1	2	6
Challengers	147	22.1	49	29	6	13	3
Open seats	45	19.5	47	31	3	15	4
Republicans	383	108.5	53	29	6	7	5
Incumbents	160	67.3	53	37	4	1	5
Challengers	182	21.4	54	11	10	22	3
Open seats	41	19.8	53	24	10	10	3

Senate, 1986

All candidates[a]	68	208.6	60	21	9	6	4
Democrats	34	90.2	56	22	8	9	5
Incumbents	9	28.2	62	26	7	2	3
Challengers	18	40.3	51	19	9	16	5
Open seats	7	21.7	60	22	8	5	5
Republicans	34	118.5	63	21	9	2	5
Incumbents	18	68.9	63	24	8	<1	5
Challengers	9	20.4	64	9	18	6	3
Open seats	7	29.1	61	22	6	2	9

House, 1988

All candidates[a]	813	249.0	46	40	4	5	5
Democrats	429	140.0	40	47	3	5	5
Incumbents	238	103.8	39	51	2	1	7
Challengers	154	23.5	46	31	7	13	3
Open seats	27	12.7	39	36	7	14	4
Republicans	384	109.0	52	31	6	6	5
Incumbents	164	73.7	51	39	3	1	6
Challengers	194	21.6	55	10	13	19	3
Open seats	26	13.7	54	21	13	12	<1

(table continues)

Table 3-8 *(continued)*

Party and candidate status	Number of candidates	Contributions plus party expenditures on behalf of candidates ($ millions)	Percentage coming from:				
			Individuals	PACs	Party (contributions plus expenditures)	Candidate to self (contributions plus loans)	Other
Senate, 1988							
All candidates[a]	66	199.4	59	22	9	5	5
Democrats	33	103.0	58	23	7	8	4
Incumbents	15	53.0	61	29	4	1	5
Challengers	12	29.1	66	16	11	3	4
Open seats	6	20.9	37	16	8	35	4
Republicans	33	96.3	61	22	11	2	4
Incumbents	12	50.8	62	26	8	<1	4
Challengers	15	27.7	63	11	18	6	2
Open seats	6	17.8	54	26	13	1	6
House, 1990							
All candidates[a]	807	257.5	44	40	3	6	7
Democrats	413	146.5	39	47	3	5	6
Incumbents	249	113.2	37	52	1	2	8
Challengers	132	16.0	44	27	9	16	4
Open seats	32	17.3	42	33	4	17	4

Republicans	394	108.8	51	32	4	7	6
Incumbents	159	70.7	50	41	2	1	6
Challengers	206	23.9	54	10	7	24	5
Open seats	29	14.1	50	24	10	12	4
Senate, 1990							
All candidates[a]	67	191.0	61	21	7	5	6
Democrats	34	90.8	63	22	6	4	5
Incumbents	17	66.7	65	25	5	0	5
Challengers	14	21.0	58	12	9	15	6
Open seats	3	3.1	50	18	11	21	<1
Republicans	33	100.2	59	21	9	5	6
Incumbents	15	58.9	65	22	7	0	6
Challengers	15	33.4	51	16	12	15	6
Open seats	3	7.9	43	36	7	0	14
House, 1992							
All candidates[a]	851	331.5	47	36	5	9	3
Democrats	427	184.7	43	43	4	6	4
Incumbents	213	122.1	40	50	2	1	7
Challengers	140	25.1	48	26	10	13	3
Open seats	74	37.5	49	30	4	17	<1

(table continues)

Table 3-8 *(continued)*

Party and candidate status	Number of candidates	Contributions plus party expenditures on behalf of candidates ($ millions)	Percentage coming from: Individuals	PACs	Party (contributions plus expenditures)	Candidate to self (contributions plus loans)	Other
Republicans	424	146.9	51	26	6	13	4
Incumbents	138	74.8	52	39	3	1	5
Challengers	216	44.5	47	9	10	22	12
Open seats	70	27.5	57	21	7	14	1
Senate, 1992							
All candidates[a]	71	214.2	58	21	13	5	3
Democrats	35	108.5	60	23	11	2	4
Incumbents	15	43.9	52	35	6	2	5
Challengers	13	43.1	68	12	14	3	3
Open seats	7	21.5	61	19	13	3	4
Republicans	36	106.9	55	19	15	7	4
Incumbents	12	59.4	58	25	13	<1	4
Challengers	17	24.0	55	9	20	14	2
Open seats	7	23.5	48	16	16	18	2

	House, 1994						
All candidates[a]	824	371.3	49	34	5	8	4
Democrats	403	196.7	43	43	5	5	4
Incumbents	226	142.4	34	50	3	1	12
Challengers	130	23.6	45	23	11	17	4
Open seats	47	30.7	47	27	8	15	3
Republicans	421	174.6	56	24	6	11	3
Incumbents	157	82.9	58	36	2	1	3
Challengers	217	58.6	56	10	10	20	4
Open seats	47	33.1	50	19	8	19	4
	Senate, 1994						
All candidates[a]	70	291.7	54	15	8	19	4
Democrats	35	124.9	55	18	10	12	5
Incumbents	16	86.4	54	18	8	14	6
Challengers	10	11.7	46	16	13	21	4
Open seats	9	26.9	60	16	14	3	7
Republicans	35	166.7	53	13	6	24	4
Incumbents	10	35.4	60	30	6	<1	4
Challengers	16	96.1	47	3	5	41	4
Open seats	9	35.2	61	21	11	1	6
	House, 1996						
All candidates[a]	873	460.8	53	33	4	6	4
Democrats	435	211.6	48	35	4	9	4
Incumbents	171	108.8	47	46	2	1	5

(table continues)

Table 3-8 *(continued)*

Party and candidate status	Number of candidates	Contributions plus party expenditures on behalf of candidates ($ millions)	*Percentage coming from:*				
			Individuals	PACs	Party (contributions plus expenditures)	Candidate to self (contributions plus loans)	Other
Challengers	211	67.3	50	24	6	17	3
Open seats	53	35.5	48	26	5	18	3
Republicans	438	249.2	57	30	4	4	4
Incumbents	213	171.3	58	37	2	1	2
Challengers	174	40.0	64	11	9	13	3
Open seats	51	35.0	53	23	8	12	3
Senate, 1996							
All candidates[a]	68	242.1	58	17	9	12	4
Democrats	34	116.2	59	13	8	16	4
Incumbents	7	36.4	74	13	4	5	4
Challengers	14	36.5	50	6	8	34	2
Open seats	13	43.3	55	18	11	9	7
Republicans	34	125.9	57	21	9	8	4
Incumbents	13	50.0	57	29	9	2	4
Challengers	8	25.6	70	14	10	3	3
Open seats	13	50.3	50	18	9	18	5

House, 1998

All candidates[a]	782	436.1	51	35	3	6	4
Democrats	390	199.6	49	38	3	6	4
Incumbents	194	130.6	47	46	2	0	5
Challengers	162	41.6	52	19	4	21	3
Open seats	34	27.4	59	27	4	6	3
Republicans	392	236.5	53	33	3	6	4
Incumbents	211	166.6	54	39	2	1	5
Challengers	149	42.3	54	15	8	17	5
Open seats	32	27.6	45	28	5	18	3

Senate, 1998

All candidates[a]	70	265.9	58	18	7	11	7
Democrats	35	126.1	58	16	8	9	9
Incumbents	15	71.9	65	22	7	0	6
Challengers	15	39.4	45	4	10	27	15
Open seats	5	14.7	59	2	9	4	26
Republicans	35	139.8	57	19	7	12	4
Incumbents	14	72.7	60	26	6	3	5
Challengers	16	52.7	52	9	8	29	3
Open seats	5	14.3	59	25	8	0	8

a. This entry excludes minor-party candidates.

Source: Federal Election Commission.

Table 3-9 Number of Registered Political Action Committees, 1974–1998

Committee type	1974	1976	1978	1980	1984	1988	1990	1992	1994	1996	1998
Corporate	89	433	784	1,204	1,682	1,816	1,795	1,735	1,660	1,642	1,567
Labor	201	224	217	297	394	354	346	347	333	332	321
Trade/membership/health[a]	318	489	451	574	698	786	774	770	792	838	821
Nonconnected	—	—	165	378	1,053	1,115	1,062	1,145	980	1,103	935
Cooperative	—	—	12	42	52	59	59	56	53	41	39
Corporation without stock	—	—	24	56	130	138	136	142	136	123	115
Total	608	1,146	1,653	2,551	4,009	4,268	4,172	4,195	3,954	4,079	3,798

Note: The data are as of December 31 for every year.

a. This category includes all noncorporate and nonlabor PACs through December 31, 1976.

Source: Federal Election Commission PAC count press release, issued annually.

Table 3-10 PAC Contributions to Congressional Candidates, 1978–1998 (in $ millions)

Type of PAC	1978	1980	1982	1984	1986	1988	1990	1992	1994	1996	1998
Labor	9.9	13.2	20.3	24.8	29.9	33.9	33.6	39.7	40.7	46.5	43.4
Corporate	9.5	19.2	27.5	35.5	46.2	50.4	53.5	64.3	64.1	69.7	71.1
Trade/membership/health	11.2	15.9	21.9	26.7	32.9	38.9	42.5	51.4	50.1	56.2	59.0
Nonconnected	2.5	4.9	10.7	14.5	18.8	19.2	14.3	17.5	17.3	22.0	27.1
Other[a]	1.0	2.0	3.2	3.8	4.9	5.4	5.9	6.6	6.6	6.8	6.2
Total	34.1	55.2	83.6	105.3	132.7	147.8	149.7	179.4	178.8	201.2	206.8

Note: The data are for contributions to all candidates for election in the year indicated that were made during the two-year election cycle.

a. This category includes cooperatives and corporations without stock.

Table 3-11 How PACs Distributed Their Contributions to Congressional Candidates, 1978–1998

| | Percentage distribution (House) | | | | | | | | Percentage distribution (Senate) | | | | | | | | | |
| | Incumbent | | Challenger | | Open seat | | Percent to chamber | Dollars to chamber (in millions) | Incumbent | | Challenger | | Open seat | | Percent to chamber | Dollars to chamber (in millions) | Total percent | Total dollars (in millions) |
	D	R	D	R	D	R			D	R	D	R	D	R				
House / Senate, 1978																		
Corporate	22	18	1	10	4	8	63	6.2	6	14	2	7	3	6	37	3.6	100	9.8
Association	27	20	2	11	7	9	76	8.6	5	8	2	4	2	3	24	2.8	100	11.3
Labor	43	2	12	<1	14	<1	72	7.5	10	2	9	<1	5	<1	28	2.8	100	10.3
Nonconnected	9	10	3	29	4	18	74	2.1	3	5	3	10	1	5	26	0.7	100	2.8
Other PACs	49	12	2	1	8	5	77	0.8	5	5	2	4	4	3	23	0.2	100	1.0
All PACs	30	14	5	9	8	7	71	25.0	6	8	4	4	3	3	29	10.2	100	35.2
House / Senate, 1980																		
Corporate	23	21	1	13	1	6	64	11.7	9	5	<1	17	1	4	36	6.4	100	18.1
Association	29	24	1	13	2	6	75	11.2	9	4	1	8	1	2	25	3.8	100	15.0
Labor	50	3	12	<1	7	<1	72	8.9	18	3	4	<1	3	<1	28	3.4	100	12.3
Nonconnected	13	9	3	26	2	8	62	2.8	8	2	<1	20	<1	5	37	1.7	100	4.5
Other PACs	40	19	2	2	3	4	72	1.4	16	4	1	5	2	2	28	0.5	100	1.9
All PACs	31	17	3	10	3	5	69	36.0	11	4	1	10	2	2	31	15.9	100	51.9
House / Senate, 1982																		
Corporate	22	31	1	6	2	6	69	18.1	8	13	5	<1	<1	4	31	8.3	100	26.4
Association	26	32	3	6	3	6	77	15.9	9	9	1	2	<1	2	23	4.9	100	20.8
Labor	40	3	21	<1	11	1	75	14.6	14	2	7	<1	2	<1	25	4.8	100	19.4

(table continues)

Table 3-11 *(continued)*

	Percentage distribution (House)								Percentage distribution (Senate)									
	Incumbent		Challenger		Open seat		Percent to chamber	Dollars to chamber (in millions)	Incumbent		Challenger		Open seat		Percent to chamber	Dollars to chamber (in millions)	Total percent	Total dollars (in millions)
	D	R	D	R	D	R			D	R	D	R	D	R				
Nonconnected	20	13	11	12	5	7	69	6.9	9	6	5	7	2	2	31	3.2	100	10.0
Other PACs	40	25	3	1	4	3	78	2.4	11	5	2	<1	<1	3	22	0.7	100	3.1
All PACs	28	22	8	5	5	5	73	57.9	9	6	5	7	2	2	27	21.8	100	79.7
	House, 1984								*Senate, 1984*									
Corporate	29	26	<1	7	4	4	67	22.9	7	19	1	2	1	4	33	11.4	100	34.3
Association	36	28	2	5	2	4	77	19.8	6	11	2	1	1	1	23	6.0	100	25.8
Labor	57	4	14	<1	5	<1	80	18.7	6	1	9	<1	4	<1	20	4.6	100	23.3
Nonconnected	26	9	5	15	3	6	63	8.6	7	10	10	4	3	2	37	5.1	100	13.7
Other PACs	48	23	2	2	1	2	78	2.9	7	10	2	1	2	1	22	0.8	100	3.7
All PACs	38	18	4	6	2	3	72	72.9	6	11	4	2	2	2	28	27.9	100	100.8
	House, 1986								*Senate, 1986*									
Corporate	26	24	1	2	1	4	58	26.4	5	20	3	3	2	9	42	19.0	100	45.3
Association	33	27	2	2	3	5	71	23.0	6	12	4	1	2	4	29	9.4	100	32.4
Labor	45	5	14	<1	10	<1	75	21.9	6	2	11	<1	6	<1	25	7.1	100	29.1
Nonconnected	21	12	8	5	7	6	59	10.7	6	11	10	2	7	5	41	7.5	100	18.2
Other PACs	36	23	1	2	2	2	67	3.2	6	15	6	1	2	3	33	1.6	100	4.8
All PACs	32	19	5	2	5	4	66	85.2	5	13	6	1	4	5	34	44.6	100	129.8
	House, 1988								*Senate, 1988*									
Corporate	31	26	1	2	1	3	63	31.6	11	14	4	1	3	5	37	18.8	100	50.4
Association	37	26	2	1	3	4	73	28.6	9	9	2	1	2	3	27	10.4	100	38.9

(continued from previous section)

PAC type	Inc. D	Inc. R	Chal. D	Chal. R	Open D	Open R	House %	House $ (mil.)	Inc. D	Inc. R	Chal. D	Chal. R	Open D	Open R	Senate %	Senate $ (mil.)	Total %	Total $ (mil.)
Labor	50	6	15	<1	9	<1	79	26.8	9	1	6	<1	4	<1	21	7.1	100	33.9
Nonconnected	25	12	8	4	6	4	59	11.4	13	9	7	3	4	4	41	7.8	100	19.2
Other PACs	41	23	1	2	2	2	72	3.8	12	9	2	1	2	2	28	1.5	100	5.3
All PACs	36	19	6	1	4	3	69	102.2	10	9	3	2	3	3	31	45.7	100	147.8

House, 1990 / Senate, 1990

PAC type	Inc. D	Inc. R	Chal. D	Chal. R	Open D	Open R	House %	House $ (mil.)	Inc. D	Inc. R	Chal. D	Chal. R	Open D	Open R	Senate %	Senate $ (mil.)	Total %	Total $ (mil.)
Corporate	32	25	1	2	2	4	66	35.4	13	11	<1	6	3	1	34	18.0	100	53.5
Association	40	25	2	2	5	5	77	32.5	9	8	1	3	2	<1	23	10.0	100	42.5
Labor	54	5	9	<1	13	<1	82	27.6	11	1	5	<1	1	<1	18	6.0	100	33.6
Nonconnected	26	13	4	4	8	5	60	8.5	20	10	2	5	1	2	40	5.7	100	14.3
Other PACs	46	21	1	2	2	2	74	4.3	13	8	1	2	2	<1	26	1.5	100	5.8
All PACs	39	19	3	1	6	4	72	108.5	11	9	2	3	2	1	28	41.2	100	149.7

House, 1992 / Senate, 1992

PAC type	Inc. D	Inc. R	Chal. D	Chal. R	Open D	Open R	House %	House $ (mil.)	Inc. D	Inc. R	Chal. D	Chal. R	Open D	Open R	Senate %	Senate $ (mil.)	Total %	Total $ (mil.)
Corporate	32	23	1	3	1	5	67	42.9	10	13	2	2	2	4	33	21.2	100	64.1
Association	35	22	3	3	7	6	76	38.7	8	8	1	2	2	3	24	12.4	100	51.1
Labor	48	3	11	<1	16	1	78	30.5	9	1	7	<1	5	<1	22	8.6	100	39.1
Nonconnected	25	11	5	5	9	1	60	10.3	12	10	6	3	6	3	40	6.9	100	17.2
Other PACs	43	19	1	2	4	3	72	4.2	11	9	2	2	2	2	28	1.6	100	5.7
All PACs	36	17	4	2	8	4	71	127.0	9	8	3	3	3	3	29	51.1	100	178.1

House, 1994 / Senate, 1994

PAC type	Inc. D	Inc. R	Chal. D	Chal. R	Open D	Open R	House %	House $ (mil.)	Inc. D	Inc. R	Chal. D	Chal. R	Open D	Open R	Senate %	Senate $ (mil.)	Total %	Total $ (mil.)
Corporate	34	22	1	4	2	5	68	43.4	9	9	2	3	2	5	32	20.6	100	64.1
Association	37	22	2	5	5	6	77	38.6	7	6	2	5	2	<1	23	11.3	100	50.0
Labor	55	3	10	<1	14	<1	82	33.3	9	<1	4	<1	5	<1	18	7.2	100	40.4

(table continues)

Table 3-11   (continued)

| | Percentage distribution (House) | | | | | | | | Percentage distribution (Senate) | | | | | | | | | |
| | Incumbent | | Challenger | | Open seat | | Percent to chamber | Dollars to chamber (in millions) | Incumbent | | Challenger | | Open seat | | Percent to chamber | Dollars to chamber (in millions) | Total percent | Total dollars (in millions) |
	D	R	D	R	D	R			D	R	D	R	D	R				
Nonconnected	31	11	4	7	7	6	66	11.6	11	7	1	3	5	5	33	5.6	100	17.3
Other PACs	43	18	2	4	4	4	74	4.0	11	5	1	1	3	4	26	1.8	100	6.6
All PACs	40	15	4	4	6	4	74	138.8	9	5	1	2	3	5	26	46.5	100	178.4
House, 1996 / Senate, 1996																		
Corporate	20	44	<1	2	2	5	74	51.3	2	11	<1	3	3	7	26	18.3	100	69.6
Association	21	40	3	3	4	6	79	44.0	2	8	1	2	3	6	22	12.0	100	56.0
Labor	41	5	25	<1	13	<1	85	39.4	3	1	3	<1	8	<1	15	6.9	100	46.3
Nonconnected	16	26	10	6	4	7	69	15.1	4	9	2	4	5	7	31	6.9	100	22.0
Other PACs	27	36	3	3	3	5	76	5.2	3	7	2	2	4	5	24	1.5	100	6.7
All PACs	25	30	8	3	5	5	76	155.0	3	7	2	2	5	5	24	45.6	100	200.6
House, 1998 / Senate, 1998																		
Corporate	21	41	0	2	1	5	70	50.3	8	14	0	3	2	3	29	20.9	100	71.1
Association	25	40	2	3	3	6	79	46.5	6	9	0	2	2	2	21	12.5	100	59.0
Labor	54	7	12	0	13	0	86	37.3	8	1	2	0	2	0	14	6.0	100	43.4
Nonconnected	18	24	5	11	5	11	74	20.0	9	9	1	3	2	2	26	7.1	100	27.1
Other PACs	31	35	1	3	2	3	76	4.7	10	9	1	2	1	1	24	1.5	100	6.2
All PACs	29	31	4	3	5	5	77	158.7	8	9	1	2	2	2	23	48.1	100	206.8

Notes: The data are for general-election candidates only. D indicates Democrat; R indicates Republican. Percentages may not add to 100 because of rounding.

Source: Federal Election Commission.

Figure 3-4 Political Party Contributions and Coordinated Expenditures for Congress, 1976–1998

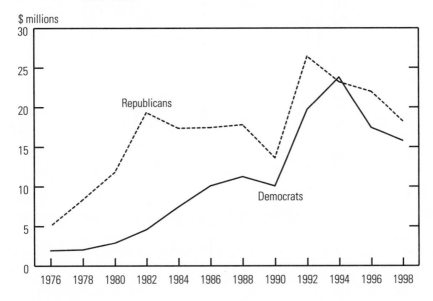

Source: Table 3-12.

Figure 3-5 Independent Expenditures in Senate and House Elections, 1978–1998

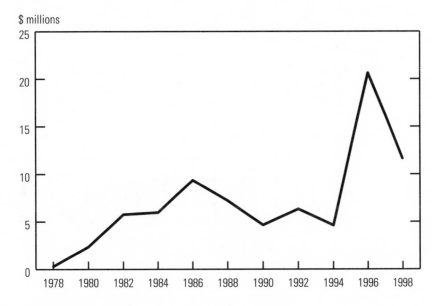

Source: Table 3-14.

Table 3-12 Political Party Contributions and Coordinated Expenditures for Congressional Candidates, 1976–1998 (in dollars)

	Senate		House		Total
	Contributions	Expenditures	Contributions	Expenditures	
1976					
Democrats	468,795	4,359	1,465,629	500	1,939,283
Republicans	930,034	113,976	3,658,310	329,583	5,031,903
1978					
Democrats	466,683	229,218	1,262,298	72,892	2,031,091
Republicans	703,204	2,723,880	3,621,104	1,297,079	8,345,267
1980					
Democrats	480,464	1,132,912	1,025,989	256,346	2,895,711
Republicans	677,004	5,434,758	3,498,323	2,203,748	11,813,833
1982					
Democrats	579,337	2,265,197	1,052,286	694,321	4,591,141
Republicans	600,221	8,715,761	4,720,959	5,293,260	19,330,201
1984					
Democrats	441,467	3,947,731	1,280,672	1,774,452	7,444,322
Republicans	590,922	6,518,415	4,060,120	6,190,309	17,359,766
1986					
Democrats	620,832	6,656,286	968,913	1,836,213	10,082,244
Republicans	729,522	10,077,902	2,520,278	4,111,474	17,439,176
1988					
Democrats	501,777	6,592,264	1,258,952	2,891,152	11,244,145
Republicans	719,006	10,260,600	2,657,069	4,162,207	17,798,882

1990					
Democrats	515,332	5,210,002	943,135	3,401,579	10,070,048
Republicans	862,621	7,725,853	2,019,279	3,012,313	13,620,066
1992					
Democrats	689,953	11,915,878	1,234,553	5,883,678	19,724,102
Republicans	807,397	16,509,940	2,197,611	6,906,729	26,421,677
1994					
Democrats	638,618	13,204,309	1,501,220	8,455,070	23,799,217
Republicans	748,011	11,561,866	2,036,712	8,851,871	23,198,460
1996					
Democrats	637,734	8,611,897	1,387,952	6,786,959	17,424,542
Republicans	772,244	10,751,093	2,462,999	7,998,844	21,985,180
1998					
Democrats	302,478	9,349,948	1,542,312	4,596,380	15,791,118
Republicans	514,657	9,334,065	2,098,276	6,310,120	18,257,118

Note: The table includes direct contributions made by party committees to congressional candidates and coordinated expenditures made on their behalf, known as 441a(d) expenditures because the legal spending limits are contained in U. S. Code, Title 2, sec. 441a(d). Under that provision, party committees are allowed to spend money on behalf of federal candidates, in addition to the money they may contribute directly.

House candidates may receive in direct contributions up to $10,000 each ($5,000 in the primary and $5,000 in the general election) from the national party, congressional campaign committee, Senate campaign committee, and state party. Senate candidates may receive in direct contributions a total of $17,500 from the national party and senatorial campaign committee and another $10,000 each from the congressional party and the state party.

The limits on 441a(d) expenditures are as follows: (a) for Senate candidates, two cents times the voting age population, or $20,000 in 1974 dollars adjusted for inflation, whichever is greater; (b) for House candidates from states with only one House district, $20,000 in 1974 dollars adjusted for inflation; and (c) for all other House candidates, $10,000 in 1974 dollars adjusted for inflation. State parties are allowed to spend equal amounts on behalf of congressional candidates, and court decisions permit state and local parties to designate a national party committee as its agent for those expenditures.

Combining the maximum national party contributions, home state party contributions, and 441a(d) expenditure limits would have given House candidates $105,100 in 1998. Senate limits ranged from a low of $167,700 in small states to a high of $3,730,374 in California.

Table 3-13   "Soft Money" Disbursements by National Party Committees from Nonfederal Accounts, 1992–1998 (in dollars)

	1992	1994	1996	1998
Democratic				
National Committee	28,388,869	45,097,098	100,483,977	57,411,879
Senatorial	506,362	416,743	14,061,273	25,858,673
Congressional	4,017,579	5,135,552	11,822,790	16,617,533
Total	32,878,310	50,383,546	121,826,562	92,987,711
Republican				
National Committee	33,601,431	42,413,166	114,401,973	74,325,722
Senatorial	7,655,641	6,527,505	29,362,653	37,283,103
Congressional	6,209,404	4,747,525	28,746,879	24,092,993
Total	46,176,476	48,387,091	149,658,099	127,730,744

Note: The data are as reported to the Federal Election Commission for each full two-year cycle.

Table 3-14   Independent Expenditures in House and Senate Elections, 1978–1998 (in dollars)

	For Democrats	Against Democrats	For Republicans	Against Republicans	Total
1978					
House	28,725	31,034	70,701	5,298	135,758
Senate	102,508	36,717	26,065	1,985	167,275
1980					
House	190,615	38,023	410,478	45,132	684,248
Senate	127,381	1,282,613	261,678	12,430	1,684,102
1982					
House	241,442	862,654	492,404	66,296	1,662,796
Senate	127,451	3,182,986	298,410	483,750	4,092,597
1984					
House	560,727	118,171	633,646	26,847	1,339,391
Senate	326,031	410,428	1,807,981	2,082,207	4,626,647
1986					
House	2,385,685	227,286	1,313,578	120,032	4,046,581
Senate	988,382	632,412	3,342,790	348,006	5,311,590
1988					
House	1,465,554	278,723	919,929	148,705	2,812,911
Senate	831,064	617,066	2,809,517	143,441	4,401,088
1990					
House	709,292	130,695	669,726	74,444	1,584,157
Senate	780,832	266,230	1,436,553	584,429	3,068,044
1992					
House	1,485,768	430,902	1,586,017	452,942	3,955,629
Senate	1,137,321	164,358	864,493	210,490	2,376,662
1994					
House	502,621	488,479	1,088,356	50,815	2,130,271
Senate	204,212	433,947	1,309,572	537,531	2,485,262
1996					
House	711,226	158,132	2,630,273	1,401,101	4,900,732
Senate	337,594	5,575,164	7,567,653	2,239,230	15,719,641
1998					
House	1,816,997	299,876	3,783,017	601,976	6,501,866
Senate	1,529,340	110,971	1,694,742	1,811,575	5,146,628

Note: An independent expenditure is defined as an "expenditure by a person for a communication expressly advocating the election or defeat of a clearly identified candidate that is not made with the cooperation or with the prior consent of, or in consultation with, or at the request or suggestion of, a candidate or any agent or authorized committee of such candidate" (11 C.F.R. 109.1[a]).

4

Committees

Congress does most of its work through the committee system. Virtually every bill passed into law has passed through at least one committee. Until 1975, committees frequently conducted their business in closed sessions. (See table 4-1.) The 106th Congress assembled over 200 committees to prepare legislation, examine presidential nominees, and oversee the federal bureaucracy.[1]

From the 1950s through the 1970s, the number of House committees and subcommittees grew erratically but persistently from around 130 panels in each body to a high of around 205. (See tables 4-2 and 4-3.) A period of stabilization and some small decline followed that growth up until the 103d Congress, which saw a significant drop in the total number of panels in the House. The decrease was due in large part to rules changes that tightened restrictions on the number of subcommittees allowed each standing committee, as well as to the elimination of the House's four select committees.

But members did not consider those reforms substantial enough. Therefore, the 103d Congress created the Joint Committee on the Organization of Congress to study the institution and introduce a comprehensive package of reforms. Unfortunately, when the particular recommendations for committee consolidation, including elimination of some panels and major changes in jurisdiction of others, were put before the full chamber, strong opposition and bickering among affected members prevented any significant reforms from being adopted. Immediately after the Republicans took over in the 104th Congress, they approved a series of committee changes as part of their agenda to reform the way the House operated. The total number of House panels dropped by 25 percent. In addition to eliminating three committees—the first decline in the number of full committees since 1955—the new rules stipulated that, with three exceptions, no committee could have more than five subcommittees. That lowered the total number of subcommittees to just above the 1955 level—an arrangement still in place in the 106th Congress.

The Senate has followed a much different pattern. (See tables 4-2 and 4-4.) In the mid-1970s the House and the Senate had roughly the same number of panels. In 1977 the upper chamber enacted comprehensive reforms and significantly cut the number of panels, particularly subcommittees. In 1976 the Senate had 205 panels compared with only 130 panels four years later. Initially, the new Republican Senate of 1980 sought a larger number of committees, but the Senate reversed course two years later and dropped back to the postreform levels. When the Republicans gained power again in 1994, they followed the House's lead and reduced the total number of panels, but not by nearly so much.

Between 1955 and 1991 the average number of assignments per member of the House more than doubled from 3 to 6.8. (See table 4-5.) The restructuring of the 104th Congress included a limitation to two standing committee and four subcommittee assignments for most members. That measure brought the average back down to under five seat assignments for each member—still much higher than the 1950s House average.

The average number of Senate assignments dropped from 17.6 in 1975 to 10.4 in 1979, following that body's restructuring. (See table 4-6.) The average began to rise again slightly until it was 11.8 in 1993 but has dropped back under 11 under the Republicans in the past three Congresses. Even with the reforms, senators average more than twice as many assignments as their House counterparts, a difference that reflects the nature of that less specialized body.

During the 1960s and 1970s the proportion of House majority party members holding chairmanships of committees and subcommittees steadily rose. (See table 4-7.) That figure stabilized at about 50 percent in the 1980s and has fallen some since then. We can directly trace that rise to the rise in the total number of panels created by each house. In 1971 the House Democrats passed a rule limiting most members to the chairmanship of only one subcommittee. The number of members with multiple chairmanships declined accordingly, and for the first time more than half of the majority party members held chairmanships of one kind or another. In the 1980s the number of members holding multiple chairmanships jumped significantly, until 1995, when the direction shifted again. The total number of majority members serving as chairs decreased under the Republicans, although the smaller majority margin kept the percentage of majority members chairing panels from falling much at all. In fact, the 106th Congress saw the percentage rise back above the 103d Congress's level. The impact of the current restrictions on "stockpiling" chairmanships is clearly seen in that only two members of the House chair more than one standing committee or subcommittee.

The number of chairmanships in the Senate is very different. (See table 4-8.) With the ratio of members to panels much smaller than in the House, few majority party senators have been denied a gavel of one sort or another since the 1950s; indeed, through the 1970s the average majority member held more than two chairs. In the 1980s that slipped under 2 and in 1999 dipped down to 1.7 per member. The Senate has always provided greater opportunities for junior members to rise to leadership positions. When the Republicans took over Congress in 1980, every single member of the party held a chair of one sort or another. Since the 100th Congress, the proportion has remained below 90 percent, until the 106th Congress, when the proportion rose again to 96.4 percent.

In the 1950s and early 1960s, Democrats from the Deep South constituted a near majority of their party—table 1-2 offers a more detailed regional breakdown—and they held an even greater share of committee chairmanships. (See table 4-9.) Their total strength in numbers, however, discouraged any challenge to the system of selecting chairmen by nonsoutherners who opposed the system's unrepresentative results. By the late 1960s, the South's share of the Democratic Party in Congress was on the wane, but its hold on chairmanships of committees, especially the most powerful committees, was more tenacious. The declining number of southern members facilitated a change in the seniority pattern for the election of chairmen in 1971. After that reform and the dramatic ouster of three southern chairmen in December 1974, the figures changed markedly. By the end of the decade, southerners were underrepresented in committee chairmanships, and while they regained some power in the 1980s, southerners failed to regain the disproportionate share of House chairmanships that they held in the 1950s and 1960s.

In 1994 the Republicans took over the South and, as a consequence, Congress. For the first time since Reconstruction, Republicans captured a majority of southern seats in the House and the Senate. Still, southerners now make up a smaller percentage of the majority and hold a smaller share of committee chairmanships than in the Democratic majority. The region is still powerful, however, because southerners chair two of the three exclusive committees in the House. Southern Republicans may hope to increase their strength if the party can retain majority status. But the term limits for committee chairs make that very uncertain.

The Senate story is very similar in that instance. Through the departure from the Senate of senior southerners and their replacement at the top rungs of committee seniority by nonsouthern Democrats, a broader and more equal regional distribution of power was achieved by the mid-1970s. Although control of the chamber shifted in the 1980s, Southerners managed to retain a disproportionate level of chairmanships; several southern Republicans had been elected already, so the region managed to retain power under both parties. In 1994 the Republicans took over the Senate again, but then the large share of southern senators in the party were new and without seniority. A quarter of the party came from the South, but only 12 percent of the chairmanships. That figure rebounded only two years later and now holds steady at 24 percent—a figure significantly lower than previous years but more in line with the southern share of the Republican Party.

Note

1. The number of subcommittees in a given Congress is a particularly nebulous figure. During any Congress, subcommittees are added or dropped, and some ad hoc or special units may be listed or omitted from the various directories. We consulted multiple sources, including current committees' websites, for each Congress to obtain the number of subcommittees.

Table 4-1 Closed House and Senate Committee Meetings, 1953–1975

Year	Total meetings	Number closed	% closed
1953	2,640	892	34
1954	3,002	1,243	41
1955	2,940	1,055	36
1956	3,120	1,130	36
1957	2,517	854	34
1958	3,472	1,167	34
1959	3,152	940	30
1960	2,424	840	35
1961	3,159	1,109	35
1962	2,929	991	34
1963	3,868	1,463	38
1964	2,393	763	32
1965	3,903	1,537	39
1966	3,869	1,626	42
1967	4,412	1,716	39
1968	3,080	1,328	43
1969	4,029	1,470	36
1970	4,506	1,865	41
1971	4,816	1,731	36
1972	4,073	1,648	40
1973	5,520	887	16
1974	4,731	707	15
1975[a]	6,325	449	7
Total	84,880	27,411	32

Note: The totals include subcommittee meetings along with full committee sessions. Open meetings followed by closed meetings were counted twice, once in each category. Joint meetings of separate committees or subcommittees were counted as one meeting for each. The tabulations exclude meetings held when Congress was not in regular session, meetings held outside Washington, D.C., informal meetings without official status, and meetings of the House Rules Committee to consider sending legislation to the floor. Meetings of the House Appropriations Committee, all reported closed until 1971, were not included in the study until 1965.

a. Figures have not been computed after 1975 because virtually all committee meetings have been open. At the start of the 104th Congress, House Republicans passed a rule that all committee and subcommittee meetings must be open unless it would pose a threat to national security.

Source: Congressional Quarterly's Guide to Congress, 2d ed. (Washington, D.C.: Congressional Quarterly, 1976), 370.

Table 4-2 Number of Committees in the Senate and the House,
84th–106th Congresses, 1955–1999

Congress		Senate	House	Total[a]
84th	(1955–1956)	133	130	242
90th	(1967–1968)	155	185	315
92d	(1971–1972)	181	175	333
94th	(1975–1976)	205	204	385
96th	(1979–1980)	130	193	314
97th	(1981–1982)	136	174	300
98th	(1983–1984)	137	172	299
99th	(1985–1986)	120	191	301
100th	(1987–1988)	118	192	298
101st	(1989–1990)	118	189	295
102d	(1991–1992)	119	185	284
103d	(1993–1994)	111	146	252
104th	(1995–1996)	92	110	198
105th	(1997–1998)	92	112	200
106th	(1999–2000)	94	111	201

Note: "Committees" include standing committees, subcommittees of standing committees, select and special committees, subcommittees of select and special committees, joint committees, and subcommittees of joint committees.

a. The total is less than for the Senate and House combined because we count joint panels only once.

Sources: Charles B. Brownson, *Congressional Staff Directory* (Washington, D.C.: Congressional Staff Directory, various years); *Congressional Quarterly Almanac* (Washington, D.C.: Congressional Quarterly, various years); *Congressional Yellow Book* (Washington, D.C.: Monitor Publishing Co., quarterly editions); Secretary of the Senate, *List of Standing Committees and Subcommittees and Select and Special Committees of the U.S. Senate,* March 25, 1991; Clerk of the House of Representatives, *List of Standing Committees and Select Committees and Their Subcommittees of the House of Representatives,* March 25, 1991; *Congressional Quarterly Committee Guide* (Washington, D.C.: Congressional Quarterly, May 1, 1993; March 25, 1995; March 22, 1997; March 13, 1999).

Table 4-3 Number and Type of House Committees, 84th–106th Congresses, 1955–1999

Congress		Standing committees	Subcommittees of standing committees	Select and special committees	Subcommittees of select and special committees	Joint committees	Subcommittees of joint committees
84th	(1955–1956)	19	83	2	5	10	11
90th	(1967–1968)	20	133	1	6	10	15
92d	(1971–1972)	21	120	3	8	8	15
94th	(1975–1976)	22	151	3	4	7	17
96th	(1979–1980)	22	149[a]	5	8	4	5
97th	(1981–1982)	22	132	3	7	4	6
98th	(1983–1984)	22	130	3	7	4	6
99th	(1985–1986)	22	142	5	12	4	6
100th	(1987–1988)	22	140[b]	6	12	4	8
101st	(1989–1990)	22	138[b]	5	12	4	8
102d	(1991–1992)	22	135[b]	5	11	4	8
103d	(1993–1994)	22	115	1	3	5	0
104th	(1995–1996)	19	84	1	2	4	0
105th	(1997–1998)	19	86	1	2	4	0
106th	(1999–2000)	19	85	1	2	4	0

a. This number includes nine budget task forces and the Welfare and Pension Plans Task Force (of the Subcommittee on Labor Management Relations of the Education and Labor Committee).

b. This number includes panels and task forces only if the committee has no subcommittees.

Sources: Congressional Staff Directory; Congressional Quarterly Almanac; Congressional Yellow Book; Clerk of the House of Representatives; *Congressional Quarterly Committee Guide,* May 1, 1993; March 25, 1995; March 22, 1997; March 13, 1999.

Table 4-4 Number and Type of Senate Committees, 84th–106th Congresses, 1955–1999

Congress		Standing committees	Subcommittees of standing committees	Select and special committees	Subcommittees of select and special committees	Joint committees	Subcommittees of joint committees
84th	(1955–1956)	15	88	3	6	10	11
90th	(1967–1968)	16	99	3	12	10	15
92d	(1971–1972)	17	123	5	13	8	15
94th	(1975–1976)	18	140	6	17	7	17
96th	(1979–1980)	15	91	5	10	4	5
97th	(1981–1982)	15	94	5	12	4	6
98th	(1983–1984)	16	103	4	4	4	6
99th	(1985–1986)	16	90	4	0	4	6
100th	(1987–1988)	16	85	5	0	4	8
101st	(1989–1990)	16	86	4	0	4	8
102d	(1991–1992)	16	87	4	0	4	8
103d	(1993–1994)	17	86	3	0	5	0
104th	(1995–1996)	17	68	3	0	4	0
105th	(1997–1998)	17	68	3	0	4	0
106th	(1999–2000)	17	68	4	0	4	0

Sources: Congressional Staff Directory; Congressional Quarterly Almanac; Walter Oleszek, "Overview of the Senate Committee System" (paper prepared for the Commission on the Operation of the Senate, 1977); *Congressional Yellow Book;* Secretary of the Senate; *Congressional Quarterly Committee Guide,* May 1, 1993; March 25, 1995; March 22, 1997; March 13, 1999.

Table 4-5 Committee Assignments for Representatives, 84th–106th Congresses, 1955–1999

Congress		Mean no. of standing committee assignments	Mean no. of subcommittees of standing committee assignments	Mean no. of other committee assignments[a]	Total
84th	(1955–1956)	1.2	1.6	0.2	3.0
92d	(1971–1972)	1.5	3.2	0.4	5.1
94th	(1975–1976)	1.8	4.0	0.4	6.2
96th	(1979–1980)	1.7	3.6	0.5	5.8
97th	(1981–1982)	1.7	3.4	0.4	5.5
98th	(1983–1984)	1.7	3.6	0.5	5.8
99th	(1985–1986)	1.8	4.0	0.8	6.6
100th	(1987–1988)	1.7	3.8	1.0[b]	6.5
101st	(1989–1990)	1.8	3.9	1.1[b]	6.8
102d	(1991–1992)	1.9	4.0	0.9[b]	6.8
103d	(1993–1994)	2.0	3.7	0.2	5.9
104th	(1995–1996)	1.8	2.9	0.1	4.8
105th	(1997–1998)	1.8	3.2	0.1	5.1
106th	(1999–2000)	1.9	3.2	0.1	5.2

a. "Other" committees include select and special committees, subcommittees of select and special committees, joint committees, and subcommittees of joint committees.
b. This number includes task forces when the committee has no other subcommittees.

Sources: Congressional Staff Directory; Congressional Quarterly Almanac; Congressional Yellow Book; Clerk of the House of Representatives; *Congressional Quarterly Committee Guide,* May 1, 1993; March 25, 1995; March 22, 1997; March 13, 1999.

Table 4-6 Committee Assignments for Senators, 84th–106th Congresses, 1955–1999

Congress		Mean no. of standing committee assignments	Mean no. of subcommittees of standing committee assignments	Mean no. of other committee assignments[a]	Total
84th	(1955–1956)	2.2	4.8	0.9	7.9
92d	(1971–1972)	2.5	9.5	3.3	15.3
94th	(1975–1976)	2.5	11.0	4.1	17.6
96th	(1979–1980)	2.3	6.6	1.5	10.4
97th	(1981–1982)	2.5	6.7	1.5	10.7
98th	(1983–1984)	2.9	7.5	1.2	11.6
99th	(1985–1986)	2.8	6.9	0.9	10.6
100th	(1987–1988)	2.9	7.0	1.2	11.1
101st	(1989–1990)	3.0	7.0	1.1	11.1
102d	(1991–1992)	2.9	7.4	1.1	11.0
103d	(1993–1994)	3.2	7.8	0.8	11.8
104th	(1995–1996)	3.1	6.2	0.7	10.8
105th	(1997–1998)	3.1	6.5	0.7	10.3
106th	(1999–2000)	3.2	6.8	0.7	10.7

a. "Other" committees include select and special committees, subcommittees of select and special committees, joint committees, and subcommittees of joint committees.

Sources: Congressional Staff Directory; Congressional Quarterly Almanac; Congressional Yellow Book; Secretary of the Senate; *Congressional Quarterly Committee Guide,* May 1, 1993; March 25, 1995; March 22, 1997; March 13, 1999.

Table 4-7   Majority Party Chairmanships of House Committees and Subcommittees, 84th–106th Congresses, 1955–1999

Congress		Party in majority	No. of majority party members in House	No. chairing standing committees and subcommittees	No. with two or more chairmanships	% chairing standing committees and subcommittees	No. chairing all committees and subcommittees[a]	No. with two or more chairmanships	% chairing all committees and subcommittees[a]
84th	(1955–1956)	D	232	63	18	27.2	75	22	32.3
90th	(1967–1968)	D	247	111	32	44.9	117	38	47.4
92d	(1971–1972)	D	254	120	25	47.2	131	31	51.6
94th	(1975–1976)	D	289	142	24	49.1	150	28	51.9
96th	(1979–1980)	D	276	144	19	52.2	149	28	54.0
97th	(1981–1982)	D	243	121	16	49.8	125	26	51.4
98th	(1983–1984)	D	267	124	23	46.4	127	33	47.6
99th	(1985–1986)	D	253	129	27	51.0	131	37	51.8
100th	(1987–1988)	D	258	128	28	49.6	132[b]	42	51.2
101st	(1989–1990)	D	260	134	26	51.5	137	38	52.7
102d	(1991–1992)	D	267	130	25	48.7	135[b]	37	50.6
103d	(1993–1994)	D	258	113	19	43.8	116	22	45.0
104th	(1995–1996)	R	230	102	1	44.3	103	4	44.8
105th	(1997–1998)	R	227	101	4	44.5	102	9	44.9
106th	(1999–2000)	R	223	100	2	44.8	101	6	45.3

a. This number includes standing committees, subcommittees of standing committees, select and special committees, subcommittees of select and special committees, joint committees, and subcommittees of joint committees.
b. This number includes task forces when the committee has no other subcommittees.

Sources: Congressional Staff Directory; Congressional Quarterly Almanac; Clerk of the House of Representatives; *Congressional Quarterly Committee Guide,* May 1, 1993; March 25, 1995; March 22, 1997; March 13, 1999.

Table 4-8 Majority Party Chairmanships of Senate Committees and Subcommittees, 84th–106th Congresses, 1955–1999

Congress		Party in majority	No. of majority party in Senate	No. chairing standing committees and subcommittees	% chairing standing committees and subcommittees	Average no. of standing committees and subcommittees chaired by majority members	No. chairing all committees and subcommittees[a]	% chairing all committees and subcommittees[a]	Average no. of all committees and subcommittees chaired by majority members[a]
84th	(1955–1956)	D	48	42	87.5	1.8	42	87.5	2.0
90th	(1967–1968)	D	64	55	85.9	1.8	58	90.6	2.1
92d	(1971–1972)	D	55[b]	51	92.7	2.6	52	94.5	2.9
94th	(1975–1976)	D	62[b]	57	91.9	2.4	57	91.9	2.9
96th	(1979–1980)	D	59[b]	58	98.3	1.8	58	98.3	2.1
97th	(1981–1982)	R	53	51	96.2	1.9	52	98.1	2.3
98th	(1983–1984)	R	54	52	96.3	1.9	52	96.3	2.5
99th	(1985–1986)	R	53	49	92.4	1.9	49	92.4	2.0
100th	(1987–1988)[c]	D	54	47	87.0	1.8	47	87.0	2.0
101st	(1989–1990)	D	55	46	83.6	1.9	46	83.6	1.9
102d	(1991–1992)	D	56	50	89.3	1.8	50	89.3	2.0
103d	(1993–1994)	D	57	46	80.7	1.8	46	80.7	1.9
104th	(1995–1996)	R	54	44	81.5	1.8	44	81.5	1.9
105th	(1997–1998)	R	55	48	87.3	1.7	48	87.3	1.9
106th	(1999–2000)	R	55	53	96.4	1.6	53	96.4	1.7

a. This number includes standing committees, subcommittees of standing committees, select and special committees, subcommittees of select and special committees, joint committees, and subcommittees of joint committees.

b. This number includes Harry Byrd, Jr., who was elected as an Independent.

c. Figures for the 100th Congress were compiled after the death of Sen. Edward Zorinsky (D-Neb.) but before the appointment of his successor and the redistribution of his chairmanships.

Sources: Congressional Staff Directory; Congressional Quarterly Almanac; Secretary of the Senate; Congressional Quarterly Committee Guide, May 1, 1993; March 25, 1995; March 22, 1997; March 13, 1999.

Table 4-9 Southern Chairmanships of House and Senate Standing Committees, 84th–106th Congresses, 1955–1999

	House				Senate			
Year	Number of southern chairmen	% of chairmanships held by southerners	% of exclusive committees[a] chaired by southerners	% of majority party[b] from the South	Number of southern chairmen	% of chairmanships held by southerners	% of exclusive committees[a] chaired by southerners	% of majority party[b] from the South
1955	12	63	67	43	8	53	50	46
1967	10	50	100	35	9	56	100	28
1971	8	38	100	31	9	53	100	30
1975	9	41	33	28	6	33	100	27
1979	5	23	33	28	4	27	50	28
1981	6	27	33	29	3	20	25	19
1983	7	32	67	30	3	19	25	20
1985	8	36	67	29	2	13	0	19
1987	7	31	67	29	7	44	75	30
1989	8	36	33	29	6	38	50	27
1991	8	36	33	29	6	38	50	27
1993	6	27	33	33	6	35	25	26
1995	4	21	67	25	2	12	50	25
1997	3	17	67	31	4	24	50	29
1999	6	32	67	32	4	24	50	25

a. In the House these include Ways and Means, Rules, and Appropriations; in the Senate these include Appropriations, Finance, Foreign Relations, and Armed Services.
b. In 1981, 1983, 1985, 1995, 1997, and 1999, the Republican Party was the majority party in the House. In 1995, 1997, and 1999, the Republican Party was also the majority party in the Senate. For all other years in the table, the Democratic Party was the majority party in both the Senate and the House.

Sources: Congressional Directory (Washington, D.C.: Government Printing Office, various years); Congressional Yellow Book; Congressional Quarterly Committee Guide, May 1, 1993; March 25, 1995; March 22, 1997; March 13, 1999.

5

Congressional Staff and Operating Expenses

Congress comprises a great deal more than elected senators and representatives. With over 23,000 employees in 1999 (see table 5-1 and figure 5-1), the legislative branch is larger than either the Departments of Energy, Labor, or Housing and Urban Development. Congress is by far the most heavily staffed legislative branch in the world. Members of Congress rely on their personal and committee staffs; Congress also employs major research agencies, such as the Congressional Research Service of the Library of Congress, and support personnel, such as mail carriers, police officers, television technicians, computer specialists, printers, carpenters, parking attendants, photographers, and laborers—all to keep the miniature city on Capitol Hill running smoothly.

The development of that large congressional establishment is a twentieth-century phenomenon. At the turn of the century, representatives had no personal staff, and senators had a total of only thirty-nine personal assistants. (See table 5-2 and figure 5-1.) By contrast, over 11,000 people served on the personal staffs of representatives and senators in 1998, and over 2,000 people were employed by congressional committees. In 1994 over 3,000 people served in congressional committees, but the GOP–controlled 104th Congress reduced the committee staff levels by more than 1,000—although the staff levels have begun to creep back up a bit since then.

The long-term enlargement of Congress's support staff reflects both the expanding role of the government in the United States and the changing role of the individual legislator. As government has done more, the congressional workload, in terms of both legislation and constituency service, has increased, and the staffing needs of Congress have expanded accordingly. The most dramatic staff growth took place in the years after World War II. The personal staffs of the House and Senate have increased more than fivefold and sixfold, respectively, since 1947. One reflection of the increased demands on legislators for constituency service and the members' encouragement of those demands for reelection purposes is the dramatic expansion of congressional staff working in constituency offices. Almost 45 percent of the personal staffs of representatives and close to one-third of each senator's staff now work in district or state offices—a dramatic increase since the early 1970s. (See tables 5-3 and 5-4.)

The staff explosion is also evident on the standing committees: even after the Republican reductions following the 1994 elections, House committee staffs are seven and a half times larger than in 1947, and Senate staffs are four times as large. (See table 5-5.) The largest increases in staff came in the 1970s. By the end of the decade, House staffs almost tripled. That growth was to a significant degree a result of the reform movement that swept the chamber. The sentiment for diluting the powers of committee chairmen extended to their nearly exclusive authority to hire and fire committee staff. Reforms allowed a much larger number of subcommittee chairmen and ranking members to hire their own staffs. In that period Senate committee staffs more than doubled, an increase traceable in part to a 1975 resolution authorizing one personal legislative assistant for each committee assignment (although those staffers were later shifted to the personal payroll during the 1977 Senate reforms).

Both chambers saw declines in 1993. In 1995 the Republicans opened Congress with a pledge to cut staffs by one-third, although the eventual cuts were not so deep. Despite that decline, congressional staffs have become the target of a good deal of the criticism aimed at Congress. Critics have portrayed congressional staffs as bloated and wasteful. While it is true that staffs grew sharply after World War II, the majority of that growth occurred from the late 1960s through the mid-1970s. That growth coincided with the decentralization movements within Congress and the increased tension between the legislative and executive branches. Staff growth has actually leveled off and declined significantly. In fact, personal congressional staff sizes are now at approximately the same level as they were twenty-five years ago.

Most congressional committees employ well over fifty persons, a far cry from the post–World War II era of small, informal committee staffs. (See tables 5-6 and 5-7.) Nonetheless, all but six House committees cut their staffs in 1993. In 1995 most committees trimmed their staffs to between forty and seventy persons, with only a few powerful committees retaining relatively large staffs. The size of a committee staff does not appear to be related uniformly to the reported power or desirability of an assignment to that committee. The powerful Senate Finance Committee, for example, is modestly staffed compared with the less influential Labor and Human Resources and Governmental Affairs Committees. Of course, some committees that are generally considered less desirable assignments may have expanded their staffs to attract new members.

A significant part of the congressional staff works for Congress's three major research agencies. (See table 5-8.) In the 1970s, Congress created two of those—the Congressional Budget Office and the Office of Technology Assessment.[1] Their creation reflected a basic factor underlying the growth of congressional staff. The expanded role of the government in domestic and international affairs had made Congress increasingly dependent on the executive branch for information. A growing distrust of the executive branch, which festered during the Johnson and Nixon administrations, convinced Congress of the necessity for congressionally controlled sources of information. Congress thus authorized those new agencies and simultaneously expanded the roles of the Congressional Research Service and the General Accounting Office. The GAO has multiple functions; its primary job is to review federal spending and management for Congress. In addition, the office offers legal opinions to government agencies, settles disputed claims by or against the United

States, and prescribes accounting standards for government-wide use. While a majority of the GAO's resources was devoted to the latter functions during the 1970s, the balance has since shifted, and today roughly 80 percent of the GAO's work is directly related to Congress.

Staff members play many roles in the legislative process. The infinite variety of staffing arrangements that exist in members' offices and on committees and the influence exercised by various staff members become apparent only through close examination of individual offices and committees. The role played by staff within individual offices may also change over time with the ebb and flow of political tides. President Reagan's ability to make Congress focus on budget issues, for example, greatly reduced the number of bills Congress passed, as did the focus President Clinton placed on health care reform in 1993. (See chapter 6 for a discussion of congressional workload.) That meant less chance for members to use their staffs as policy entrepreneurs. Still, although the number of bills passed declined in the early 1990s, most committees claimed some jurisdiction over the health care reform issue and had their staffers working on it fervently. Today, dozens of members have staff members researching their own social security plans and variations on each other's plans. In short, it is difficult, if not impossible to generalize about staffing roles and patterns solely on the basis of gross figures.

Increased employment has meant increased cost, and Congress is now a more than $2 billion enterprise. Although that may appear small when compared with the executive branch, Congress has grown at a spectacular rate over the same period as the staff growth. In the years between 1946 and 1998, legislative branch appropriations increased 4,231.9 percent. Over the same period, the consumer price index went up "only" 834.2 percent. (See table 5-9.) As recently as the mid-1960s, the cost of operating Congress was less than one-ninth of what it is today. Recent years have seen more legislative self-control: in the years between fiscal year 1976, when Congress first approached the billion-dollar threshold, and fiscal year 1994, legislative branch appropriations increased by only 140 percent, while the consumer price index increased by 160 percent. Republicans have been even more economical: the fiscal year 1998 budget reflected a $158.4 million decrease since 1992.[2]

The figures summarizing legislative branch appropriations include much more than the cost of House and Senate operations (although that is the largest single share by far). (See table 5-10.) The figures also include the expenses of such agencies as the Library of Congress, the Government Printing Office, the General Accounting Office, the Botanic Garden, and the Copyright Royalty Commission, which make up a large portion of the spending. In fact, actual House and Senate appropriations comprise under 50 percent of total legislative branch appropriations. And while total spending has fluctuated significantly through the years, figures within those other components have remained relatively stable over the past decade of greater fiscal restraint.

Members are given an allowance for operating their offices. In 1973 the Senate consolidated office expenses into one account to give members greater flexibility. The House followed suit in 1978. In 1995 the House GOP went one step further by consolidating all expenses into one account for each member. (See tables 5-11 and 5-12.) Because Congress is a labor-intensive enterprise, however, the largest share of the congressional allowance has always been for staff.

One of the perquisites of office available to members of Congress is use of the frank to send materials pertaining to the official business of Congress through the U.S. mails. In 1993 the cost of the congressional franking privilege was $67.7 million. (See table 5-13.) Until 1981, the main reasons for the growing use of the frank were a more liberal law, permitting members of Congress to send mail (including newsletters and questionnaires) addressed to "occupant," and the increased value that legislators attach to communications with their constituents. The rules have now changed to limit use of the frank and to prevent members from using the frank as a campaign tool. Those changes also make it harder to calculate the "cost" of franked mail.

Notes

1. In 1995 Congress abolished the Office of Technology Assessment.

2. In the source notes to the tables in this chapter, two kinds of frequently cited legislative appropriations documents are abbreviated as follows: (1) *House LBA Hearings for 19xx* = U.S. Congress, House of Representatives, Committee on Appropriations, Subcommittee on Legislative Branch Appropriations, *Hearings on Legislative Branch Appropriations for 19xx.* (2) *Senate LBA Hearings for 19xx* = U.S. Congress, Senate, Committee on Appropriations, *Hearings on Legislative Branch Appropriations for 19xx.* The year in the citation is the fiscal year covered by the appropriation hearing, not the calendar year that may appear in the table.

Table 5-1 Congressional Staff, 1979–1999

	1979	1981	1983	1985	1987	1989	1991	1993	1995	1997	1999
House											
Committee staff[a]	2,027	1,917	2,068	2,146	2,136	2,267	2,321	2,147[b]	1,266	1,276	1,267
Personal staff	7,067	7,487	7,606	7,528	7,584	7,569	7,278	7,400	7,186	7,282	7,216
Leadership staff[c]	162	127	135	144	138	133	149	132	134	126	179
Officers of the House, staff[d]	1,487	1,686	1,728	1,818	1,845	1,215	1,293	1,194	1,327	1,146	974
Subtotal, House	10,743	11,217	11,537	11,636	11,703	11,184	11,041	10,878	9,913	9,830	9,636
Senate											
Committee staff[a]	1,410	1,150	1,176	1,178	1,207	1,116	1,154	994	796	1,216	910
Personal staff	3,593	3,945	4,059	4,097	4,075	3,837	4,294	4,138	4,247	4,410	4,272
Leadership staff[c]	91	106	120	118	103	105	125	132	126	148	219
Officers of the Senate, staff[d]	828	878	948	976	904	926	1,092	1,165	994	958	990
Subtotal, Senate	5,922	6,079	6,303	6,369	6,289	5,984	6,665	6,429	6,163	6,732	6,391
Joint committee staffs	138	126	123	131	132	138	145	145	108	120	104
Support agencies[e]											
General Accounting Office	5,303	5,182	4,960	5,042	5,016	5,063	5,054	4,958	4,342	3,500	3,275
Congressional Research Service	847	849	853	860	860	860	831	814	746	747	747
Congressional Budget Office	207	218	211	222	226	226	226	230	214	232	232
Office of Technology Assessment	145	130	130	143	143	143	143	143	n.a.[f]	n.a.	n.a.
Subtotal, support agencies	6,502	6,379	6,154	6,267	6,245	6,292	6,254	6,145	5,302	4,479	4,254
Miscellaneous											
Architect	2,296	1,986	2,061	2,073	2,412	2,088	2,099	2,060	2,151	1,854	2,012
Capitol Police[g]	1,167	1,163	1,148	1,227	1,250	1,259	1,265	1,159	1,076	1,076	1,251
Subtotal	3,463	3,149	3,209	3,300	3,662	3,347	3,364	3,219	3,227	2,930	3,263
Total	26,768	26,950	27,326	27,703	28,031	26,945	27,469	26,816	24,713	24,091	23,648

(table continues)

Table 5-1 *(continued)*

Note: The totals reflect the number of full-time paid employees.

a. This includes select and special committee staffs. Therefore, the figures do not agree with those in table 5-5.

b. In addition to the staffs (twenty-nine members) of the Permanent Select Committee on Intelligence and the Joint Committee on the Organization of Congress, which retained twenty-nine staff members, three other select committees were in operation in 1993: the Select Committee on Aging, the Select Committee on Children, Youth, and Families, and the Special and Select Committee on Funerals. The 104th Congress did not reauthorize those committees, but the committees stayed on for a few months to complete previous business. Although the committees did little business in 1993, it should be noted that they retained small staffs during that time.

c. This includes legislative counsels' offices.

d. These include doorkeepers, parliamentarians, sergeants-at-arms, the clerk of the House, Senate majority and minority secretaries, and postmasters.

e. This edition makes adjustments to reflect the current division of labor among the various support agencies. Today, approximately 80 percent of the GAO's work is done directly for Congress; the Congressional Research Service is the branch of the Library of Congress that serves Congress most directly.

f. The Office of Technology Assessment was eliminated in 1995.

g. This includes sworn officers only.

Sources: For 1979, *Report of the Clerk of the House,* July 1, 1979–September 30, 1979; *Report of the Secretary of the Senate,* April 1, 1979–September 30, 1979; U.S. Office of Personnel Management, Work Force Analysis and Statistics Branch, *Federal Civilian Workforce Statistics,* monthly release, October 31, 1979, 6. For 1981, U.S. Congress, House, Committee on Appropriations, Subcommittee on Legislative Branch Appropriations, *Hearings on Legislative Branch Appropriations for 1983,* pt. 1, 24–28; U.S. Congress, Senate, Committee on Appropriations, *Hearings on Legislative Branch Appropriations for 1982,* 117, 253, 266; Senate Committee on Rules and Administration, *Senate Committee Funding,* 97th Cong., 1st sess., 1981, Committee Print 2; *Report of the Secretary of the Senate,* October 1, 1981–March 31, 1982, 1–23. For 1983, *House LBA Hearings for 1985,* pt. 1, 23–27; Office of the Clerk of the House; Senate Committee on Rules and Administration, *Senate Committee Funding,* 98th Cong., 2d sess., 1984, Committee Print 3; *Senate LBA Hearings for 1984,* 47, 276; Office of the U.S. Capitol Police. For 1985, *House LBA Hearings for 1987,* pt. 1, 22–27; *Report of the Clerk of the House,* October 1, 1985–December 31, 1985; Senate Committee on Rules and Administration, *Senate Committee Funding,* 99th Cong., 2d sess., 1986, Committee Print 2; *Senate LBA Hearings for 1986: Report of the Secretary of the Senate,* October 1, 1985–March 31, 1986; Office of the U.S. Capitol Police. For 1987, *House LBA Hearings for 1989,* pt. 2; Office of the Clerk of the House; *Senate LBA Hearings for 1988: Report of the Secretary of the Senate,* October 1, 1987–March 31, 1988; Bureau of the Census, *Statistical Abstract of the United States 1989* (Washington, D.C.: Government Printing Office, 1989), 252; Office of the Architect of the Capitol; Office of the U.S. Capitol Police. For 1989, *House LBA Hearings for 1991,* pt. 1; Office of the Clerk of the House; *Senate LBA Hearings for 1990: Report of the Secretary of the Senate,* October 1, 1989–March 31, 1990. For 1991, *House LBA Hearings for 1993,* pt. 1; *Report of the Clerk of the House,* October 1, 1991–December 31, 1991; *Senate LBA Hearings for 1992: Report of the Secretary of the Senate,* October 1, 1991–March 31, 1992. For 1993, *House LBA Hearings for 1995,* pt. 1; *Report of the Clerk of the House,* October 1, 1993–December 31, 1993; House Office of Finance; *Senate LBA Hearings for 1994: Report of the Secretary of the Senate,* October 1, 1993–March 31, 1994. For 1995, *Legislative Branch Appropriations for 1997; Report of the Secretary of the Senate,* October 1, 1995–March 31, 1996; House Office of Finance. For 1997, *Statement of Disbursements of the House,* January 1, 1997–March 31, 1997; *Report of the Secretary of the Senate,* October 1, 1996–March 31, 1997; *Legislative Branch Appropriations for 1998.* For 1999, *Statement of Disbursements of the House,* January 1, 1999–March 31, 1999; *Report of the Secretary of the Senate,* October 1, 1998–March 31, 1999; *Legislative Branch Appropriations for 2000.*

Table 5-2   Staffs of Members of the House and the Senate, 1891–1999

Year	Employees in House	Employees in Senate	Year	Employees in House	Employees in Senate
1891	n.a.	39	1984	7,385	3,949
1914	n.a.	72	1985	7,528	4,097
1930	870	280	1986	7,920[a]	3,774[a]
1935	870	424	1987	7,584	4,075
1947	1,440	590	1988	7,564	3,977
1957	2,441	1,115	1989	7,569	3,837
1967	4,055	1,749	1990	7,496	4,162
1972	5,280	2,426	1991	7,278	4,294
1976	6,939	3,251	1992	7,597	4,249
1977	6,942	3,554	1993	7,400	4,138
1978	6,944	3,268	1994	7,390	4,200
1979	7,067	3,593	1995	7,186	4,247
1980	7,371	3,746	1996	7,288	4,151
1981	7,487	3,945	1997	7,282	4,410
1982	7,511	4,041	1998	7,269	4,281
1983	7,606	4,059	1999	7,216	4,272

Notes: The totals reflect the number of full-time paid employees.

n.a. = not available.

a. Senate figures reflect the period immediately after Gramm-Rudman mandated staffing cuts. House figures are for the entire fiscal year, thus averaging post–Gramm-Rudman staffing levels with previous, higher levels.

Sources: For 1891 through 1976, Harrison W. Fox, Jr., and Susan W. Hammond, *Congressional Staffs: The Invisible Force in American Lawmaking* (New York: Free Press, 1977), 171. For 1977 and 1978, Judy Schneider, "Congressional Staffing, 1947–78," Congressional Research Service, Library of Congress, August 24, 1979, reprinted in U.S. Congress, House, Select Committee on Committees, *Final Report*, 96th Cong., 2d sess., 1980, 540. For 1977, 1978, and 1979 House, *Report of the Clerk of the House*. For 1979 Senate, *Report of the Secretary of the Senate*. For 1980, *House LBA Hearings for 1982*, pt. 1, 25; *Senate LBA Hearings for 1981*, pt. 1, 26. For 1981, *House LBA Hearings for 1983*, pt. 1, 24–28; *Report of the Secretary of the Senate*, October 1, 1981–March 31, 1982. For 1982, *House LBA Hearings for 1984*, pt. 1, 25; *Report of the Secretary of the Senate*, October 1, 1982–March 31, 1983. For 1983, *House LBA Hearings for 1985*, pt. 1, 24; *Report of the Secretary of the Senate*, October 1, 1983–March 31, 1984. For 1984, *House LBA Hearings for 1986*, pt. 1, 22; *Report of the Secretary of the Senate*, October 1, 1984–March 31, 1985. For 1985–1986, *House LBA Hearings for 1987*, pt. 1, 23; *Report of the Secretary of the Senate*, October 1, 1985–March 31, 1986. For 1987, *House LBA Hearings for 1989*, pt. 2; *Senate LBA Hearings for 1988*; *Report of the Secretary of the Senate*, October 1, 1987–March 31, 1988. For 1988, *House LBA Hearings for 1990*, pt. 2; *Report of the Secretary of the Senate*, April–September 1989, pt. 1. For 1989, *House LBA Hearings for 1991*, pt. 2; *Report of the Secretary of the Senate*, October 1, 1989–March 31, 1990. For 1990, *House LBA Hearings for 1992*, pt. 2; *Report of the Secretary of the Senate*, October 1, 1990–March 31, 1991. For 1991, *House LBA Hearings for 1993*, pt. 2; *Report of the Secretary of the Senate*, October 1, 1991–March 31, 1992. For 1992, House Appropriations Committee; *Report of the Secretary of the Senate*, October 1, 1992–March 31, 1993. For 1993, House Office of Finance; *Report of the Secretary of the Senate*, October 1, 1993–March 31, 1994. For 1994, House Office of Finance; *Report of the Secretary of the Senate*, October 1, 1995–March 31, 1996. For 1998, *Statement of Disbursements of the House*, January 1, 1998–March 31, 1998; *Report of the Secretary of the Senate*, October 1, 1998–March 31, 1999. For 1999, *Statement of Disbursements of the House*, January 1, 1999–March 31, 1999; *Report of the Secretary of the Senate*, October 1, 1998–March 31, 1999.

Figure 5-1 Staff of Members and of Committees in Congress, 1891–1999

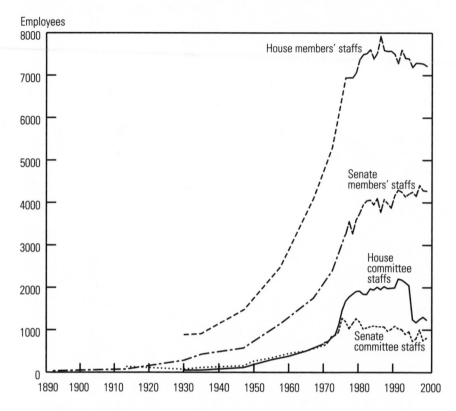

Employees

House members' staffs

Senate members' staffs

House committee staffs

Senate committee staffs

Source: Tables 5-2 and 5-5.

Table 5-3 House Staff Based in District Offices, 1970–1999

Year	Employees	Percentage of total personal staffs in district offices
1970	1,035	n.a.
1971	1,121	n.a.
1972	1,189	22.5
1973	1,347	n.a.
1974	1,519	n.a.
1975	1,732	n.a.
1976	1,943	28.0
1977	2,058	29.6
1978	2,317	33.4
1979	2,445	34.6
1980	2,534	34.4
1981	2,702	36.1
1982	2,694	35.8
1983	2,785	36.6
1984	2,872	38.9
1985	2,871	38.1
1986	2,940	43.6
1987	2,503	33.0
1988	2,954	39.6
1989	2,916	38.5
1990	3,027	40.4
1991	3,022	41.5
1992	3,128	41.2
1993	3,130	42.3
1994	3,335	45.1
1995	3,459	48.1
1996	3,144	43.1
1997	3,209	44.1
1998	3,214	44.2
1999	3,192	44.2

Notes: The totals reflect the number of full-time paid employees.
n.a. = not available.

Sources: For 1970–1978, "Congressional Staffing, 1947–78." For 1979–1988, Charles B. Brownson, *Congressional Staff Directory* (Washington, D.C.: Congressional Staff Directory, annual editions). For 1989–1999, Ann Brownson, *Congressional Staff Directory* (Washington, D.C.: Congressional Staff Directory, annual editions).

Table 5-4   Senate Staff Based in State Offices, 1972–1999

Year	Employees	Percentage of total personal staffs in state offices
1972	303	12.5
1978	816	25.0
1979	879	24.4
1980	953	25.4
1981	937	25.8
1982	1,053	26.1
1983	1,132	27.9
1984	1,140	28.9
1985	1,180	28.8
1986	1,249	33.1
1987	1,152	28.3
1988	1,217	30.6
1989	1,200	31.3
1990	1,293	31.1
1991	1,316	30.6
1992	1,368	32.2
1993	1,335	32.3
1994	1,345	32.0
1995	1,278	30.1
1996	1,290	31.1
1997	1,366	31.0
1998	1,381	32.3
1999	1,414	33.2

Note: The totals reflect the number of full-time paid employees.

Source: Congressional Staff Directory and *Report of the Secretary of the Senate.*

Table 5-5   Staffs of House and Senate Standing Committees, 1891–1999

Year	Employees in House	Employees in Senate	Year	Employees in House	Employees in Senate
1891	62	41	1981	1,843	1,022
1914	105	198	1982	1,839	1,047
1930	112	163	1983	1,970	1,075
1935	122	172	1984	1,944	1,095
1947	167	232	1985	2,009	1,080
1950	246	300	1986	1,954	1,075
1955	329	386	1987	2,024	1,074
1960	440	470	1988	1,976	970
1965	571	509	1989	1,986	1,013
1970	702	635	1990	1,993	1,090
1971	729	711	1991	2,201	1,030
1972	817	844	1992	2,178	1,008
1973	878	873	1993	2,118	897
1974	1,107	948	1994	2,046	958
1975	1,460	1,277	1995	1,246	732
1976	1,680	1,201	1996	1,177	793
1977	1,776	1,028	1997	1,250	1,002
1978	1,844	1,151	1998	1,305	747
1979	1,909	1,269	1999	1,238	805
1980	1,917	1,191			

Notes: The totals reflect the number of full-time paid employees.

Figures for 1947–1986 are for the statutory and investigative staffs of standing committees. They do not include select committee staffs, which varied between 31 and 238 in the House and between 62 and 172 in the Senate during the 1970s. For that reason, the numbers do not agree with those in table 5-1. In an attempt to provide further accuracy, we have counted certain individuals as .5 of a staff member on the basis of the length of employment and salary received. Rounding of those numbers then means that figures in this table do not necessarily equal those of the individual committees in tables 5-6 and 5-7.

Sources: For 1891–1935, *Congressional Staffs,* 171. For 1947–1978, "Congressional Staffing, 1947–78." For 1979–1980 Senate, U.S. Congress, Senate, Committee on Rules and Administration, *Senate Inquiries and Investigations,* 96th Cong., 2d sess., 1980, Committee Print 2, March 5, 1980. For 1981–1986 Senate, U.S. Congress, Senate, Committee on Rules and Administration, *Senate Committee Funding,* annual committee prints. For 1981 House, *House LBA Hearings for 1983,* pt. 2, 107. For 1982 House, *House LBA Hearings for 1984,* pt. 2, 77. For 1983–1984 House, Office of the Clerk of the House. For 1985 House, *Report of the Clerk of the House,* October 1, 1985–December 31, 1985. For 1986 House, *Report of the Clerk of the House,* October 1, 1986–December 31, 1986. For 1987, *Report of the Clerk of the House,* October 1, 1987–December 31, 1987; Senate, Committee on Rules and Administration. For 1988, *Report of the Clerk of the House,* October 1, 1988–December 31, 1988; *Report of the Secretary of the Senate,* April–September 1989, pt. 1. For 1989, *Report of the Clerk of the House,* October 1, 1989–December 31, 1989; *Report of the Secretary of the Senate,* October 1, 1989–March 31, 1990, pt. 1. For 1990, *Report of the Clerk of the House,* October 1, 1990–December 31, 1990; *Report of the Secretary of the Senate,* October 1, 1990–March 31, 1991. For 1991, *Report of the Clerk of the House,* October 1, 1991–December 31, 1991; *Report of the Secretary of the Senate,* October 1, 1991–March 31, 1992. For 1992, *Report of the Clerk of the House,* October 1, 1992–December 31, 1992; *Report of the Secretary of the Senate,* October 1, 1992–March 31, 1993. For 1993, *Report of the Clerk of the House,* October 1, 1993–December 31, 1993; *Report of the Secretary of the Senate,* October 1, 1993–March 31, 1994. For 1994, *Report of the Clerk of the House,* October 1, 1994–December 31, 1994; *Report of the Secretary of the Senate,* October 1, 1994–March 31, 1995. For 1995, *Report of the Clerk of the House,* October 1, 1995–December 31, 1995; *Report of the Secretary of the Senate,* April 1, 1995–September 30, 1995. For 1996, *Statement of Disbursements of the House,* October 1, 1996–December 31, 1996; *Report of the Secretary of the Senate,* October 1, 1996–March 31, 1997. For 1997, *Statement of Disbursements of the House,* January 1, 1997–March 31, 1997; *Report of the Secretary of the Senate,* October 1, 1996–March 31, 1997. For 1998, *Statement of Disbursements of the House,* January 1–March 31, 1998; *Report of the Secretary of the Senate,* October 1, 1998–March 31, 1999. For 1999, *Statement of Disbursements of the House,* January 1–March 31, 1999; *Report of the Secretary of the Senate,* October 1, 1998–March 31, 1999.

Table 5-6 Staffs of House Standing Committees, 1947–1999

Committee	1947	1960	1970	1975	1981	1985	1987	1989	1991	1993	1994	1995	1996	1997	1998	1999
Appropriations	29	59	71	98	127	182	188	196	218	227	202	126	143	156	152	158
Government Reform and Oversight (Government Operations)	9	54	60	68	84	86	80	82	90	86	82	75	100	120	161	129
Commerce (Energy and Commerce)	10	45	42	112	151	162	153	138	155	140	139	67	93	94	91	90
Transportation and Infrastructure (Public Works)	6	32	40	88	86	84	83	83	97	89	87	70	74	84	75	80
Economic and Educational Opportunities (Education and Labor)	10	25	77	114	121	119	127	114	117	112	114	66	75	77	94	74
Judiciary	7	27	35	69	75	81	81	80	71	75	74	47	61	85	74	70
Resources (Natural Resources)[a]	4	10	14	57	70	73	71	67	85	71	66	56	62	71	66	69
Budget	—[b]	—[b]	—[b]	67	93	109	124	96	101	98	98	61	67	61	67	68
International Relations (Foreign Affairs)	10	14	21	54	84	97	101	98	104	96	98	62	69	73	66	68
Ways and Means	12	22	24	63	91	99	108	94	94	142	122	60	67	65	67	66
Banking and Financial Services (Banking)	4	14	50	85	87	90	99	108	112	100	98	46	56	64	52	59
Science (Science, Space and Technology)	—[b]	17	26	47	74	78	78	79	84	87	86	48	56	63	57	59
National Security (Armed Services)	10	15	37	38	49	64	70	66	82	76	78	44	70	60	58	57
Agriculture	9	10	17	48	62	67	69	69	69	70	66	48	50	62	53	48
House Oversight (House Administration)[c]	7	4	25	217	252	275	228	275	317	317	316	270	33	36	41	35
Rules	4	2	7	18	43	45	43	41	49	48	47	37	36	41	36	35
Small Business	—[b]	—[b]	—[b]	27	54	53	62	54	53	45	40	24	28	40	32	30
Veterans' Affairs	7	18	18	26	34	32	44	41	44	46	45	28	28	27	25	30

Committee															
Standards of Official Conduct	—b	—b	5	5	9	9	11	8	11	9	9	10	9	11	12	13
Post Office and Civil Service	9	9	46	61	74	83	85	83	87	76	76	70	6	—d	—d	—d
Merchant Marine and Fisheries	8	8	21	28	82	79	77	74	76	75	75	75	6	—d	—d	—d
District of Columbia	7	8	15	43	41	42	42	39	40	34	34	36	6	—d	—d	—d

Notes: The totals reflect the number of full-time paid employees. Many of the committee names and jurisdictions changed in the 104th Congress. For continuity, we have included the old committee names in parentheses. The committees are ranked in order of their staff size in 1999. Through 1991, numbers ending in .5 are rounded up.

a. In 1993 the Natural Resources Committee was created out of the old Interior Committee. The staff figures for 1947–1991 are actually those of the Interior Committee.
b. This is not a standing committee.
c. After 1972, the figures include employees of House Informations Systems, the House of Representatives' central computer facility.
d. These three committees were eliminated in the first few weeks of the 104th Congress. The jurisdictions of the Post Office and Civil Service Committee and District of Columbia Committee became part of the Government Reform and Oversight Committee. The jurisdiction of the Merchant Marine and Fisheries Committee was divided among several other committees.

Sources: For 1947–1975, "Congressional Staffing, 1947–78." For 1979, *House LBA Hearings for 1979*, pt. 2, 136. For 1981, *House LBA Hearings for 1981*, pt. 2, 136. For 1983, *House LBA Hearings for 1983*, pt. 2, 107. For 1983, Office of the Clerk of the House. For 1985, *Report of the Clerk of the House*, October 1, 1985–December 31, 1985. For 1987, *Report of the Clerk of the House*, October 1, 1987–December 31, 1987. For 1989, *Report of the Clerk of the House*, October 1, 1989–December 31, 1989. For 1991, *Report of the Clerk of the House*, October 1, 1991–December 31, 1991. For 1993, *Report of the Clerk of the House*, October 1, 1993–December 31, 1993. For 1994, *Report of the Clerk of the House*, October 1, 1994–December 31, 1994. For 1995, *Report of the Clerk of the House*, October 1, 1995–December 31, 1995. For 1996, *Statement of Disbursements of the House*, October 1, 1996–December 31, 1996. For 1997, *Statement of Disbursements of the House*, January 1, 1997–March 31, 1997. For 1998, *Statement of Disbursements of the House*, January 1–March 31 1998. For 1999, *Statement of Disbursements of the House*, January 1, 1999–March 31, 1999.

Table 5-7 Staffs of Senate Standing Committees, 1947–1999

Committee	1947	1960	1970	1975	1979	1981	1985	1989	1993	1994	1995	1996	1997	1998	1999
Judiciary	19	137	190	251	223	134	141	127	108	110	74	100	141	90	122
Appropriations	23	31	42	72	80	79	82	80	72	70	60	59	76	70	79
Governmental Affairs	29	47	55	144	179	153	131	111	96	95	66	63	147	70	75
Labor and Human Resources	9	28	69	150	155	119	127	122	108	117	80	83	94	76	73
Commerce, Science, and Transportation	8	52	53	111	96	78	93	76	68	70	56	65	68	53	56
Foreign Relations	8	25	31	62	75	59	61	58	54	58	42	50	54	47	50
Armed Services	10	23	19	30	31	36	48	51	50	45	43	49	49	45	48
Finance	6	6	16	26	67	50	54	55	46	54	46	49	51	41	44
Budget	—[a]	—[a]	—[a]	90	91	82	81	66	58	66	46	46	48	41	42
Energy and Natural Resources (Interior)	7	26	22	53	55	50	57	50	46	47	39	37	39	36	41
Environment and Public Works	10	11	34	70	74	56	56	50	40	44	37	34	39	35	36
Banking, Housing, and Urban Affairs	9	22	23	55	48	39	38	51	51	58	44	47	51	45	29
Agriculture	3	10	7	22	34	34	34	42	29	35	28	33	47	27	28
Rules and Administration	41	15	13	29	37	31	28	27	24	24	20	25	27	16	23
Small Business	—[a]	—[a]	—[a]	—[a]	—[a]	—[a]	24	22	24	26	20	20	27	21	22
Veterans' Affairs	—[a]	—[a]	—[a]	32	24	22	25	25	24	14	14	17	21	22	21
Indian Affairs	—[a]	—[a]	—[a]	—[a]	—[a]	—[a]	—[a]	—[a]	—[a]	22	15	16	23	12	16

Notes: The totals reflect the number of full-time paid employees.

Committees are ranked in the order of their staff size in 1999. Through 1991, numbers ending in .5 are rounded up.

a. The committee was not in existence.

Sources: For 1947–1975, "Congressional Staffing, 1947–78." For 1979–1987, U.S. Congress, Senate, Committee on Rules and Administration, *Senate Committee Funding* (this annual committee print lists the number of positions authorized for each committee; the number actually employed at any one time may be less). For 1989, *Report of the Secretary of the Senate,* October 1, 1989–March 31, 1990, pt. 1. For 1991, *Report of the Secretary of the Senate,* October 1, 1991–March 31, 1992, pt. 1. For 1993, *Report of the Secretary of the Senate,* October 1, 1993–March 31, 1994, pt. 1. For 1996–1997, *Report of the Secretary of the Senate,* October 1, 1996–March 31, 1997. For 1998–1999, *Report of the Secretary of the Senate,* October 1, 1998–March 31, 1999.

Table 5-8   Staffs of Congressional Support Agencies, Fiscal Years 1946–1999

Year	Library of Congress	Congres- sional Research Service only[a]	General Accounting Office[b]	Congres- sional Budget Office	Office of Technology Assessment[c]
1946	—	—	14,219	—	—
1947	1,898	160	10,695	—	—
1950	1,973	161	7,876	—	—
1955	2,459	166	5,776	—	—
1960	2,779	183	5,074	—	—
1965	3,390	231	4,278	—	—
1970	3,848	332	4,704	—	—
1971	3,963	386	4,718	—	—
1972	4,135	479	4,742	—	—
1973	4,375	596	4,908	—	—
1974	4,504	687	5,270	—	10
1975	4,649	741	4,905	193	54
1976	4,880	806	5,391	203	103
1977	5,075	789	5,315	201	139
1978	5,231	818	5,476	203	164
1979	5,390	847	5,303	207	145
1980	5,047	868	5,196	218	122
1981	4,799	849	5,182	218	130
1982	4,803	849	5,027	218	130
1983	4,815	853	4,960	211	130
1984	4,802	858	4,985	210	139
1985	4,809	860	5,042	222	143
1986	4,806	860	5,019	222	143
1987	4,983	860	5,016	226	143
1988	4,874	825	5,042	211	143
1989	4,793	860	5,063	226	143
1990	4,659	797	5,066	226	143
1991	5,043	831	5,054	226	143
1992	5,050	838	5,062	218	143
1993	5,033	814	4,958	230	143
1994	4,701	740	4,572	218	143
1995	4,572	746	4,572	214	143[c]
1996	4,399	747	3,677	232	—[c]
1997	4,299	747	3,341	232	—[c]
1998	4,275	747	3,225	232	—[c]
1999	4,317	767	3,325	232	—[c]

Note: The totals reflect the number of full-time paid employees.

a. This was called the Legislative Reference Service through 1970.
b. Before 1950 the GAO was responsible for auditing all individual federal transactions and keeping a record of them. Legislation in 1950 transferred those responsibilities to the executive branch. The staff reductions through 1965 result from that 1950 change. *See* Frederich C. Mosher, *The GAO: The Quest for Accountability in American Government* (Boulder, Colo.: Westview Press, 1979), 124.
c. The Office of Technology Assessment's research activities were terminated at the end of fiscal year 1995. For fiscal year 1996, the OTA was given an appropriation sufficient to conduct agency closeout activities and the authority to employ seventeen staff members for that purpose.

Sources: For the Library of Congress and the Congressional Research Service 1946–1993, Library of Congress, *Annual Reports of the Librarian of Congress.* For the GAO 1946–1965, *Annual Reports of the Comptroller General of the United States.* For the Congressional Budget Office 1975, Joel Havemann, *Congress and the Budget* (Bloomington: Indiana University Press, 1978), 109. (Data are as of October 1975. The CBO's director took office on February 24, 1975.) For the OTA 1974–1976, *Appendixes of the Budget of the United States,* fiscal year 1976, 18; 1977, 18; 1978, 40. For the GAO 1970–1978, CBO 1976–1978, and OTA 1977–1978, "Congressional Staffing, 1947–78"; for 1979–1999, see the sources in table 5-1.

Table 5-9 Legislative Branch Appropriations and the Consumer Price Index, 1946–1998

Year	Appropriation (dollars)	Increase (percent)	Consumer price index[a]	Increase (percent)
1946	54,065,614	—	58.5	—
1947	61,825,020	14.4	66.9	14.4
1948	62,119,714	0.5	72.1	7.8
1949	62,057,678	−0.1	71.4	−1.0
1950	64,313,460	3.6	72.1	1.0
1951	71,888,244	11.8	77.8	7.9
1952	75,673,896	5.3	79.5	2.2
1953	77,670,076	2.6	80.1	0.8
1954	70,925,361	−8.7	80.5	0.5
1955	86,304,923	21.7	80.2	−0.4
1956	94,827,986	9.9	81.4	1.5
1957	120,775,798	27.4	84.3	3.6
1958	107,785,560	−10.8	86.6	2.7
1959	136,153,580	26.3	87.3	0.8
1960	131,055,385	−3.7	88.7	1.6
1961	140,930,781	7.5	89.6	1.0
1962	136,686,715	−3.0	90.6	1.1
1963	150,426,185	10.1	91.7	1.2
1964	168,467,869	12.0	92.9	1.3
1965	221,904,318	31.7	94.5	1.7
1966	197,965,307	−10.8	97.2	2.9
1967	221,715,643	12.0	100.0	2.9
1968	282,003,322	27.2	104.2	4.2
1969	311,542,399	10.5	109.8	5.4
1970	361,024,327	15.9	116.3	5.9
1971	443,104,319	22.7	121.3	4.3
1972	564,107,992	27.3	125.3	3.3
1973	645,127,365	14.4	133.1	6.2
1974	662,180,668	2.6	147.7	11.0
1975	785,618,833	18.6	161.2	9.1
1976[b]	947,185,778	20.6	170.5	5.8
1977	963,921,185	1.8	181.5	6.5
1978	1,009,225,350	4.7	195.4	7.7
1979	1,124,766,400	11.4	217.4	11.3
1980	1,199,061,463	6.6	246.8	13.5
1981	1,285,943,826	7.2	272.4	10.4
1982	1,365,272,433	6.2	289.1	6.1
1983	1,467,318,263	7.5	298.4	3.2
1984	1,644,160,600	12.0	311.1	4.3
1985	1,599,977,138	−2.7	322.2	3.6
1986	1,783,255,000	11.4	328.4	1.9
1987	1,635,190,214	−8.3	340.4	3.6
1988	1,745,201,500	6.7	354.3	4.1
1989	1,804,624,000	3.4	371.3	4.8

Year	Appropriation (dollars)	Increase (percent)	Consumer price index[a]	Increase (percent)
1990	1,968,441,000	9.1	391.4	5.4
1991	2,161,367,000	9.8	408.0	4.2
1992	2,303,844,000	6.6	420.3	3.0
1993	2,302,924,000	−0.1	432.7	3.0
1994	2,269,558,000	−1.4	444.0	2.6
1995	2,390,600,000	5.3	456.5	2.8
1996	2,125,000,000	−11.1	469.9	2.9
1997	2,165,400,000	1.9	480.5	2.3
1998	2,288,000,000	5.7	488.0	1.6
1946–98	—	4,231.9	—	834.2

Note: Appropriations include supplementals, except for 1986; appropriations are for fiscal years, but the consumer price index is the year average for calendar years.

a. The CPI base is 1967 = 100.

b. From fiscal year 1946 through fiscal year 1976, the fiscal year began on July 1. Beginning with fiscal year 1977, the start of the fiscal year was shifted to October 1. During the transition quarter of July 1–September 30, 1976, the amount appropriated for legislative branch operations was $207,391,365. We have not included that amount.

Sources: For 1946–1976, U.S. Congress, House, Committee on House Administration, *Studies Dealing with Budgetary, Staffing, and Administrative Activities of the U.S. House of Representatives, 1947–78,* 95th Cong., 2d sess., 1978. For 1977–1979, *Congressional Quarterly Almanac* (Washington, D.C.: Congressional Quarterly, 1977–1980). For 1980, *House LBA Hearings for 1981,* pt. 1, 10–11; *Senate LBA Hearings for 1981,* pt. 1, 15–23; Public Law 96–304 (July 8, 1980); Public Law 97-51 (October 1, 1981). For 1981, *House LBA Hearings for 1982,* pt. 1, 15–23; *Senate LBA Hearings for 1982,* 268; U.S. Congress, Senate, Committee on Appropriations, *Comparative Statement of New Budget Authority and Outlays—Fiscal Year 1983,* 97th Cong., 2d sess., 1982 (unpublished committee document), 3; Public Law 97-12 (June 5, 1981). For 1982–1986, House Committee on Appropriations, *Comparative Statement of New Budget Authority* (unpublished committee documents). For 1987–1998, *Congressional Quarterly Almanac.* For the consumer price index, 1946–1986, *Economic Report of the President,* January 1989. For 1987–1998, U.S. Department of Labor, Bureau of Labor Statistics.

Table 5-10 Legislative Branch Appropriations, by Category,
Fiscal Years 1984–1998 (in thousands of dollars)

	1984	1985	1986[a]	1987	1988	1989
Senate	255,856	285,930	308,834	307,658	337,314	340,677
House of Representatives	419,784	439,398	455,431	463,907	513,786	506,068
Joint items[b]	128,933	96,415	155,804	103,136	94,981	120,983
Architect of the Capitol[c]	82,021	85,181	112,191	101,633	107,306	103,640
Botanic Garden	2,158	2,080	2,197	2,062	2,221	2,521
Congressional Budget Office	16,723	17,541	18,455	17,251	17,886	18,361
Congressional Research Service	36,700	39,833	38,963	39,602	43,022	44,684
Copyright Royalty Commission[d]	210	217	227	123	129	123
General Accounting Office	271,710	299,704	339,639	304,910	329,847	347,339
Government Printing Office[c]	125,700	122,704	122,268	94,956	89,521	85,731
Library of Congress	228,715	228,242	242,829	183,670	191,998	199,650
Office of Technology Assessment	14,831	15,692	17,000	15,532	16,901	17,937
Office of Compliance	—	—	—	—	—	—

Note: The figures include supplemental appropriations, except for 1986.

a. The figures for 1986 are before Gramm-Rudman-Hollings sequestration.
b. This category includes such items as joint committees and the Capitol Police. Before 1991, official mail costs were also included in this category.
c. The figures for the Architect of the Capitol and the Government Printing Office include appropriations for legislative activities only.
d. The commission was abolished after fiscal year 1994. Its duties have been taken over by a Copyright Office Panel; therefore, there is no further appropriation.

Sources: For 1982–1986, House Committee on Appropriations, *Comparative Statement of New Budget Authority.* For 1987, *Congressional Quarterly Almanac,* vol. 43 (1988). For 1988, *Congressional Quarterly Almanac,* vol. 44 (1989). For 1989, *Congressional Quarterly Almanac,* vol. 45 (1990). For 1990, *Congressional Quarterly Almanac,* vol. 46 (1991). For 1991, *Congressional Quarterly Almanac,* vol. 47 (1992). For 1992, *Congressional Quarterly Almanac,* vol. 48 (1993). For 1993, *Congressional Quarterly Almanac,* vol. 49 (1994). For 1994, *Congressional Quarterly Almanac,* vol. 50 (1995). For 1995, *Congressional Quarterly Almanac,* vol. 51 (1996). For 1996, *Congressional Quarterly Almanac,* vol. 52 (1997). For 1997, *Congressional Quarterly Almanac,* vol. 53 (1998). For 1998, *Congressional Quarterly Almanac,* vol. 54 (1999).

1990	1991	1992	1993	1994	1995	1996	1997	1998
373,761	437,223	449,568	451,451	443,315	460,600	426,900	441,200	461,100
537,207	647,675	693,970	699,109	684,696	728,700	671,600	684,000	708,700
170,454	114,187	80,716	80,476	78,750	86,200	86,800	85,300	86,700
116,221	139,806	151,633	149,613	150,223	159,700	143,000	139,800	164,700
2,638	3,519	2,862	4,906	3,008	3,200	3,100	2,900	3,000
19,580	21,183	22,542	22,542	22,317	23,200	24,300	24,500	24,800
46,895	52,743	56,583	57,291	56,718	60,100	60,100	62,600	64,600
101	127	130	130	128	—	—	—	—
364,720	419,130	442,647	435,167	430,815	449,400	374,000	332,500	339,500
98,018	79,615	91,591	89,591	29,082	32,200	83,800	81,700	29,000
211,100	239,924	248,308	252,808	250,813	263,100	264,600	269,100	281,800
18,900	19,557	21,025	21,025	21,315	22,000	—	—	—
—	—	—	—	—	—	—	2,600	2,500

Table 5-11 Allowances for Representatives, 1977–1999

Category	1977	1981	1983	1985
Clerk-hire	$238,580	$336,384	$366,648	$394,680
Postage	$211	—[c]	—[c]	—[c]
Stationery	$6,500	—[c]	—[c]	—[c]
Travel (round trips)	33	—[c]	—[c]	—[c]
Telephone/telegraph	$5,200 for equipment 15,000 long-distance minutes	—[c]	—[c]	—[c]
District and state offices rental	2,500 sq. ft.	—[c]	—[c]	—[c]
Furnishings (one-time)	$27,000	—[c]	—[c]	—[c]
Official expenses	$7,000	$66,200– 248,601	$588,850– 279,470	$105,513– 306,509
Constituent communications (begun in 1975	$5,000	—[c]	—[c]	—[c]
Equipment lease	$9,000	—[c]	—[c]	—[c]
Members' representational allowance	—[b]	—[b]	—[b]	—[b]

a. Each member is entitled to an annual clerk-hire allowance of the designated amount for a staff not to exceed twenty-two employees, four of whom must fit into five categories: (1) shared payroll—employees, such as computer experts, who are shared by members; (2) interns; (3) employees on leave without pay; (4) part-time employees; (5) temporary employees—employees hired for a specific purpose for not more than ninety days.

b. On September 1, 1995, members' three former expense allowances (clerk-hire, official expenses, and official mail allowances) were consolidated into one members' representational allowance (MRA). Although the MRA is calculated on the basis of those three components, members may spend the MRA as they see fit. Within the MRA, each member's expenditures for franked mail may not exceed the total amount allocated by the Committee on House Oversight for official mail expenses, plus an additional $25,000, transferable within the MRA at the member's discretion according to the procedures under the previous allowance structure. The 1997 mean MRA was $901,771.

c. As of January 3, 1978, previous individual allowances for travel, office equipment lease, district office lease, stationery, telecommunications, mass mailings, postage, computer services, and other official expenses were consolidated in a single allowance category—the official expenses allowance. Members may budget funds for each category as they see fit. The average allowance for 1995 was $193,000.

d. Each member is entitled to a base official expenses allowance of $122,500. In addition, three variables determine the total amount allotted for official expenses: (1) transportation costs, (2) telecommunications costs, and (3) cost of office space. The amount allotted for travel is computed as follows: 64 multiplied by the rate per mile multiplied by the mileage between the District of Columbia and the farthest point in the member's district. The minimum amount allotted for travel in 1995 was $6,200 per member.

The amount allotted for telecommunications is computed as follows: 15,000 times the highest long-distance rate per minute from the District of Columbia to the member's district. The minimum amount allotted for telecommunications in 1995 was $6,000 per member. If the member has elected to use WATS or a similar service in his office, the 15,000-minute multiplier will be reduced by one-half.

The amount allotted for office space costs is computed as follows: 2,500 square feet multiplied by the highest applicable rate per square foot charged by the administrator of the General Services Administration to federal agencies in the district for rental of office space.

The official expenses allowance may not be used for:

(1) expenses relating to the hiring and employment of individuals, including, but not limited to, employment service fees, transportation of interviewees to and from employment interviews, and cost of relocation upon acceptance or termination of employment;

(2) items purchased from other than the House stationery store that have a useful life greater than the current term of the member and that would have a residual value of more than $25 upon the expiration of the current term of the member;

(3) holiday greeting cards, flowers, and trophies;

(4) personal advertisements (other than meeting or appearance notices);

(5) donations of any type, except flags of the United States flown over the Capitol and items purchased for use as gifts when on official travel;

(6) dues other than to legislative support organizations as approved by the Committee on House Administration;

(7) educational expenses for courses of study or information or training programs unless the benefit accrues primarily to the House and the skill or knowledge is not commonly available;

(8) purchases of radio and television time; and

(9) parking for member and employees at district offices, except when included as an integral part of the lease or occupancy agreement for the district office space.

1987	1989	1991	1993	1995	1997	1999
$406,560	$431,760[a]	$475,000[a]	$557,400[a]	568,560[a]	—[b]	—[b]
—[c]	—[c]	—[c]	—[c]	—[c]	—[b]	—[b]
—[c]	—[c]	—[c]	—[c]	—[c]	—[b]	—[b]
—[c]	—[c]	—[c]	—[c]	—[c]	—[b]	—[b]
—[c]	—[c]	—[c]	—[c]	—[c]	—[b]	—[b]
—[c]	—[c]	—[c]	—[c]	—[c]	—[b]	—[b]
$105,513–306,509[d]	$108,400–306,500	$135,000–317,000	$152,128–302,008	152,128–334,629	—[b]	—[b]
—[c]	—[c]	—[c]	—[c]	—[c]	—[b]	—[b]
—[c]	—[c]	—[c]	—[c]	—[c]	—[b]	—[b]
—[b]	—[b]	—[b]	—[b]	—[b]	$814,090–1,233,780	$858,707–1,311,594

Each member may allocate up to $40,000 from the clerk-hire allowance to supplement the official expenses allowance. A member also may allocate up to $40,000 from the official expenses allowance to supplement the clerk-hire allowance, provided that monthly clerk-hire disbursements not exceed 10 percent of the total clerk-hire allowance.

Sources: For 1977 and 1979, Committee on House Administration, *Studies Dealing with Budgetary, Staffing, and Administrative Activities of the U.S. House of Representatives, 1946–1978.* For 1981, 1983, and 1985, U.S. House of Representatives, *Congressional Handbook.* For 1987, "Salaries and Allowances: The Congress," Congressional Research Service, Library of Congress, Washington, D.C., July 15, 1987, update. For 1989, Office of the Clerk of the House. For 1991 and 1993, Committee on House Administration. For 1995, House Oversight Committee. For 1997, *Congressional Handbook,* 104th Congress, Committee on House Oversight. For 1999, *Congressional Handbook*, 105th Congress, Committee on House Oversight.

Table 5-12 Allowances for Senators, 1977–1999

Category	1977	1979	1981	1983	1985
Clerk-hire	$311,577–588,145[a]	$508,221–1,021,167[a]	$592,608–1,190,724[a]	$645,897–1,297,795[a]	$695,244–1,396,947[a]
Legislative assistance	n.a.	$157,626[b]	$183,801[b]	$200,328[b]	$215,634[b]
Postage	$1,215–1,520	—[c]	—[c]	—[c]	—[c]
Stationery	$3,600–5,000	—[c]	—[c]	—[c]	—[c]
Travel (round trips)	20–22	—[c]	—[c]	—[c]	—[c]
District and state offices rental	n.a.	4,800–8,000 sq. ft.[d]	4,800–8,000 sq. ft.[d]	4,800–8,000 sq. ft.[d]	4,800–8,000 sq. ft.[d]
Furnishings, state offices	n.a.	$22,550–31,350	$22,550–31,350	$22,550–31,350	$22,550–31,350
Official office expense account	n.a.	$33,000–143,000[f]	$33,000–143,000[f]	$36,000–156,000[f]	$36,000–156,000[f]

Note: n.a. = not applicable.

a. There is no limit on the number of employees a senator may hire. He or she must, however, use only the clerk-hire or legislative assistance allowance to pay staff salaries. The clerk-hire allowance varies according to state population.

b. In addition to clerk-hire, each senator has a legislative assistance allowance worth $385,050 in 1997. That allowance is reduced for any committee chairman or ranking minority member of a committee. It is also reduced for any other senator authorized by a committee chairman to recommend or approve any individuals for appointment to the committee staff who will assist that senator "solely and directly" in his duties as a member of the committee. The reduction requirements were waived for the 99th and 100th Congresses.

c. This allowance is one of the allocations of the consolidated office expense allowance. Before January 1, 1973, senators were authorized individually controlled allowances for six expense categories as follows: transportation expenses for the senator and his staff; stationery; air mail and special delivery postage; long-distance telephone calls; telegram charges; and home state expenses, which include home state office expenses; telephone service charges incurred outside Washington, D.C.; subscriptions to newspapers, magazines, periodicals, and clipping or similar services; and home state office rent (repealed effective July 1, 1974).

Effective January 1, 1973, the Supplemental Appropriations Act, 1973, provided for the consolidation of those same allowances to give senators flexibility in the management of the same dollars allocated for their expense allowances. That authorization imposed no limit on any expense category. The allowance was designated as the consolidated office expense allowance. Effective January 1, 1977, the Legislative Branch Appropriation Act redesignated the consolidated office expense allowance as the official office expense account.

d. Effective July 1, 1974, the Legislative Branch Appropriations Act, 1975, provided a formula for the allowable aggregate square feet of office space in the home state of a senator. There is no limit on the number of offices that a senator may establish in his home state, but the designated square footage may not be exceeded. The cost of office space in the home state is not chargeable to the official office expense account.

e. An aggregate furniture and furnishings allowance is provided through the General Services Administration for one or more state offices in either federal or privately owned buildings. The $30,000 minimum allowance for office space not greater than 4,800 square feet is increased by $734 for each authorized increase of 200 square feet of space.

f. The expense account may be used for the following expenses (2 U.S.C. 58[a], as amended):

(1) official telegrams and long-distance phone calls and related services;
(2) stationery and other office supplies purchased through the stationery room for official business;
(3) costs incurred in the mailing or delivery of matters relating to official business;
(4) official office expenses in home state, other than equipment or furniture (purchase of office equipment beyond stated allocations may be made through 10 percent of the funds listed under item 9 below);
(5) official telephone charges incurred outside Washington, D.C.;
(6) subscriptions to newspapers, magazines, periodicals, or clipping or similar services;
(7) travel expenses incurred by a senator or staff member, subject to certain limitations;
(8) expenses incurred by individuals selected by a senator to serve on panels or other bodies making recommendations for nominees to service academies or federal judgeships; and
(9) other official expenses as the senator determines are necessary, including (a) additional office equipment for Washington, D.C., or state offices; (b) actual transportation expenses incurred by the senator and employees for official business in the Washington metropolitan area (this is also allowed to employees assigned to a state office for actual transportation expenses in the general vicinity of the office to which assigned but is not available for a change of assignment within the state or for commuting between home and office).

1987	1989	1991	1993	1995	1997	1999
$716,102–1,438,856[a]	$754,000–1,636,000[a]	$814,000–1,760,000[a]	$1,540,000–1,914,000[a]	$1,660,000–1,935,000[a]	$1,087,597–1,974,051[a]	$1,210,467–2,157,222
$243,543[b]	$248,000[b]	$269,000[b]	$374,000[b]	$377,400[b]	$385,050	$396,477
—[c]	—[c]	—[c]	—[c]	—[c]	—[c]	—[c]
—[c]	—[c]	—[c]	—[c]	—[c]	—[c]	—[c]
—[c]	—[c]	—[c]	—[c]	—[c]	—[c]	—[c]
4,800–8,000 sq. ft.[d]	4,800–8,000 sq. ft.[d]	4,800–8,000 sq. ft.[d]	4,800–8,000 sq. ft.[d]	4,800–8,000 sq. ft.[d]	4,800–8,000 sq. ft.[d]	4,800–8,000 sq. ft.[d]
$30,000–41,744	$30,000–41,744[e]	$30,000–41,744[e]	$30,000–41,744[e]	$30,000–41,744[e]	$30,000–41,744[e]	$30,000–41,744[e]
$36,000–156,000	$33,000–156,000[f]	$47,000–122,000[f]	$44,000–200,000[f]	$90,000–250,000[f]	$95,825–245,000[f]	$127,384–470,272

The total reimbursement expense for the calendar year may not exceed 10 percent of the total official office expense account.

Beginning with fiscal year 1981, each senator was also allowed to transfer funds from the administrative, clerical, and legislative assistance allowances to the official office expense account.

Sources: For 1977, *Senate LBA Hearings for 1980.* For 1979–1985, U.S. Senate, *Congressional Handbook.* For 1987, "Salaries and Allowances: The Congress." For 1989, Office of the Secretary of the Senate; Office of the Sergeant-at-Arms. For 1991 and 1993, Senate Disbursing Office. For 1995, Senate Disbursing Office and Sergeant-at-Arms. For 1997, *Senate Legislative Branch Appropriations.* For 1999, 2 U.S.C., Sec. 59; Appropriations Committee.

Table 5-13 Costs of Official Mail, 1971–1993

Year	Appropriations (dollars)	Average unit cost of franked mail (cents)
1971	11,244,000	8.0
1972	14,594,000	8.0
1972 supplement	18,400,000	
1973	21,226,480	9.0
1974	30,500,000	9.9
1975	38,756,015	11.4
1976	46,101,000	13.2
Transition period[a]	11,525,000	
1976 supplement	16,080,000	
1977	46,904,000	13.4
1978	48,926,000	11.4
1979	64,944,000	12.8
1980[b]	50,707,000	13.4
1981	52,033,000	12.4
1982	75,095,000	13.9
1983	93,161,000	13.1
1984	117,277,000	12.8
1985	85,797,000	12.6
1986	95,700,000	12.6
1987	91,423,000	18.4
1988	82,163,000	14.1
1989	85,262,000[c]	14.9
1990	99,016,000	15.3[d]
1991	88,834,000	15.7
1992	112,000,000	14.9
1993	67,700,000	15.5

Note: See table 6-8 for the number of pieces of franked mail.

a. This reflects the change in the fiscal year from July 1 to October 1.

b. The lower figure reflects the decrease in bulk mail rates.

c. This is adjusted to reflect the fiscal year 1989 shortfall in the mail account.

d. In 1990 the U.S. Postal Service altered its method for calculating the average unit cost. Average figures before 1990 are combined House and Senate figures. Figures for 1990 and later are for the House only.

Sources: For 1971–1987, Office of the Clerk of the House. For 1988–1989, Congressional Research Service Report for Congress, "U.S. Congress Official Mail Costs: FY1972 to FY1991," July 20, 1990. For 1990–1991, Congressional Research Service. For 1992–1993, U.S. Postal Service.

6

Workload

Measuring "work" in Congress is not simple. Although many quantitative indicators exist—from bills introduced to hours in session—they do not necessarily provide a precise sense of what Congress as an institution does or what individual members do nor do they enable a qualitative assessment of the work product. Workload numbers can, however, give us a sense of patterns of activity over time and the relative emphasis each Congress places on its legislative workload. Over the past several decades, several distinct ebbs and flows in work and work product have been evident.

Bills Introduced

The number of bills introduced in the House has had several pronounced increases and decreases. (See table 6-1.) Bills introduced ranged from an average of about 10,000 per Congress in the 1940s and early 1950s to around 14,000 in the mid-1950s and rose to 20,000 in the mid-1960s. In the 1970s that trend reversed, and bills introduced declined by about 25 percent, owing in part to changes in the rules regarding cosponsorship, which reduced the need to introduce multiple numbers of an identical bill. The numbers dropped dramatically in the Ninety-sixth Congress—by 42 percent—and continued to decline to under 5,000 in the 104th Congress. In the 105th Congress the number rebounded slightly to 5,014. It has remained well under 10,000 since 1980.

The Senate has no distinct ebbs and flows in legislation introduced. (See table 6-2.) Rather, there has been a general, if unsteady, trend downward since the 1970s. As with the House, the Senate's modern low came in the 104th Congress, when senators introduced only 2,226 bills—roughly half the average of the 1970s, but that was quickly followed by the 105th Congress, which introduced 3,160 bills.

Bills Passed

An examination of number of bills passed in both houses shows a definite decline in the 1960s and again in the 1970s. That level stabilized in the 1980s at roughly half the total of the 1950s. In general, the number of bills passed in each house fell from a rough average of 2,000 per Congress in the 1950s to 1,000 in the 1980s. That pattern abruptly changed with the Republican majority, when the next two Congresses passed 611 and 710 bills, respectively.

The ratio of bills passed to bills introduced serves as a useful measure of comparison over time. (See figure 6-1.) We should not, however, overstate the significance of that measure because some bills are introduced by more than one member and some that are passed may originally have been introduced in the other body. With that caveat, it is clear that the proportion of bills passed has steadily declined since 1947 (although the trend reversed slightly in the mid-1980s). Today, a bill has roughly half the chance of passing that it would have had in the Eightieth Congress under President Truman.

In recent years we can in part trace the decline in the number of bills passed to the domination of one issue in each session of Congress. In 1993 the Clinton economic package took up an enormous amount of Congress's time and energy. The same thing happened in 1994 with the Clinton health care proposals, in 1995 and 1996 with the intensely partisan budget battles, and again in 1998, when Congress spent the second half of the year focused on presidential scandal.

Recorded Votes

The number of recorded votes remained quite low in the House through the 1940s and 1950s, increased in the 1960s, and then jumped dramatically in the 1970s. (See tables 6-1 to 6-3 and figure 6-2.) A rules change in 1971, which permitted recorded teller votes and thereby expanded the opportunities for recorded votes on amendments, was clearly the major factor in increasing the number of recorded votes in the House. The Senate also showed a marked, though smaller, increase in 1971, despite the fact that members introduced no comparable procedural reform. In the 104th Congress the number was sharply up again and reflected not only the increased partisanship but also an almost frenetic early pace in the newly Republican Congress. But the number dropped back a bit in the 105th Congress.

When we break down recorded votes by year, we find a small but relatively steady decline in the votes in the Senate since 1977, with steep decreases in the late 1970s and again in the 1980s. (See table 6-3 and figure 6-2.) The House rates declined significantly in 1979 and 1980, dropped sharply in 1981 to levels of a decade earlier, then increased somewhat to a rough average of 450 per year. Although long-term future trends are difficult to discern, it seems likely that the number of recorded votes in both chambers will stabilize at levels below the peak years of the mid-1970s but above those of the 1960s. In the 104th Congress, the fast, early pace, the crowded agenda, and the use of more open rules in the House prompted a jump in the number of recorded votes; the numbers in the 105th Congress suggest that it might prove a temporary phenomenon.

Time in Session

The number of days per session per Congress has fluctuated substantially, without a sharp pattern until recently. (See tables 6-1 and 6-2.) In the 104th Congress, a slow upward trend showed a distinct shift: both houses of Congress are now in session for fewer days but for distinctly longer hours. The House went from an average of 4.2 hours per day in the 1950s to 4.4 in the 1960s and 5.3 in the 1970s, with an average of 5.8 hours per day in 1979–1980. The numbers increased in the 101st through the

103d Congresses to an average of just over 6.5 hours per day, then jumped sharply to 8.5 hours per day in the 104th Congress and 8 hours per day in the 105th Congress.

In the Senate, where floor procedures have always been looser and more informal to allow extended debate and individual prerogatives, filibusters have periodically extended the time in session. Sessions in the 1970s and 1980s were consistently long and only once fell below 2,000 hours. In the earlier period the length of sessions demonstrated considerably more fluctuation, with only five of the twelve sessions between 1947 and 1970 running over 2,000 hours. The average hours per day in session jumped in the Ninety-ninth Senate to 8.1 and reached the highest level in at least forty-six years (8.6 hours) in the 103d Senate. In the 104th Senate the average length of sessions dropped slightly to 8.4 hours and then again to 7.4 hours in the 105th Congress.

Committee and Subcommittee Meetings

The number of committee and subcommittee meetings and hearings rose consistently in the House of Representatives beginning in 1965–1966. The most substantial increases occurred in the middle to late 1970s, by which time the figure was more than double that of the 1950s. The expansion of power and initiative of subcommittees and the wider distribution of chairmanships probably accounted for much of that change. But the figures for the 1980s and early 1990s indicate a marked cutback in committee and subcommittee activity to levels of a decade or more earlier, with another steep decline in the Republican 104th Congress.

The Senate numbers also increased but then peaked and declined earlier than in the House. The number of meetings and hearings jumped substantially in the late 1960s and early 1970s, beginning especially with the famous "Great Society" Eighty-ninth Congress (1965–1966) and reaching a peak a decade later—70 percent higher than in the 1950s. After the committee system reorganization of 1977, the number began to decline steadily down to under 2,000 in the 104th and 105th Congresses—less than half the total of the Ninety-third Congress.

Laws and Other Output

Since the assent of both Houses of Congress and the president is required for a bill to become a law, bills that pass in either chamber do not necessarily become law. (See tables 6-1, 6-2, and 6-4.) The number of bills that became laws fluctuated from Congress to Congress, but broad patterns are evident. (See figure 6-3.) An average of 900 or so bills in the 1950s went to 700 or so bills in the 1960s and 600 or so in the 1970s and 1980s. The numbers dropped significantly in the 102d through 105th Congresses. The modern low was in the 104th Congress, which enacted only 333 laws (85 in the first session). As the number of laws decreased, however, the average length of each bill has increased. From the 1950s through the mid-1960s, the average number of pages per statute was approximately 2.5 pages, doubling by the mid-1970s to 5 pages and then steadily increasing through the 1980s and 1990s until in the 104th Congress the average was 19.1 pages per statute. Divided government, when fewer bills have a chance of being enacted, often results in the inclusion of various issues and interests in a single piece of legislation that has a reasonable likelihood of becoming law. It is important to understand that a handful of those omnibus measures accounts for a large proportion of total statute pages.

Actions of Congress, in votes and laws, affect the workload, job difficulty, and output of the federal executive as well. As the average length of statutes increased in

Congress in the 1970s, the number of pages in the *Federal Register*—which among other things displays regulations mandated by those statutes—jumped accordingly. (See table 6-5.) In 1981, as deregulation proceeded in the Reagan administration and the number of substantive bills declined, the total pages in the *Federal Register* dropped by 27 percent—to the level of 1977–1978 at the beginning of the Carter administration—and reached a level of 47,418 pages in 1986, the lowest in twelve years. The page count then rose during the Bush administration and has continued to rise. Although the number of bills enacted fell during the 104th Congress, the number of pages exceeded 69,000 and then in the 105th Congress jumped to over 70,000 for the first time.

Presidential Vetoes

President Truman exercised his veto power far more than any of his successors; he vetoed seventy-five bills in the so-called Do-Nothing Eightieth Congress. (See table 6-6.) The number of vetoes is generally higher when presidents face Congresses with opposition party majorities, although such arrangements can also become quite productive partnerships of the sort seen in late 1996 between Bill Clinton and the new Republican Congress. And despite the fact that Ronald Reagan seldom used the veto power (but often its threat), he actually vetoed more legislation under the split Congresses of 1983–1984 and 1985–1986 than he did in the final two years of his term, after the Senate swung back to the Democrats.

Presidents Nixon and Ford faced the greatest resistance from Congress. The Ninety-third and Ninety-fourth Congresses attempted a much higher number of veto overrides than any of the other Congresses in the previous thirty years, and a large number of their attempts were successful. The first three Congresses under Reagan did not show any particular inclination to override his vetoes, but the last picked up a bit and overrode 37.5 percent of Reagan's vetoes. President Bush's use of the veto was numerically in line with his predecessors, but he often reserved the veto for crucial pieces of legislation, such as the Civil Rights Act of 1990, and had impressive success in having his vetoes sustained in his first two years.

President Clinton became the first president since 1853 not to veto a single bill during an entire Congress. Having a Democratic House and Senate certainly diminished his need or willingness to use the veto, yet zero vetoes is highly unusual. Clinton seemed to be a president much more prone to compromise than to confrontation. But that tendency did not last for long. The Republican takeover of Congress in 1994 transformed executive-congressional relations and ensured a substantial number of vetoes during the 104th Congress, although still fewer applied than during the Reagan or Bush administration. The numbers dropped considerably in the 105th Congress.

Filibusters

The filibuster or threat of filibuster is a regular fact of legislative life in the contemporary Senate. (See table 6-7.) The record shows that the filibuster (measured by the number of cloture votes) was a Senate privilege rarely exercised until it jumped from one or two to six or seven per Congress in the 1960s. In the 1970s Majority Leader Mike Mansfield introduced a "two-track" system to enable the Senate to conduct other business as a filibuster proceeded. The increased use of filibusters on a wider variety of issues led the Senate to amend the rules in 1975 by changing the number of votes required to invoke cloture from two-thirds of those present and voting to three-fifths of the total Senate. That change did not reduce the number of attempted filibusters, but the success rate for cloture votes clearly increased. Except for the Nixon-Ford years, filibusters are generally more prevalent in the second session of a Congress, when delaying tactics have a greater likelihood of succeeding because of the strong incentive to finish the languishing business of the session. Republicans routinely used filibusters in the 103d Congress to frustrate President Clinton's agenda, and Democrats immediately adopted the tactic in the 104th Congress to slow work on the Contract with America.

Volume of Mailings

From the 1960s through the 1980s, the amount of franked mail generated by Congress increased tremendously and averaged approximately 700 million pieces by the late 1980s. (See table 6-8.)[1] In light of those escalating numbers, Congress came under considerable pressure in 1990 to adopt reforms in an attempt to curb the use of franked mail. The House imposed a requirement that each member adhere to an individual, publicly disclosed mail budget. Both the total cost and the amount of mail sent fell 54 percent during the following year. Despite that reduction, the pattern of sending more mail in election years is quite apparent. In 1992 the number jumped up 76 percent over the previous year, only to decline a year later.

Note

1. The system for counting franked mail has changed so much that reliable data can no longer be compiled; thus, the table ends with data for 1993.

Table 6-1 House Workload, 80th–105th Congresses, 1947–1998

Congress		Bills introduced[a]	Average no. of bills introduced per member	Bills passed	Ratio of bills passed to bills introduced	Recorded votes[b]	Time in session Days	Time in session Hours	Hours per day in session	Committee, subcommittee meetings[c]
80th	(1947–48)	7,611	17.5	1,739	0.228	159	254	1,224	4.8	n.a.
81st	(1949–50)	10,502	24.1	2,482	0.236	275	345	1,501	4.4	n.a.
82d	(1951–52)	9,065	20.8	2,008	0.222	181	274	1,163	4.2	n.a.
83d	(1953–54)	10,875	25.0	2,129	0.196	147	240	1,033	4.3	n.a.
84th	(1955–56)	13,169	30.3	2,360	0.179	147	230	937	4.1	3,210
85th	(1957–58)	14,580	33.5	2,064	0.142	193	276	1,147	4.2	3,750
86th	(1959–60)	14,112	32.4	1,636	0.116	180	265	1,039	3.9	3,059
87th	(1961–62)	14,328	32.9	1,927	0.134	240	304	1,227	4.0	3,402
88th	(1963–64)	14,022	32.2	1,267	0.090	232	334	1,251	3.7	3,596
89th	(1965–66)	19,874	45.7	1,565	0.079	394	336	1,547	4.6	4,367
90th	(1967–68)	22,060	50.7	1,213	0.055	478	328	1,595	4.9	4,386
91st	(1969–70)	21,436	49.3	1,130	0.053	443	350	1,613	4.6	5,066
92d	(1971–72)	18,561	42.7	970	0.052	649	298	1,429	4.8	5,114
93d	(1973–74)	18,872	43.4	923	0.049	1,078	318	1,487	4.7	5,888
94th	(1975–76)	16,982	39.0	968	0.057	1,273	311	1,788	5.7	6,975
95th	(1977–78)	15,587	35.8	1,027	0.066	1,540	323	1,898	5.9	7,896

96th	(1979–80)	9,103	20.9	929	0.102	1,276	326	1,876	5.8	7,033
97th	(1981–82)	8,094	18.6	704	0.087	812	303	1,420	4.7	6,078
98th	(1983–84)	7,105	16.3	978	0.137	906	266	1,705	6.4	5,661
99th	(1985–86)	6,499	14.9	973	0.150	890	281	1,794	6.4	5,272
100th	(1987–88)	6,263	14.4	1,061	0.169	939	298	1,659	5.6	5,388
101st	(1989–90)	6,683	15.4	968	0.145	915	281	1,688	6.0	5,305
102d	(1991–92)	7,771	17.9	932	0.120	932	277	1,795	6.5	5,152
103d	(1993–94)	6,647	15.3	749	0.113	1,122	265	1,887	7.1	4,304
104th	(1995–96)	4,542	10.4	611	0.134	1,340	289	2,444	8.5	3,796
105th	(1997–98)	5,014	11.5	710	0.142	1,187	251	2,001	8.0	3,624

Note: n.a. = not available.

a. This number includes all bills and joint resolutions introduced.

b. This number includes all quorum calls, yea and nay votes, and recorded votes.

c. Figures do not include the House Appropriations Committee for the Eighty-fourth to Eighty-eighth Congresses. House Appropriations Committee meetings included in subsequent Congresses numbered 584 in the Eighty-ninth Congress, 705 in the Ninetieth, 709 in the Ninety-first, 854 in the Ninety-second, and 892 in the Ninety-third.

Sources: Arthur G. Stevens, "Indicators of Congressional Workload and Activity," staff report, Congressional Research Service, Library of Congress, Washington, D.C., May 30, 1979; U.S. Congress, *Congressional Record—Daily Digest,* various issues; *Congressional Quarterly Almanac* (Washington, D.C.: Congressional Quarterly, various years); Roger H. Davidson and Carol Hardy, "Indicators of Congressional Workload and Activity," staff report, Congressional Research Service, Library of Congress, Washington, D.C., 1989; Office of the Official Reporters to House Committees, U.S. House of Representatives.

Table 6-2 Senate Workload, 80th–105th Congresses, 1947–1998

Congress		Bills introduced[a]	Average no. of bills introduced per member	Bills passed	Ratio of bills passed to bills introduced	Recorded votes[b]	Time in session		Hours per day in session	Committee, subcommittee meetings[c]
							Days	Hours		
80th	(1947–48)	3,186	33.2	1,670	0.524	248	257	1,462	5.7	n.a.
81st	(1949–50)	4,486	46.7	2,362	0.527	455	389	2,410	6.2	n.a.
82d	(1951–52)	3,665	38.2	1,849	0.505	331	287	1,648	5.7	n.a.
83d	(1953–54)	4,077	42.5	2,231	0.547	270	294	1,962	6.7	n.a.
84th	(1955–56)	4,518	47.1	2,550	0.564	224	224	1,362	6.1	2,607
85th	(1957–58)	4,532	47.2	2,202	0.486	313	271	1,876	6.9	2,748
86th	(1959–60)	4,149	42.3	1,680	0.405	422	280	2,199	7.9	2,271
87th	(1961–62)	4,048	40.5	1,953	0.482	434	323	2,164	6.7	2,532
88th	(1963–64)	3,457	34.6	1,341	0.388	541	375	2,395	6.4	2,493
89th	(1965–66)	4,129	41.3	1,636	0.396	497	345	1,814	5.3	2,889
90th	(1967–68)	4,400	44.0	1,376	0.313	595	358	1,961	5.5	2,892
91st	(1969–70)	4,867	48.7	1,271	0.261	667	384	2,352	6.1	3,264
92d	(1971–72)	4,408	44.1	1,035	0.235	955	348	2,294	6.6	3,559
93d	(1973–74)	4,524	45.2	1,115	0.246	1,138	334	2,028	6.1	4,067
94th	(1975–76)	4,114	41.1	1,038	0.252	1,290	320	2,210	6.9	4,265
95th	(1977–78)	3,800	38.0	1,070	0.282	1,151	337	2,510	7.4	3,960

96th (1979–80)	3,480	34.8	977	0.281	1,043	333	2,324	7.0	3,790
97th (1981–82)	3,396	34.0	803	0.236	966	312	2,158	6.9	3,236
98th (1983–84)	3,454	34.5	936	0.271	673	281	1,951	6.9	2,471
99th (1985–86)	3,386	33.9	940	0.278	740	313	2,531	8.1	2,373
100th (1987–88)	3,325	33.3	1,002	0.301	799	307	2,342	7.6	2,493
101st (1989–90)	3,669	36.7	980	0.267	638	274	2,254	8.2	2,340c
102d (1991–92)	4,245	42.5	947	0.223	550	287	2,291	8.0	2,039
103d (1993–94)	3,177	31.8	682	0.215	724	291	2,513	8.6	2,043
104th (1995–96)	2,266	22.7	518	0.229	919	343	2,876	8.4	1,601
105th (1997–98)	2,718	27.2	586	0.216	622	296	2,188	7.4	1,954

Note: n.a. = not available.

a. This number includes all bills and joint resolutions introduced.

b. This number includes all yea and nay votes.

c. Where final legislative calendars were not available, we compiled figures from *Congressional Information Service Abstracts* and the *Congressional Record.*

Sources: "Indicators of Congressional Workload and Activity" (1987); "Resume of Congressional Activity," *Daily Digest,* various issues; *Congressional Quarterly Almanac,* various years; final legislative calendars for each committee, 100th and 101st Congresses.

Figure 6-1 Ratio of Bills Passed to Bills Introduced, 80th–105th Congresses, 1947–1998

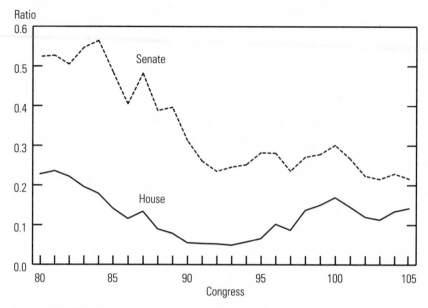

Sources: Tables 6-1 and 6-2.

Figure 6-2 Recorded Votes in the House and the Senate, 80th–105th Congresses, 1947–1998

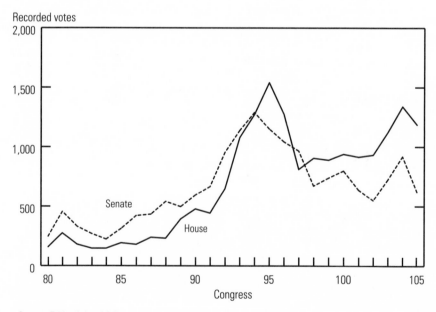

Sources: Tables 6-1 and 6-2.

Table 6-3 Recorded Votes in the House and the Senate, 80th–105th Congresses, 1947–1998

Year	House	Senate		Year	House	Senate
1947	84	138		1973	541	594
1948	75	110		1974	537	544
1949	121	226		1975	612	602
1950	154	229		1976	661	688
1951	109	202		1977	706	635
1952	72	129		1978	834	516
1953	71	89		1979	672	497
1954	76	181		1980	604	546
1955	73	88		1981	353	497
1956	74	136		1982	459	469
1957	100	111		1983	498	381
1958	93	202		1984	408	292
1959	87	215		1985	439	381
1960	93	207		1986	451	359
1961	116	207		1987	488	420
1962	124	227		1988	451	379
1963	119	229		1989	379	312
1964	113	312		1990	536	326
1965	201	259		1991	444	280
1966	193	238		1992	488	270
1967	245	315		1993	615	395
1968	233	280[a]		1994	507	329
1969	177	245		1995	885	613
1970	266	422		1996	455	306
1971	320	423		1997	640	304
1972	329	532		1998	547	318

Note: House figures reflect the total number of quorum calls, yea and nay votes, and recorded votes, while Senate figures include only yea and nay votes.

a. This figure does not include one yea and nay vote that was ruled invalid for lack of a quorum.

Sources: "Resume of Congressional Activity," *Congressional Record—Daily Digest,* various issues; *Congressional Quarterly Almanac,* various years; *Congressional Monitor,* October 7, 1996, 5.

Table 6-4 Congressional Workload, 80th–105th Congresses, 1947–1998

		Public bills			Private bills		
Congress		No. of bills enacted	Total pages of statutes	Average pages per statute	No. of bills enacted	Total pages of statutes	Average pages per statute
80th	(1947–48)	906	2,236	2.5	458	182	0.40
81st	(1949–50)	921	2,314	2.5	1,103	417	0.38
82d	(1951–52)	594	1,585	2.7	1,023	360	0.35
83d	(1953–54)	781	1,899	2.4	1,002	365	0.36
84th	(1955–56)	1,028	1,848	1.8	893	364	0.41
85th	(1957–58)	936	2,435	2.6	784	349	0.45
86th	(1959–60)	800	1,774	2.2	492	201	0.41
87th	(1961–62)	885	2,078	2.3	684	255	0.37
88th	(1963–64)	666	1,975	3.0	360	144	0.40
89th	(1965–66)	810	2,912	3.6	473	188	0.40
90th	(1967–68)	640	2,304	3.6	362	128	0.35
91st	(1969–70)	695	2,927	4.2	246	104	0.42
92d	(1971–72)	607	2,330	3.8	161	67	0.42
93d	(1973–74)	649	3,443	5.3	123	48	0.39
94th	(1975–76)	588	4,121	7.0	141	75	0.53
95th	(1977–78)	633	5,403	8.5	170	60	0.35
96th	(1979–80)	613	4,947	8.1	123	63	0.51
97th	(1981–82)	473	4,343	9.2	56	25	0.45
98th	(1983–84)	623	4,893	7.8	54	26	0.48
99th	(1985–86)	664	7,198	10.8	24	13	0.54
100th	(1987–88)	713	4,839	6.8	48	29	0.60
101st	(1989–90)	650	5,767	8.9	16	9	0.56
102d	(1991–92)	590	7,544	12.8	20	11	0.55
103d	(1993–94)	465	7,542	16.2	8	9	1.10
104th	(1995–96)	333	6,369	19.1	4	4	1.00
105th	(1997–98)	394	7,269	18.4	10	11	0.91

Sources: "Indicators of Congressional Workload and Activity"; *U.S. Code Congressional and Administrative News,* volumes for 97th, 98th, 99th, and 100th Congresses; Office of the Law Revision Counsel, U.S. House of Representatives. For the 101st, 102d, and 103d Congresses, Office of the Law Revision Counsel; *Federal Register*, Statutes Branch.

Table 6-5 Pages in the *Federal Register,* 1936–1998

Year	Pages	Year	Pages	Year	Pages
1936	2,355	1977	63,629	1988	53,376
1946	14,736	1978	61,261	1989	53,821
1956	10,528	1979	77,497	1990	53,618
1966	16,850	1980	87,012	1991	67,715
1969	20,464	1981	63,554	1992	62,919
1971	25,442	1982	58,493	1993	69,684
1972	28,920	1983	57,703	1994	68,107
1973	35,586	1984	50,997	1995	68,108
1974	45,422	1985	53,479	1996	69,368
1975	60,221	1986	47,418	1997	68,530
1976	57,072	1987	49,654	1998	72,356

Figure 6-3   Public Bills in the Congressional Workload, 80th–105th Congresses, 1947–1998

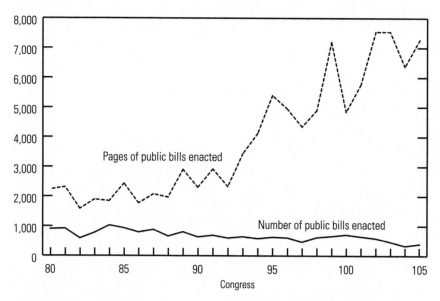

Source: Table 6-4.

Table 6-6 Vetoes and Overrides, 80th–105th Congresses, 1947–1998

Congress		Total no. of presidential vetoes	No. of regular vetoes	No. of pocket vetoes	Vetoes overridden		House attempts to override vetoes	Senate attempts to override vetoes
					Total	Percentage of regular vetoes		
80th	(1947–48)	75	42	33	6	14.3	8	8
81st	(1949–50)	79	70	9	3	4.3	5	5
82d	(1951–52)	22	14	8	3	21.4	4	4
83d	(1953–54)	52	21	31	0	—	0	0
84th	(1955–56)	34	12	22	0	—	1	1
85th	(1957–58)	51	18	33	0	—	1	1
86th	(1959–60)	44	22	22	2	9.1	5	6
87th	(1961–62)	20	11	9	0	—	0	0
88th	(1963–64)	9	5	4	0	—	0	0
89th	(1965–66)	14	10	4	0	—	0	0
90th	(1967–68)	8	2	6	0	—	0	0
91st	(1969–70)	11	7	4	2	28.6	4	4
92d	(1971–72)	20	6	14	2	33.3	3	4
93d	(1973–74)	39	27	12	5	18.5	12	10
94th	(1975–76)	37	32	5	8	25.0	17	15
95th	(1977–78)	19	6	13	0	—	2	0

96th	(1979–80)	12	7	5	2	28.6	2	2
97th	(1981–82)	15	9	6	2	22.2	4	3
98th	(1983–84)	24	9	15	2	22.2	2	2
99th	(1985–86)	20	13	7	2	15.4	3	3
100th	(1987–88)	19	8	11	3	37.5	5	4
101st	(1989–90)	21	16	5	0	—	9	5
102d	(1991–92)	25	15	10[a]	1	6.7	3	3
103d	(1993–94)	17	0	0	0	0	0	0
104th	(1995–96)	8	17	0	1	5.9	6	1
105th	(1997–98)	8	8	0	0	0	1	1

Note: This table does not include line-item vetoes. After President Clinton excised several Pentagon programs from the 1998 budget, both houses of Congress, under the line-item veto law, passed legislation restoring some of the programs (H.R. 2631). President Clinton subsequently vetoed that bill, and both houses of Congress passed legislation overriding his veto. Subsequently, the Supreme Court declared the line-item veto unconstitutional.

a. President Bush asserted that he had pocket-vetoed S. 1176, although some members in Congress dispute that assertion on the grounds that bills can be pocket-vetoed only after Congress has adjourned, not during a recess.

Sources: "Indicators of Congressional Workload and Activity." For 1989–1990, Congressional Quarterly Research Query Service. For 1991–1992, *Congressional Quarterly Weekly Report,* December 19, 1992, 3925–26. For 1993–1994, *Congressional Quarterly Weekly Report,* December 31, 1994, 3623. For 1995–1996, *Congressional Quarterly Weekly Report,* December 14, 1996, 3386. For 1997–1998, *Congressional Quarterly Weekly Report,* various issues.

Table 6-7 Attempted and Successful Cloture Votes in the Senate, 1919–1998

	1st session		2d session		Total	
Congress	attempted	successful	attempted	successful	attempted	successful
66th (1919–20)	1	1	0	0	1	1
67th (1921–22)	1	0	1	0	2	0
68th (1923–24)	0	0	0	0	0	0
69th (1925–26)	0	0	2	1	2	1
70th (1927–28)	5	2	0	0	5	2
71st (1929–30)	0	0	0	0	0	0
72d (1931–32)	0	0	0	0	0	0
73d (1933–34)	1	0	0	0	1	0
74th (1935–36)	0	0	0	0	0	0
75th (1937–38)	0	0	2	0	2	0
76th (1939–40)	0	0	0	0	0	0
77th (1941–42)	0	0	1	1	1	1
78th (1943–44)	0	0	1	1	1	1
79th (1945–46)	0	0	4	0	4	0
80th (1947–48)	0	0	0	0	0	0
81st (1949–50)	0	0	2	0	2	0
82d (1951–52)	0	0	0	0	0	0
83d (1953–54)	0	0	1	0	1	0
84th (1955–56)	0	0	0	0	0	0
85th (1957–58)	0	0	0	0	0	0
86th (1959–60)	0	0	1	0	1	0
87th (1961–62)	1	0	3	1	4	1
88th (1963–64)	1	0	2	1	3	1
89th (1965–66)	2	1	5	0	7	1
90th (1967–68)	1	0	5	1	6	1
91st (1969–70)	2	0	4	0	6	0
92d (1971–72)	10	2	10	2	20	4
93d (1973–74)	10	2	21	7	31	9
94th (1975–76)	23	13	4	4	27	17
95th (1977–78)	5	1	8	2	13	3
96th (1979–80)	4	1	17	9	21	10
97th (1981–82)	7	2	20	7	27	9
98th (1983–84)	7	2	12	9	19	11
99th (1985–86)	9	1	14	9	23	10
100th (1987–88)	24	6	20	6	44	12
101st (1989–90)	9	6	15	5	24	11
102d (1991–92)	21	9	28	14	49	23
103d (1993–94)	20	4	22	10	42	14
104th (1995–96)	21	4	29	5	50	9
105th (1997–98)	23	7	28	11	51	18

Note: The number of votes required to invoke cloture was changed on March 7, 1975, from two-thirds of those present and voting to three-fifths of the total Senate membership, as Rule XXII of the standing rules of the Senate was amended.

Sources: "Indicators of Congressional Workload and Activity." For 1989–1992, Congressional Research Service, Library of Congress-Government Division. For 1993, *Congressional Quarterly Almanac,* 1994, 14. For 1994–1996, *Congressional Monitor*, October 11, 1994, 17; October 7, 1996, 24. For 1997–1998, Senate Bill Clerk.

Table 6-8   Congressional Mailings, 1954–1993

Fiscal year	Millions of pieces	Increase or decrease (%)
1954	43.5	—
1955	45.6	4.8
1956	58.2	27.6
1957	59.6	2.4
1958	65.4	9.7
1959	86.5	32.3
1960	108.0	24.9
1961	85.1	−21.2
1962	110.1	29.4
1963	94.7	−14.0
1964	110.5	16.7
1965	120.9	9.4
1966	197.5	63.4
1967	192.9	−2.3
1968	178.2	−7.6
1969	190.0	6.6
1970	201.0	5.8
1971	238.4	18.6
1972	308.9	29.6
1973	310.6	0.6
1974	321.0	3.3
1975	312.4	−2.7
1976	401.4	28.5
Transition quarter	159.9	—
1977	293.3	−26.9
1978	430.2	46.7
1979	409.9	−4.7
1980	511.3	24.7
1981	395.6	−22.6
1982	771.8	95.1
1983	556.8	−27.9
1984	924.6	60.3
1985	675.0	−27.9
1986	758.7	12.4
1987	494.7	−34.8
1988	804.9	62.7
1989	598.6	−25.6
1990	564.2	−5.7
1991	259.8	−54.0
1992	458.0	76.3
1993	200.7	−56.3

Sources: For 1954–1978, U.S. Congress, House, Committee on Appropriations, Subcommittee on Legislative Branch Appropriations, *Hearings on Legislative Branch Appropriations for 1980,* pt. 2. For 1979, *House LBA Hearings for 1981,* pt. 2. For 1980–1983, Office of the Clerk of the House. For 1984, *House LBA Hearings for 1986,* pt. 2. For 1985, *House LBA Hearings for 1987,* pt. 2. For 1986, *House LBA Hearings for 1988,* pt. 2. For 1987, *House LBA Hearings for 1989,* pt. 2. For 1988, *House LBA Hearings for 1990,* pt. 2. For 1989, Congressional Research Service Report for Congress, "U.S. Congress Official Mail Costs: FY1972 to FY1991." For 1990–1991, Congressional Research Service, "U.S. Congress Official Mail Costs: FY1972 to FY1993 (Est.)." For 1992–1993, U.S. Postal Service.

7

Budgeting

The Constitution gives Congress the power to levy taxes and to appropriate money. Accordingly, the executive branch can raise and spend money only to the extent and in the manner authorized by Congress. In addition to its taxing and appropriating power, Congress makes financial decisions through its authorizations and budget processes. The authorizations process is anchored in the rules of the House and, to a lesser extent, those of the Senate that require agencies and programs to be authorized in law before funds are appropriated for them. The Congressional Budget Act of 1974 established the current budget process. That act required Congress to adopt two budget resolutions each year to coordinate the numerous fiscal decisions made in separate revenue, spending, and debt legislation. Successive reforms have not altered the basics.

In recent years, however, Congress has adopted only a single budget resolution. The process itself came under reexamination in the past few years with proposed legislation for biennial budgeting and a constitutional amendment requiring a balanced budget. The 104th Congress actually passed one reform: a statutory line-item veto. When President Clinton excised several military programs from the 1998 budget, the GOP cried foul and, under the format laid out by the law, promptly reinstated some of the programs over the president's veto. Shortly after that, the Supreme Court ruled the entire law unconstitutional; that decision disappointed proponents, who continue to look for ways to restore the power to the president. The entire experience seems to have dampened enthusiasm for the line-item veto, however, and supporters are unlikely to be successful, given the political climate and legal restrictions.

Although budget deficits have turned to surpluses, instead of easing budget problems, the surplus presents members with difficult choices about future spending and taxation—made more difficult by spending "caps" implemented by the 1990 and 1997 budget agreements. Because virtually all issues before Congress have spending or tax implications, the budget will remain one of the most contentious issues.

Budget Resolutions

In 1998, for the first time since the 1974 reforms, Congress failed to adopt a budget resolution. While each house passed a resolution, the two versions were so far apart that Congress never seriously tried to reconcile the differences in a conference committee. Divided by politics and preoccupied by scandal, each house was forced to accept much of the president's spending—along with more by the congressmen. The partisan nature of 1998 was drastic but hardly unprecedented. Since the inception of the congressional budget process, voting on the resolutions has reflected a sharp split in the House between the Democratic and Republican parties. (See table 7-1.) Typically, in that period the Democrats controlled the process, but rarely with enough unity to keep Republicans from scoring victories and occasionally seizing control of the process under President Reagan. Another factor was the diversity of the Democratic party. Occasionally, the liberal and conservative wings of the Democratic Party would oppose the party's position and force revisions to the budget resolutions.

In the 1970s and 1980s Republicans were much more unified: approximately 95 percent of the House GOP voted against adoption of those budget resolutions. For fiscal years 1982 and 1983, the Republicans gained control of the process (despite their minority status in the House), and most of them voted for those budgets, proposed in large part by Ronald Reagan. But in 1984 Democrats regained control of the process, and Republicans were forced back into opposition for the rest of the decade. GOP unity wavered in 1989 and 1990 and created a new bipartisan coalition for the budget proposals. Republicans more or less maintained their solidarity in the 1990s, however: not a single Republican voted for the 1993, 1994, or 1995 budget resolutions. The 1993 budget vote was extremely close (209–207), with the Speaker casting a rare floor vote. The 1994 budget was based on the first proposals from a Democratic president in twelve years, and the party rallied around Bill Clinton and quickly passed the resolution by a wide margin. But the real test came with the deficit-reduction package, and there Clinton faced a difficult test of his authority. The cliff-hanger vote passed by a single vote in each chamber, without any Republican support.

After the Republican takeover, the pattern simply reversed with nearly unanimous GOP support and Democratic opposition to the 1996 and 1997 budget resolutions. After the 1996 elections, in which the voters returned both the Republican Congress and the Democratic president, the two parties cooperated and produced a budget that received overwhelming support (333–99 in the House and 78–22 in the Senate). Both sides trumpeted that vote as a victory, and in fiscal year 1998—with the advent of the surplus—budget politics seemed to be getting easier.

The Senateís pattern was different in the 1970s. (See table 7-2.) Large, bipartisan coalitions passed the budget resolutions until 1982 and 1983, when a majority of Senate Democrats voted against the resolution. From that point the Senateís debate remained partisan, although not in comparison with the House debate. After the Democrats regained control of the chamber, the GOP increased its opposition to Democratic budgets. The pattern again reversed itself when the Republicans regained control of the Senate. Both parties were often split, so occasionally bipartisan coalitions, such as the one for the fiscal year 1998 agreement, surfaced.

The fiscal year 1998 agreement was not a harbinger of the future, however. As Congress debated the fiscal year 1999 budget, the process broke down. Conservative House Republicans would not abandon their hopes for a large tax cut and deep spending cuts. The more moderate Senate wanted a bill closely aligned with the five-year plan laid out in the previous budget. Ultimately, when the two chambers could not agree, Clinton's political leverage allowed him to emerge from the budget battles the clear victor. In 1999 the Republican Congress quickly passed a joint budget resolution, but few believed that the appropriators could live with its tight spending caps.

In each budget resolution, Congress goes on record with respect to both the aggregate budget and the specific allocations for various departments and programs. (See table 7-3.) In the 1970s actual spending and the deficit tended to be below those set by Congress in the budget resolutions. Beginning in 1980, the pattern reversed, and the final results began to show much higher spending. In the 1991 budget Congress projected the deficit at $64 billion, but it was actually $268.7 billion. Congress passed the Budget Enforcement Act, forcing budget writers to make more realistic deficit projections in subsequent years. In 1993 deficit politics began to change drastically: the actual deficit as well as all key budget aggregates were below those of Congress's resolution for the first time since the trend began in 1980. Five years of strong economic growth and surprisingly high tax revenues combined to produce a surplus by 1998.

Congressional Control of the Budget

Although Congress holds the power of the purse, the rise of uncontrollable spending— programs not regulated by annual appropriations—has hampered members' ability to exercise that power effectively. During fiscal years 1967–1992 "relatively uncontrollable" outlays soared from less than $100 billion to more than $1 trillion and from less than 60 percent of total outlays to nearly 80 percent. (See table 7-4.) In the 1990s that growth stabilized as a strong, low-inflation economy kept outlays for Social Security, Medicare, and Medicaid at roughly 80 percent of the total budget. By fiscal year 1998, the uncontrollable portion still remained above 80 percent of the total budget.

Most uncontrollables are in the form of entitlements: provisions of law that mandate payments to eligible recipients. Most entitlements are open-ended and cannot be controlled through the budget or appropriations bills. Moreover, many entitlements are indexed to the rate of inflation, so that payments are adjusted to increases in the cost of living without congressional action. Congress can control entitlements only by changing the laws that mandate the payments, as it did in 1996 when it passed welfare reform. Congress developed the reconciliation process in 1980 as a means of reducing certain entitlements that would then, lawmakers hoped, bring expenditures for them in line with congressional budget decisions. But that method proved ineffective, and as deficit reduction became a greater national priority, the massive growth of entitlement spending, especially that of Social Security, Medicare, and Medicaid, gained much attention.

In 1993 and 1994, Medicare and Medicaid spending came under intense scrutiny during the debate over health care reform. But when discussion of cuts began, legislators were quickly reminded of the wide public support of those programs. The future of Social Security expenditures brought much contention to the 1995 debate requiring a balanced federal budget. Senate Democrats demanded that legislation proposed by Republicans include a measure protecting Social Security from budget cuts. Both those measures were a prelude for the all-out warfare of government shutdowns. The controversy cooled in the wake of the 1997 balanced-budget deal, which formed a bipartisan commission on Medicare and Medicaid. But even surpluses have not been able to solve the thorny issues surrounding those entitlements, and the Medicare Commission failed to find consensus for reforms.

The Appropriations Process

A budget resolution is advisory. Government agencies cannot spend funds pursuant to the amounts set in a resolution. The actual provision of funds occurs in appropriations bills, of which there are supposed to be thirteen regular bills and a number of supplemental measures each year.

The Appropriations Committees see themselves as guardians of the Treasury, a role that is reflected in their determination to appropriate less money than the president has requested. In almost every year, the total amount appropriated is below the presidentís budget request. (See table 7-5.) Those figures do not include permanent appropriations (which the Appropriations Committees do not review) or ìbackdoorî authority provided in other legislation.

Although the Appropriations Committees provide less money than the president requests, they also enact sizable supplemental appropriations each year. (See table 7-6.) Supplemental appropriations are made for a number of reasons: to provide for agencies not funded in the regular appropriations bills, to pay for the salary increases of federal employees, to supplement the funds for agencies facing a deficiency, to finance new or expanded programs, to pay for natural disasters like floods or hurricanes, and, as in 1999, to finance major military operations such as the Yugoslavia bombing. The number of supplemental bills and their amounts rose after the congressional budget process was introduced but then declined in the early 1990s. In 1995 Republicans and conservative Democrats demanded and received offsets in other spending areas for all supplemental spending. Supplemental appropriations show signs of increasing use, however. The fiscal year 1999 budget process included several nonemergency measures in the supplemental appropriations bill for disaster reliefóin direct violation of the 1997 budget agreement.

Historically, the budget cutting has been concentrated in the House, which, under long-standing precedent, considers appropriations bills before the Senate takes them up. That role depends largely on the ability of the House Appropriations Committee to protect its bills against floor amendments to provide additional funds. But from 1965 through 1980 the number of amendments proposed and the number agreed to by the House increased steadily. (See table 7-7.)

One important factor in that upward trend was the Legislative Reorganization Act of 1970, which provided for recorded votes in the Committee of the Whole, where most House action on appropriations bills (and other measures) takes place. Another reason for the increase in floor amendments has been the practice of attaching "limitations" to appropriations bills. Although the rules bar insertion of legislation in appropriations bills, limitations that restrict the use of appropriated funds are permissible. The House adopted three times as many limitation amendments in the 1970s as it did in the 1960s. Some of the most contentious issues, such as U.S. policy in Vietnam, aid to Nicaraguan contras, school busing, and abortions, have been considered as limitations in appropriations bills.

A change in rules adopted by the House at the start of the Ninety-eighth Congress in 1983 appears to have caused downturn in the number of limiting amendments. The new rule makes it easier for the House to avoid consideration of those amendments, but if a House majority wants to do so, it can still use appropriations bills as an effective means of controlling government policy by limiting the use of appropriated funds.

The Congressional Budget Act of 1974 established a timetable designed to ensure enactment of all regular appropriations bills by October 1, when the new fiscal year begins. Despite the legislative schedule laid out in the act, Congress has had difficulty in completing its work on regular appropriations bills by the start of the fiscal year. As a consequence, Congress has been compelled to provide stopgap funding through continuing appropriations. (See table 7-8.) In only four fiscal years—1977, 1989, 1995, and 1998—has Congress not needed to rely on continuing appropriations. Often Congress has acted on only a few of the appropriations bills by the beginning of the fiscal year—failing to enact any bills at the beginning of fiscal years 1986–1988 and 1990–1991. The fiscal year 1989 aberration came when Congress decided to put off all difficult spending issues until after the presidential election of 1988. A similar dynamic emerged in 1995, although it appears that such practices are single-year events and not apparently part of a trend. The budget battles of the 104th Congress intensified the old passions, and the future is likely to be turbulent again.

The Budgetary Work of Congress

To an extraordinary degree the business of Congress, particularly the House, revolves around the budget. Between 1955 and 1982 the number of House and Senate roll call votes dealing with the budget increased markedly. (See tables 7-9 and 7-10.) Budget-related votes include all roll calls on appropriations bills, tax legislation (other than treaties and tariffs), budget resolutions, and reconciliation bills, as well as votes pertaining to the level of authorizations. The number of budget-related votes has escalated in both chambers over the past thirty years, although more so in the Senate. In most years slightly under 50 percent of House roll call votes each year have been budget-related; such votes reached 59 percent in 1993 but then declined to 38 percent in 1998. In the Senate, budget-related roll call votes hit a high of 71 percent in 1981 and then fluctuated between 50 and 70 percent until 1998, when the number peaked again at 74 percent.

One interesting pattern has emerged regarding the congressional budget process: Congress still gives a great deal of attention to authorizations, appropriations, and tax legislation. Congressional budget activity—especially in the Senate—was extraordinary during the 1981 session, which coincided with Ronald Reagan's first year in office. The new president organized his domestic agenda around the federal budget and called for major changes in economic policies and spending priorities. Inevitably, Congress increased its budget activity. In subsequent years, budget activity was more normal but was still the dominant issue of each Congress. Since 1993 the budget has remained central to virtually all major debates in Congress.

Rescissions and Deferrals

One of the key purposes of the congressional budget process is to ensure that congressional spending priorities prevail when they are in conflict with those of the president. To achieve that end, the Impoundment Control Act established procedures for congressional review of presidential proposals to defer or rescind funds provided by Congress. When a president proposes rescission, Congress has a forty-five-day period during which it can pass a bill rescinding the funds; if Congress fails to act during that period, the president is required to make the funds available for the expenditure. The deficit-control mentality of the 1990s led many members, most Republicans, to call for passage of a presidential line-item veto. The 104th Congress passed a line-item veto provision, which was actually more an enhanced rescission that allowed the president to veto specific sections of appropriations bills. Congress had to overturn any such rescissions by a two-thirds margin. When President Clinton excised several programs in the fall of 1997, he ironically angered Republicans, who had ardently advocated the line-item veto, and they then voted with many Democrats to restore the programs. In 1998 the Supreme Court ruled the line-item veto unconstitutional.

The use of the rescission varies sharply from year to year. (See table 7-11.) For instance, President Ford proposed billions of dollars in rescissions, but Congress actually rescinded less than 10 percent of his requests. During President Carter's administration, rescissions dropped sharply. Reagan resorted to rescissions to implement his budget policy, however, and in 1981, 90 percent of his request was rescinded—although he was less successful later. President Bush proposed only seventeen rescissions in his first two years, but Congress rescinded less than 1 percent of the funds he requested. Bush relied on rescissions to a much greater extent in the second half of his term. In 1992, 26 percent of the $8 billion he requested was approved. Under Clinton, Congress has generally been very receptive to proposed rescissions and has often exceeded his requests. In 1995 the new Republican Congress forced the president to accept more than $16 billion in rescissions.

When a president proposes deferrals, either the House or the Senate can approve an "impoundment resolution" compelling the release of the affected funds. (See table 7-12.) The June 1983 decision of the Supreme Court that invalidated all legislative vetoes questioned the constitutional status of that procedure. Because the president now proposes only nonpolicy deferrals, Congress usually disapproves only a small portion of them. In fact, from 1988 through 1996, Congress accepted all the president's proposed deferrals.[1]

Note

1. Changes in the way House Appropriations Committee counts rescissions and deferrals prevented us from including the two most recent years in this edition.

Table 7-1 House Votes on Adoption of Budget Resolutions, by Party, Fiscal Years 1976–1999

Fiscal year	Resolution	Total Yes	Total No	Democrats Yes	Democrats No	Republicans Yes	Republicans No
1976	First	200	196	197	68	3	128
	Second	225	191	214	67	11	124
1977	First	221	155	208	44	13	111
	Second	227	151	215	38	12	113
	Third	239	169	225	50	14	119
1978	First (first round)	84	320	82	185	2	135
	First (second round)	213	179	206	58	7	121
	Second	199	188	195	59	4	129
1979	First	201	197	198	61	3	136
	Second	217	178	215	42	2	136
1980	First	220	184	211	50	9	134
	Second (first round)	192	213	188	67	4	146
	Second (second round)	212	206	212	52	0	154
	Third[a]	241	174	218	45	23	129
1981	First	225	193	203	62	22	131
	Second	203	191	201	45	2	146
1982	First	270	154	84	153	186	1
	Second	206	200	70	150	136	50
1983	First	219	206	63	174	156	32
1984	First	229	196	225	36	4	160
1985	First	250	168	229	29	21	139
1986	First	258	170	234	15	24	155
1987	First	245	179	228	19	17	160
1988	First	215	201	212	34	3	167
1989	First	319	102	227	24	92	78
1990	First	263	157	157	96	106	61
1991	First	218	208	218	34	0	174
1992	First	239	181[b]	231	25	8	155
1993	First	209	207[b]	209	47	0	159
1994	First	243[b]	183	242	11	0	172
1995	First	223[b]	175	222	11	0	164
1996	First	238	194[b]	8	191	230	1
1997	First	216	211[b]	4	191	212	19
1998	First	333	99[b]	132	72	201	26
1999	First[c]	216	204[b]	3	194	213	9

Note: These votes are on passage of the resolutions in the House, not on adoption of the conference report. Beginning with the 1983 fiscal year, Congress has adopted only one budget resolution each year, rather than the two originally prescribed by the Congressional Budget Act.

a. The third resolution for fiscal 1980 was part of the first resolution for the 1981 fiscal year, but it was voted on separately in the House.
b. The total includes Bernard Sanders (I-Vt.).
c. Although both chambers passed a 1999 budget resolution, the two different versions were so far apart that Congress never seriously attempted to reconcile the two bills, so that 1999 was the first year under the budgeting act that Congress did not pass a budget resolution.

Sources: Congressional Record; Congressional Quarterly Almanac (Washington, D.C.: Congressional Quarterly, various years); *Congressional Quarterly Weekly Report,* various issues.

Table 7-2 Senate Votes on Adoption of Budget Resolutions, by Party,
Fiscal Years 1976–1999

		Total		Democrats		Republicans	
Fiscal year	Resolution	Yes	No	Yes	No	Yes	No
1976	First	69	22	50	4	19	18
	Second	69	23	50	8	19	15
1977	First	62	22	45	6	17	16
	Second	55	23	41	5	14	18
	Third	72	20	55	3	17	17
1978	First	56	31	41	14	15	17
	Second	63	21	46	8	17	13
1979	First	64	27	48	8	16	19
	Second	56	18	42	6	14	12
1980	First	64	20	44	5	20	15
	Second	62	36	45	14	17	22
1981	First	68	28	49	6	19	22
	Second	48	46	33	21	15	25
1982	First	78	20	28	18	50	2
	Second	49	48	2	44	47	4
1983	First	49	43	3	41	46	2
1984	First	50	49	29	17	21	32
1985	First	41	34	1	31	40	3
1986	First	50	49	1	45	49[a]	4
1987	First	70	25	38	6	32	19
1988	First	53	46	50	3	3	43
1989	First	69	26	44	6	25	20
1990	First	68	31	38	17	30	14
1991	First[b]	—	—	—	—	—	—
1992	First	57	41	49	7	8	34
1993	First	52	41	36	16	16	25
1994	First	54	45	54	2	0	43
1995	First	57	40	55	0	2	40
1996	First	57	42	3	42	54	0
1997	First	53	46	0	46	53	0
1998	First	78	22	37	8	41	14
1999	First[c]	57	41	3	44	54	0

Note: These votes are on passage of the resolutions in the Senate, not on adoption of the conference report. Beginning with the 1983 fiscal year, Congress has adopted only one budget resolution each year, rather than the two originally prescribed by the Congressional Budget Act.

a. Vice President George Bush cast the deciding vote for the Republicans.
b. The Senate Budget Resolution (S. Con. Res. 110) was approved by voice vote on June 14, 1990.
c. Although both chambers passed a 1999 budget resolution, the two different versions were so far apart that Congress never seriously attempted to reconcile the two bills, so that 1999 was the first year under the budgeting act that Congress did not pass a budget resolution.

Sources: Congressional Record; Congressional Quarterly Almanac, various years; *Congressional Quarterly Weekly Report,* various issues.

Table 7-3 Budgeted and Actual Revenues, Budget Authority, Outlays, and Deficits, Fiscal Years 1976–2000 (billions of dollars)

Fiscal year	Revenues	Budget authority	Budget outlays	Budget deficit/surplus
1976				
President's budget	297.7	385.8	349.4	−51.7
First budget resolution	298.2	395.8	367.0	−68.8
Second budget resolution	300.8	408.0	374.9	−74.1
Actual	300.0	415.3	366.4	−66.4
1977				
President's budget	351.3	433.4	394.2	−42.9
First budget resolution	362.5	454.2	413.3	−50.8
Second budget resolution	362.5	451.6	413.1	−50.6
Third budget resolution	347.7	472.9	417.5	−69.8
Fourth budget resolution	356.6	470.2	409.2	−52.6
Actual	357.8	464.4	402.7	−44.9
1978				
Ford budget	393.0	480.4	440.0	−47.0
Carter budget	401.6	507.3	459.4	−57.8
First budget resolution	396.3	503.5	461.0	−64.7
Second budget resolution	397.0	500.1	458.3	−61.3
Actual	402.0	500.4	450.8	−48.8
1979				
President's budget	439.6	568.2	500.2	−60.6
First budget resolution	447.9	568.9	498.8	−50.9
Second budget resolution	448.7	555.7	487.5	−38.8
Third budget resolution	461.0	559.2	494.5	−33.5
Actual	465.9	556.7	493.6	−27.7
1980				
President's budget	502.6	615.5	531.6	−29.0
First budget resolution	509.0	604.4	532.0	−23.0
Second budget resolution	517.8	638.0	547.6	−29.8
Third budget resolution	525.7	658.9	572.7	−47.0
Actual	520.0	658.8	579.6	−59.6
1981				
President's budget	600.0	696.1	615.8	−15.8
Revised budget	628.0	691.3	611.5	16.5
First budget resolution	613.8	697.2	613.6	0.2
Second budget resolution	605.0	694.6	632.4	−27.4
Third budget resolution	603.3	717.5	661.4	−58.1
Actual	599.3	718.4	657.2	−57.9
1982				
Carter budget	711.8	809.8	739.3	−27.5
Reagan budget	650.3	772.4	695.3	−45.0
Budget resolution	657.8	770.9	695.5	−37.7
Revised resolution	628.4	777.7	734.1	−105.7
Actual	617.8	779.9	728.4	−110.6

(table continues)

Table 7-3 *(continued)*

Fiscal year	Revenues	Budget authority	Budget outlays	Budget deficit/surplus
1983				
President's budget	666.1	801.9	757.6	–91.5
Budget resolution	665.9	822.4	769.8	–103.9
Actual	600.6	866.7	796.0	–195.4
1984				
President's budget	659.7	900.1	848.5	–188.8
Budget resolution[a]	679.6	919.5	849.5	–169.9
		928.7	858.9	–179.3
Revised resolution	672.9	918.9	845.6	–172.7
Actual	666.5	949.8	851.8	–185.3
1985				
President's budget	745.1	1,006.5	925.5	–180.4
Budget resolution	750.9	1,021.4	932.1	–181.2
Actual	734.1	1,074.1	946.3	–212.2
1986				
President's budget	793.7	1,060.0	973.7	–180.0
Budget resolution	795.7	1,069.7	967.6	–171.9
Actual	769.1	1,072.8	989.8	–220.7
1987				
President's budget	850.4	1,102.0	994.0	–143.6
Budget resolution	852.4	1,093.4	995.0	–142.6
Actual	854.1	1,099.9	1,003.8	–149.7
1988				
President's budget	916.6	1,142.2	1,024.4	–107.8
Budget resolution	921.6	1,153.2	1,055.5	–133.9
Actual	909.0	1,185.5	1,064.0	–155.0
1989				
President's budget	964.7	1,222.1	1,094.2	–129.5
Budget resolution	964.3	1,232.0	1,098.2	–133.9
Actual	990.7	1,309.9	1,144.1	–153.4
1990				
President's budget	1,059.3	1,331.2	1,151.8	–92.5
Budget resolution	1,065.5	1,350.9	1,165.3	–99.8
Actual	1,031.3	1,368.5	1,251.7	–220.4
1991				
President's budget	1,170.2	1,396.5	1,233.3	–63.1
Budget resolution	1,172.9	1,485.6	1,236.9	–64.0
Actual	1,054.3	1,398.2	1,323.0	–268.7
1992				
President's budget	1,172.2	1,579.3	1,442.2	–270.0
Budget resolution	1,169.2	1,590.1	1,448.0	–278.8
Actual	1,091.7	1,469.2	1,381.9	–290.2

Fiscal year	Revenues	Budget authority	Budget outlays	Budget deficit/surplus
1993				
President's budget	1,171.2	1,516.8	1,503.0	−331.8
Budget resolution	1,173.4	1,516.4	1,500.0	−326.6
Actual	1,153.5	1,473.6	1,408.7	−255.1
1994				
President's budget	1,242.1	1,512.6	1,500.6	−258.5
Budget resolution	1,241.8	1,507.1	1,495.6	−253.8
Actual	1,257.7	1,528.4	1,460.9	−203.2
1995				
President's budget	1,353.8	1,537.0	1,518.9	−165.1[b]
Budget resolution	1,338.2	1,540.7	1,513.6	−175.4
Actual	1,351.8	1,543.3	1,515.7	−163.9
1996				
President's budget	1,415.5	1,613.8	1,612.1	−196.7
Budget resolution	1,417.2	1,591.7	1,587.5	−170.3
Actual	1,453.1	1,581.1	1,560.3	−107.3
1997				
President's budget	1,495.2	1,638.4	1,635.3	−140.1
Budget resolution	1,469.0	1,633.0	1,622.0	−153.4
Actual	1,579.3	1,642.9	1,601.2	−21.9
1998				
President's budget	1,566.8	1,709.6	1,687.5	−120.6
Budget resolution	1,602.0	1,703.8	1,692.0	−90.0
Actual	1,721.8	1,692.3	1,652.6	69.2
1999				
President's budget[c]	1,742.7	1,751.0	1,733.2	9.5
2000				
President's budget[c]	1,883.0	1,781.1	1,765.7	117.3

a. Larger figures for authority, outlays, and deficit assumed enactment of programs in a reserve fund.
b. This figure assumed enactment of the president's health care reforms.
c. President Clinton indicated in his fiscal year 1999 and 2000 *Budget Proposals* that the surplus would be reserved for the Social Security trust fund, pending a legislative solution. So, while the budget did not call the remainder a surplus, we treated it as such in this table.

Sources: Congressional Budget Office; *The Budget of the United States Government* for fiscal years 1984–2000; *Congressional Quarterly Almanac,* vols. 39–40; *Congressional Quarterly Weekly Report,* 1985–1987, and March 26, 1988; *Congressional Record,* vol. 136, no. 131, October 7, 1990. For 1992, *Congressional Quarterly Weekly Report,* May 25, 1991. For 1993, Congressional Budget Office. For 1994, *Congressional Quarterly Weekly Report,* April 3, 1993. For 1995, *Congressional Quarterly Weekly Report,* May 7, 1994. For 1996, *Congressional Quarterly Weekly Report,* February 11, 1995; May 20, 1995. For 1997, *Congressional Quarterly Weekly Report,* March 23, 1996; *U.S. Budget History,* tables 1.1 and 5.1, fiscal year 1998 and fiscal year 1999. For 1998, Congressional Budget Office and House Budget Committee. For 1999, *President's Budget Fiscal Year 1999.* For 2000, *President's Budget Fiscal Year 2000.*

Table 7-4 Relatively Uncontrollable Federal Outlays under Present Law, Fiscal Years 1967–1999 (billions of dollars)

Fiscal year	Social Security and other retirement	Medical care	Other payments to individuals	Net interest	Outlays from prior obligations	Other uncon-trollables	Total uncon-trollables	Percent budget uncontrollable
1967	26.3	4.6	10.7	10.3	37.0	4.7	93.5	59.1
1968	29.1	7.2	11.4	11.1	42.3	6.2	107.3	60.0
1969	33.1	8.9	12.9	12.4	41.9	6.9	116.1	63.1
1970	36.9	9.9	15.4	14.4	41.5	7.6	125.7	64.0
1971	43.8	11.2	22.3	14.8	40.2	8.0	140.4	66.4
1972	49.2	13.4	25.8	15.5	39.2	10.4	153.5	66.2
1973	63.6	14.1	18.3	17.3	41.4	13.9	168.6	68.7
1974	72.5	17.2	21.4	21.4	46.0	11.9	190.4	70.8
1975	86.7	21.6	34.3	23.2	53.3	9.3	228.4	70.4
1976	97.2	26.3	43.5	26.7	53.7	10.1	257.5	70.7
1977	111.5	31.4	39.6	29.9	58.8	12.4	283.5	70.8
1978	122.8	35.9	36.9	35.4	76.9	15.8	323.7	72.2
1979	136.7	41.6	46.5	42.6	85.3	12.0	364.7	72.3
1980	156.5	49.0	47.0	52.5	103.2	16.2	424.4	73.6
1981	183.7	59.3	51.5	68.7	108.6	13.2	485.0	73.8
1982	201.8	65.6	53.2	85.0	121.5	15.1	542.1	74.4
1983	219.1	73.5	61.2	89.8	128.7	21.3	593.6	74.6
1984	228.3	79.9	49.2	111.1	145.3	10.3	624.1	73.3
1985	238.2	91.0	49.7	129.4	162.2	17.3	689.5	72.9
1986	252.8	97.8	52.0	136.0	181.3	25.5	745.4	76.2
1987	263.8	105.6	52.1	138.6	185.2	23.8	769.1	76.6
1988	279.6	114.7	53.7	151.7	186.8	20.9	807.4	76.5
1989	285.9	133.4	52.3	169.1	210.4	16.9	868.0	75.9
1990	304.8	155.8	57.4	184.2	231.6	12.0	945.8	75.6

1991	329.2	175.7	69.9	194.5	233.8	15.2	1,018.3	77.0
1992	349.7	208.5	84.7	199.4	233.8	15.2	1,091.3	79.0
1993	368.8	230.0	87.8	198.8	236.7	20.4	1,142.5	81.1
1994	386.6	251.9	75.0	203.0	228.2	15.1	1,159.8	79.4
1995	405.7	275.3	77.9	232.2	233.2	9.8	1,234.1	81.2
1996	418.1	293.6	76.9	241.1	227.9	9.2	1,266.8	81.2
1997	441.1	313.9	75.9	244.0	228.8	9.0	1,312.7	82.0
1998	453.0	324.3	77.0	243.4	228.0	12.2	1,337.8	81.0
1999 (est.)	469.2	348.1	85.2	227.2	243.9	21.5	1,339.5	80.8

Note: From time to time, the Office of Management and Budget reclassifies or redefines uncontrollables; hence, the figures in this table may not be consistent with those published in some budget documents.

Sources: For the 1967–1972 fiscal years, *The Budget of the United States Government Fiscal Year 1977*, table 16. For the 1973–1981 fiscal years, *The Budget of the United States Government Fiscal Year 1983*. For the 1982–1983 fiscal years, *The Budget of the United States Government Fiscal Year 1985*, table 20. For the 1984–1985 fiscal years, *The Budget of the United States Government Fiscal Year 1986*, table 18. For the 1986 fiscal year, *The Budget of the United States Government Fiscal Year 1987*, table 16. For the 1987 fiscal year, *The Budget of the United States Government Fiscal Year 1989*, table 16. For the 1988–1989 fiscal years, *The Budget of the United States Government Fiscal Year 1990*, table 14. For the 1990–1991 fiscal years, *The Budget of the United States Government Fiscal Year 1992*, tables 1-1 and 1-2. For the 1992–1993 fiscal years, *The Budget of the United States Government Fiscal Year 1994*, appendix. For the 1994–1995 fiscal years, *The Budget of the United States Government, Analytical Perspectives*, table 6-2. For the 1996–1999 fiscal years, *The Budget of the United States Government*.

Table 7-5 President's Budget Requests and Congressional Appropriations, 1968–1998 (thousands of dollars)

Year	Budget requests	Appropriations	Appropriations compared with requests
1968	147,908,613	133,339,869	−14,568,744
1969	142,701,346	134,431,463	−8,269,883
1970	147,765,358	144,273,529	−3,491,830
1971	167,874,625	165,225,662	−2,648,963
1972	185,431,805	178,960,107	−6,471,698
1973	177,959,504	174,901,434	−3,058,070
1974	213,667,190	204,012,312	−9,654,878
1975	267,224,774	259,852,322	−7,372,452
1976	282,142,432	282,536,695	394,263
1977	364,867,240	354,025,781	−10,841,459
1978	348,506,125	337,859,467	−10,646,658
1979	397,653,766	386,822,093	−10,831,673
1980	340,339,447	333,695,164	−6,644,283
1981	440,398,235	442,215,128	1,816,893
1982	507,740,133	514,832,375	7,092,242
1983	542,956,652	551,620,505	8,663,853
1984	576,343,258	559,151,835	−17,191,422
1985	588,698,503	583,446,885	−5,251,618
1986	590,345,199	577,279,102	−13,066,097
1987	595,071,473	584,399,770	−10,671,703
1988	607,213,694	606,443,182[a]	−770,511
1989	652,138,432	666,211,681	14,073,249
1990	704,510,962	697,257,740	−7,253,222
1991[b]	720,178,246	712,696,380	−7,481,866
1992[b,c]	736,231,270	715,697,705	−20,533,566
1993	798,046,000	782,150,000	−15,896,000
1994	782,753,000	779,375,000	−3,378,000
1995	804,207,430	761,097,096	−43,110,334
1996	801,214,439	793,403,352	−7,811,087
1997	799,196,397	787,614,002	−11,582,395
1998	859,790,825	864,003,763	4,212,938

Note: The years are calendar, not fiscal, years. The amounts shown are for budget authority provided in appropriations acts and do not include permanent appropriations or budget authority provided in legislative acts.

a. This figure includes the defense rescission of $3,531,030.
b. This figure excludes Desert Shield/Desert Storm contributed funds.
c. This figure includes the rescission of Desert Shield/Desert Storm funds.

Source: House Committee on Appropriations.

Table 7-6 Supplemental Appropriations, Fiscal Years 1964–1998

Fiscal year	Number of supplemental bills[a]	Amount of budget authority[b] (millions of dollars)
1964	1	290
1965	4	5,645
1966	4	21,889
1967	3	19,420
1968	5	8,218
1969	4	5,835
1970	2	5,993
1971	4	9,870
1972	7	11,599
1973	5	11,371
1974	5	14,796
1975	7	27,587
1976	5	24,636
1977	5	49,835
1978	9	16,053
1979	1	13,845
1980	6	19,683
1981	2	20,960
1982	4	27,442
1983	2	22,655
1984	4	16,307
1985	3	14,804
1986	3	8,191
1987	1	9,400
1988	1	672
1989	1	3,294
1990	1	4,344
1991	3	48,639
1992	2	9,786
1993	5	11,957
1994	2	9,291
1995	0	—[c]
1996	1[d]	2,125
1997	1	8,900
1998	1	6,100

a. The number of supplemental bills does not include regular and continuing appropriations in which supplemental budget authority was provided.

b. The amount of budget authority does include, for fiscal year 1976 and subsequent years, supplementals provided in regular or continuing appropriations bills. The figure represents supplemental spending after accounting for offsetting cuts.

c. All 1995 supplemental spending was offset.

d. The supplementals fell under ten regular appropriations bills but were lumped into the omnibus fiscal year 1996 appropriations bill (H.R. 3019).

Sources: For the 1964–1969 fiscal years, Louis Fisher, "Supplemental Appropriations History, Controls, Recent Record," Congressional Research Service, Library of Congress, Washington, D.C., April 12, 1979. For the 1970–1980 fiscal years, Congressional Budget Office, *Supplemental Appropriations in the 1970s,* staff working paper, July 1981. For the 1981–1983 and 1987–1988 fiscal years, *Congressional Quarterly Almanac.* For the 1984–1988 fiscal years, House Committee on Appropriations. For the 1989–1994 fiscal years, *Congressional Quarterly Weekly Report,* June 30, 1989; November 3, 1990; December 7, 1991; November 5, 1994. For the 1992–1994 fiscal years, House Committee on Appropriations. For the 1995 fiscal year, *Congressional Quarterly Almanac.* For the 1996 fiscal year, *Congressional Quarterly Weekly Report,* May 25, 1996, 1488. For the 1997–1998 fiscal years, *Congressional Quarterly Almanac.*

Table 7-7 House Amendments to Appropriations Bills, 1963–1982

Year	Total amendments	Amendments adopted	Limitation amendments[a]	Limitation amendments adopted
1963	47	15	17	7
1964	27	9	11	2
1965	26	9	11	1
1966	56	10	8	1
1967	70	15	16	4
1968	75	24	20	7
1969	89	27	20	10
1970	51	11	13	1
1971	83	34	23	7
1972	89	15	26	5
1973	99	31	31	12
1974	109	53	34	15
1975	106	52	34	12
1976	122	68	33	13
1977	107	54	44	24
1978	135	61	44	25
1979	165	74	52	31
1980	168	100	74	57
1981	143	87	47	33
1982	59	33	21	14

Note: The years are calendar, not fiscal, years. No new data are available after 1982.

a. Limitation amendments are amendments that bar the use of appropriated funds for specified purposes.

Sources: For 1963–1977, Democratic Study Group, Special Report No. 95-12, Washington, D.C., February 14, 1978. For 1978–1982, Richard S. Beth, Daniel P. Strickland, and Stanley Bach, "Limitation and Other House Amendments to General Appropriation Bills: Fiscal Years 1979–1983," Congressional Research Service, Library of Congress, Washington, D.C., December 28, 1982. The two sources may not be completely consistent in their scope and definition of amendments.

Table 7-8 Continuing Appropriations, Fiscal Years 1972–1999

Fiscal year	Regular appropriation bills not enacted by start of fiscal year[a]	Continuing resolutions enacted for fiscal year
1972	5	5
1973	4	5
1974	10	2
1975	6	4
1976	11	3
1977[b]	0[c]	2
1978	4	3
1979	8	1
1980	10	2
1981	12	2
1982	13	5
1983	12	2
1984	9	4
1985	9	4
1986	13	5
1987	13	1
1988	13	5
1989	0[d]	0
1990	13	3
1991	13	5
1992	10	3
1993	12	1
1994	11	3
1995	0	0
1996	11	14
1997	0	0
1998	13	6
1999	9	3

a. In calendar year 1976, the start of the fiscal year was changed from July 1 to October 1.
b. Although all regular appropriation bills were enacted by the start of the fiscal year, continuing appropriations were needed for certain items not provided for in those bills.
c. The appropriation was signed into law on the first day of the fiscal year.
d. Congress cleared and sent all bills to the president by the beginning of the fiscal year, but he did not sign all the bills until the following day.

Sources: Robert A. Keith, "An Overview of the Use of Continuing Appropriations," Congressional Research Service, Library of Congress, Washington, D.C., September 26, 1980; Congressional Budget Office, "Consideration of Appropriation Bills," unpublished memorandum, August 21, 1979. Data for the 1980–1989 fiscal years are taken from the House calendars. Data for the 1990–1999 fiscal years come from *Congressional Quarterly Weekly Report,* various issues.

Table 7-9 Budget-Related Roll Call Votes in the House, Selected Years, 1955–1998

Measure	1955	1960	1965	1970	1975	1980	1981	1983	1985
Authorizations	27	28	78	77	147	105	70	129	95
Appropriations	6	16	21	39	94	111	85	112	82
Tax legislation	3	3	3	1	48	14	7	9	11
Budget resolutions	—	—	—	—	12	30	13	4	10
Reconciliation bills	—	—	—	—	—	6	12	2	10
Debt ceilings	1	2	2	2	11	7	2	3	11
Miscellaneous	0	1	0	2	8	4	7	3	1
Total budget-related roll calls	37	50	104	121	320	277	196	262	220
Total roll calls	76	93	201	266	612	604	353	498	439
Percentage budget-related	49	54	52	45	52	46	56	53	50

Sources: For 1955–1982, Allen Schick, "Legislation, Appropriations, and Budgets: The Development of Spending Decision-Making in Congress," Congressional Research Service, Library of Congress, Washington, D.C., 1984. For 1983–1986, House Appropriations Committee. For 1987–1998, the numbers are based on the Congressional Quarterly roll call vote index.

1987	1989	1990	1991	1992	1993	1994	1995	1996	1997	1998
118	68	116	83	38	94	94	57	40	82	51
86	95	110	101	129	176	121	294	146	147	119
0	0	0	11	21	6	6	20	18	9	15
8	7	8	9	10	8	9	23	8	10	4
6	14	5	0	0	9	0	9	8	12	0
7	3	6	0	0	0	1	13	10	0	0
2	0	8	4	16	12	34	65	11	9	23
227	187	253	208	214	305	265	481	241	269	212
488	359	497	414	459	513	500	885	455	640	547
46	52	51	50	47	59	53	54	53	42	38

Table 7-10 Budget-Related Roll Call Votes in the Senate, Selected Years, 1955–1998

Measure	1955	1960	1965	1970	1975	1980	1981	1983	1985
Authorizations	22	48	87	83	96	82	55	58	67
Appropriations	12	28	27	77	87	128	130	107	59
Tax legislation	2	10	10	6	48	10	56	13	7
Budget resolutions	—	—	—	—	8	50	26	34	39
Reconciliation bills	—	—	—	—	—	4	63	2	23
Debt ceilings	0	2	1	3	3	6	12	15	29
Miscellaneous	1	0	0	1	4	3	2	9	6
Total budget-related roll calls	37	88	125	170	246	283	344	238	230
Total roll calls	87	207	258	418	602	531	483	381	381
Percentage budget-related	42	42	48	41	41	53	71	62	60

a. The number 597 is the total number of roll call votes listed in the *Congressional Quarterly Weekly Report* index. It does not accord with "yeas" and "nays" according to the *Congressional Record* and Congressional Quarterly's final vote number. That number was 613.

Sources: For 1955–1982, "Legislation, Appropriations, and Budgets." For 1983–1986, Senate Appropriations Committee. For 1987–1998, the numbers are based on the Congressional Quarterly roll call vote index.

1987	1989	1990	1991	1992	1993	1994	1995	1996	1997	1998
84	42	81	73	20	27	68	38	33	33	38
66	75	58	66	64	114	108	113	80	82	81
0	5	0	5	41	27	3	27	10	18	37
17	8	1	12	14	46	15	56	42	22	34
8	2	6	0	0	6	0	48	31	51	0
17	0	1	0	0	0	0	4	2	0	0
3	6	10	3	9	16	9	58	15	3	6
195	138	157	159	148	236	203	344	213	209	234
420	302	337	287	267	383	330	597[a]	308	304	318
46	46	46	55	55	62	62	58	69	69	74

Table 7-11 Rescissions, Fiscal Years 1975–1996

Fiscal year	Number of rescissions	Amount proposed ($ thousands)	Amount approved ($ thousands)	Amount rescinded (percent)	Proposals approved, wholly or in part (percent)
1975	91	3,328,500	391,295	12	43
1976[a]	50	3,608,363	138,331	4	14
1977	21	1,835,602	1,271,040	69	48
1978	8	644,055	55,255	9	38
1979	11	908,692	723,609	80	80
1980	59	1,618,061	778,127	48	58
1981	208	16,204,936	14,509,878	90	67
1982	34	9,484,941	5,974,966	63	21
1983	21	1,569,015	0	0	0
1985	244	1,855,000	212,000	11	39
1986	83	10,121,548	18,876,367[b]	188[b]	—
1987	73	5,835,800	36,090	1	3
1988	0	0	0	—	—
1989	6	143,096	2,053	1	17
1990	11	554,258	0	0	0
1991	30	4,859,300	0	0	0
1992	128	7,879,500	2,066,900	26	20
1993	7	356,000	2,411,587[b]	677	—
1994	65	3,172,180	3,667,895[b]	116	—
1995	25	1,199,824	19,713,689	1,643	—
1996	16	963,500	4,170,246	433	—

a. Fiscal year 1976 data include the transition quarter. A proposal to rescind or defer funds in both fiscal year 1976 and the transition quarter counted as a single proposal.

b. Some approved amounts are higher than proposals because Congress added its own rescissions.

Sources: House Appropriations Committee; Senate Budget Committee.

Table 7-12 Deferrals, Fiscal Years 1975–1996

Fiscal year	Number of deferrals	Amount proposed ($ thousands)	Amount disapproved ($ thousands)	Number of deferrals disapproved	Amount disapproved (percent)	Deferrals disapproved (percent)
1975	159	24,574,236	9,318,217	16	38	10
1976[a]	119	9,209,780	393,081	24[b]	4	20
1977	68	6,831,194	25,600	3	0.4	4
1978	66	4,910,114	69,531	6	1	9
1979	70	4,696,056	13,852	2	0.3	3
1980	73	9,846,235	3,663,448	2	37	3
1981	131	7,535,493	367,359	15	5	12
1982	267	7,562,078	386,347	15	5	6
1983	87	9,957,186	4,119,590	16	41	19
1985	78	8,476,000	0	0	0	0[c]
1986	70	24,767,151	2,828,276	—[c]	11.4	—[c]
1987	57	11,494,600	174,300	—[c]	1.5	
1988	22	9,320,100	0	0	0	0
1989	14	9,156,174	0	0	0	0
1990	28	11,071,540	0	0	0	0
1991	11	10,347,800	0	0	0	0
1992	12	5,791,800	0	0	0	0
1993	12	2,921,080	0	0	0	0
1994	12	7,334,903	0	0	0	0
1995	7	3,525,000	0	0	0	0
1996	6	3,700,000	0	0	0	0

a. Fiscal year 1976 data include the transition quarter. A proposal to rescind or defer funds in both fiscal year 1976 and the transition quarter counted as a single proposal.
b. Two fiscal year 1976 deferrals that both the House and the Senate disapproved are counted here once each.
c. We cannot list the figures because in many cases Congress deferred only partial amounts.

Sources: House Appropriations Committee; Senate Budget Committee.

8

Voting Alignments

Three important patterns to track congressional voting are support for the president, the cohesion of the parties, and the strength of the ideological coalitions that cut across party lines. This chapter describes the dynamics of those forces in congressional decisionmaking since the 1950s by using the measures that Congressional Quarterly compiles annually.

Presidential Success and Support

To measure presidential support, Congressional Quarterly determines on which votes the president took clear-cut positions by analyzing his messages to Congress, press conference remarks, and other public statements. The measure combines the significant and the trivial, the controversial and the consensual; moreover, it reflects the position of the president at the time of a vote, although that position may reflect a major concession from an earlier stand.

Despite those limitations, the measure does give a rough indication of the state of relations between the president and Congress. Presidential success seems mainly to be a function of the number of congressional seats his party holds. (See table 8-1 and figure 8-1.) When one party controls both branches, success never drops below 75 percent; with divided government, presidents average well below that level of success.

With the Democrats in control of the House, Senate, and presidency during Bill Clinton's first two years in office, presidential success scores reached 86.4 percent, the highest since Lyndon Johnson's Great Society. In 1993 the president and the Democratic Congress achieved many genuine legislative victories. But we can largely attribute the president's high rate of success in 1994 to the fact that most of his controversial legislation became so stymied that it never reached a vote. The second Congress of Clinton's presidency was not nearly so supportive. In 1995, amid budget and policy battles, the Republican House and Senate supported the president only 36 percent of the time, the lowest rate since those scores have been recorded. That decline fits with the pattern of previous presidencies. President Eisenhower's score dropped twenty-four percentage points after the Democratic victory in the 1958 elections. President Johnson achieved a modern high of 93 percent in the session following the 1964 elections, but that score dropped significantly in later years. And, after President Reagan's smashing victory in 1980, he enjoyed a level of support seven percentage points higher than President Carter's during his first year in office. But Reagan's support plummeted in the Senate after the Democrats regained control in 1986.

Success rates usually deteriorate over the course of a presidency (Johnson, Nixon, Reagan, and Bush), but at times they remain relatively stable (Carter) or even increase (Kennedy). We should note that we cannot measure presidential success by the outcome of roll call votes alone. They do not account for the many other ways in which a president can influence the legislative process. For example, on numerous occasions President Bush effectively used the veto and the threat of vetoes to affect legislative outcomes. Clinton, who did not use the veto during his first two years, subsequently wielded it skillfully in his battles with the Republicans.

President Bush won an average of only 51.6 roll call votes on which he took a stand over the course of his term. That marked the lowest score of any first-term president since Congressional Quarterly began keeping track in 1953. Bush's low point was in 1992, when he could claim victory on only 43 percent of the votes on which he held a clear position. But Congress and the president can work together across party lines, as in 1981, when President Reagan won on 82.3 percent of the issues on which he took a stand. For President Clinton, that pattern of cooperation emerged in the second half of the 104th Congress. Although still low compared with previous years, the support was nearly double that of 1995. We can attribute some of that cooperation to avoiding votes on the difficult issues and waiting for an election to resolve them, but we can attribute more to congressional resolve to go into the election looking cooperative, not confrontational.

The base for computing presidential scores varies widely, from a low of 34 House votes in 1953 and 1956 to a high of 185 Senate votes in 1973. The average number of votes on which presidents have taken clear-cut positions has increased over time, but the percentage has declined. In 1979 President Carter made his position known on only 22 percent of all House recorded votes and 19 percent of Senate votes. The comparable figures for President Eisenhower's third year are 56 percent in the House and 59 percent in the Senate. The congressional liaison workload of the White House has increased, but so too has the relative independence of Congress.

Ideologically, southerners of both parties have been more conservative than their party's mainstream. Southern Democrats have long been a group considered pivotal for building majorities. That distinct nature makes them worthy of specific examination with respect not only to presidential support but to two other measures discussed. Senate Republicans have usually been more supportive of presidents, Republican and Democratic, than their House counterparts. (See table 8-2.) No such consistent pattern is evident among Democrats. Whereas Democrats in the Senate were more supportive of Carter than their party colleagues in the House, the pattern was just the opposite under Presidents Kennedy and Johnson. That change at least partially comes from the voting of southern Democrats. Among southern Democratic members, President Kennedy fared better in the House than in the Senate, but President Carter received more support from among the Senate members.

The sharpest trend in presidential support scores is the decline in support for Republican presidents among southern Democrats, particularly in the House. The steady decline in success by President Reagan after 1981 mirrors the collapse in support for his proposals by House Democrats south of the Mason-Dixon line. While Bush regained some support among southern Democrats in both houses during his first year in office, that support eroded over time and, in fact, reached a low point in the Senate in 1992. In 1993 Clinton received the highest support score recorded among southern Democrats in the House and Senate, in part because of his own southern roots and in part because of the changing nature of southern Democrats. But the House support score among southern Democrats dropped almost fifteen percentage points in 1994, foreshadowing the Republican takeover of the South. Clinton's scores among Republicans were lower than for most Democratic presidents. The relatively higher scores in the Senate for 1994 were somewhat artificial because many items did not come to a vote. Clinton's scores with Republicans are much better reflected in the last two years of his first term, when the Republicans supported him only 22 percent of the time in the House and only 29 percent in the Senate in 1995. Facing an election with their majorities at stake, Republicans agreed to compromises that slightly raised Clinton's scores in 1996. The generally lower scores continued in 1997 and 1998, with one notable exception. Senate Republican support was considerably higher than House Republican support, by a margin of about twenty to thirty points, reflecting that body's more moderate view of the president and his policies.

Party Unity

One important component of the structure of congressional voting is party-line voting. Congressional Quarterly defines its measure of party-line voting as the percentage of all votes when a majority of voting Democrats opposes a majority of voting Republicans. In the House the trend in that measure had been downward beginning with Johnson's troubles with the war in Vietnam. (See table 8-3.) Under both President Nixon and President Ford, about 35 percent of roll call votes produced a party split, down from the midfiftieth percentile under Eisenhower. The number rose to 40 percent under Carter but then dropped back to 37 percent in Reagan's first year. By 1983 the scene changed, and the House took on a distinctly partisan cast. By 1987 the percentage of party votes in the House reached its highest point in the postwar period at 64 percent. The Senate by that time was also showing signs of a partisan increase, and the percentage of party votes climbed in the same year to a historically high 53 percent. After a dip, both percentages trended up again in 1993, reaching 65 percent in the House and 67 percent in the Senate, under the first Democratic Congress and president in twelve years. By 1994, the scores dipped, but that was also deceptive because a Congress so divided could not bring several measures to the floor. In 1995 partisanship rose to 73 percent in the House under the Republicans and 69 percent in the Senate, but partisanship then receded back to the midfiftieth percentile in subsequent years, when an unpopular Congress wished to avoid the appearance of obstructionism.

An election-year cycle is apparent in those figures, especially in recent years. The percentage of party votes increases in off years and declines in subsequent election years. That may reflect the efforts of congressional leaders during election years to avoid sharply partisan votes that may hurt members back home or an effort by members to put party interests aside and vote with their constituents' interests in mind.

The other information needed to gauge the level of party voting is the cohesion of the parties on those votes that elicit a party split. (See table 8-4.) Parties are generally quite cohesive on those partisan votes. After Kennedy and Johnson, both Democratic and Republican cohesion declined in the House by about ten percentage points and in the Senate by about five percentage points. By 1980 cohesion increased. The GOP senators reached a postwar high of 85 percent in 1981. Reagan may have galvanized Democrats as well, for they reached similar highs. Both parties generally held that high level of cohesion throughout the 1980s. Since 1992, GOP unity scores in both chambers have been well over 80 percent and poking above 90 percent. Democrats are at slightly lower levels, in part because of lower scores among southern Democrats.

However important the decline in party voting during the 1960s or the post-1980 resurgence, it pales in significance when compared with the long-term decline in party voting. From 1890 to 1910, two-thirds of all votes evoked a party split, and in several sessions more than half the roll calls found 90 percent of one party opposing 90 percent of the other. Since 1946 the percentage of votes showing such extreme partisan division has not gone above 10 percent.

Conservative Coalition

One reason for the decline in cohesion among the Democrats was the emergence in the late 1930s of a set of issues that brought together southern Democrats and Republicans and pitted them against northern Democrats. Since then, the "conservative coalition" has proven itself a formidable opponent to Democratic presidents. Congressional Quarterly defines that coalition as a majority of voting southern Democrats and a majority of voting Republicans opposing a majority of voting northern Democrats.

Over the past several decades, the coalition appeared more often in the Senate than in the House, although the record of success for the coalition was no greater in the Senate than the House (with the important exception of the Reagan era of split-party control of Congress). (See table 8-5.) The coalition's percentage of success reached an all-time low in the House during the Eighty-ninth Congress (after the 1964 Democratic landslide) and a modern-day high in 1981—rivaling its record in the 1940s and 1950s. Much more significant is the virtual disappearance of the coalition during the last two years of the Reagan presidency. That trend has continued in the 1990s with the coalition's appearing on no more than 14 percent of roll call votes in either house since 1987. As one political scientist put it, "The conservative coalition as a working political force is really a statistical artifact."[1] By 1998 the conservative coalition appeared on only 8 of 314 Senate votes, far too few to be statistically significant. On the other side of Capitol Hill, the Republicans could garner only four southern Democratic defectors to vote for one or more articles of impeachment, a result symbolizing the coalition's drastically decreased significance. Consequently, Congressional Quarterly has decided that it will no longer analyze the scores in future years (although it will continue to collect and publish the data). Ironically, the virtual disappearance of the coalition has been accompanied by success rates reaching 100 percent in the 1990s in both chambers.

Northern Democrats began voting in support of the coalition in greater numbers in the 1970s and again in the late 1980s and early 1990s and reached a high of 39 percent in 1994. (See table 8-6.) (By definition northern Democratic support cannot go above 50 percent.) Among southern Democrats, support has declined from what it once was in the 1950s and 1960s. Today, it hovers around 60 percent among southern Democrats.

Conservative coalition support scores are most useful for gauging how ideologically representative smaller groups of members are of their party and of the entire chamber. (See table 8-7, figure 8-2, table 8-8, and figure 8-3.) Scores reflecting the average conservative coalition support among all members in the chamber and in each party caucus provide a view of the relative conservatism of each committee. The absolute scores are less reliable than the relative standing of the committees and their parent chamber over time.

The ideological makeup of some committees changed dramatically, even before the shift in party control. In the House, the District of Columbia Committee, one of the most conservative committees in 1959, became one of the most liberal—in 1991 Democrats had a mean support score of 6 percent. Not surprisingly, that committee was one of the first the Republicans eliminated after the 1994 elections. (Its duties have been folded into the Government Reform and Oversight Committee.) A similar though less dramatic drift to the left occurred in the Ways and Means and Commerce Committees. The Education Committee grew more conservative. Other committees did not transform their philosophical base but moved further toward the ideological poles. Armed Services, always conservative, became the single most conservative committee in the House. After 1995, most committees have moved in a more conservative direction. The Rules and Appropriations Committees have moved the most, probably not by accident.

Similar patterns exist in the Senate, at least before the 1980 elections. Between 1959 and 1979, the Finance and the Appropriations Committees moved from right to center, and the Energy and Public Works Committees moved from left to center. The Armed Services and Agriculture Committees remained more conservative than the Senate as a whole; the Foreign Relations and Labor Committees continued to be more liberal. The infusion of conservative Republicans in 1980 shifted the Senate and every single committee to the right. In 1981 nine Senate committees were still more liberal than the average, but two-thirds of those were more conservative than the average in the previous Congress. Even the liberal Labor and Human Resources Committee had shifted by fifteen percentage points in a more conservative direction, and its average score was more than 50 percent for the first time in at least three decades. The GOP fueled that change as the Democratic ideology shifted from 43 to 44 percent in coalition support while GOP support went from 74 to 84 percent. The ideological gap grew on many committees but became most significant among the most prestigious committees like Appropriations, Finance, Budget, and Foreign Relations. Some already polarized committees, such as Labor, Banking, and Energy and Environment, became even more polarized.

After the 1986 elections, the Senate again shifted left and remained fairly constant through 1993. Three-fourths of the committees either became more liberal or remained at the same level. All committees reflected increased conservatism via support from the conservative coalition in 1995 with the Republican takeover. Some committees' support scores showed particularly noticeable change by the 105th Congress: Finance went from 58 percent in 1993 to 78 percent in 1997; Environment and Public Works went from 52 to 66 percent; and Rules and Administration went from 60 to 75 percent. Across the board, committee scores have reached some of their highest levels ever and have made the 106th Congress one of the most conservative in the past few generations.

Note

1. Burdett Loomis, quoted in *Congressional Quarterly Weekly Report,* December 28, 1991, 3759.

Table 8-1 Presidential Victories on Votes in Congress, 1953–1998

President and year	House and Senate (%)	House (%)	No. of votes	Senate (%)	No. of votes
Eisenhower					
1953	89.2	91.2	34	87.8	49
1954	82.8	n.a.	n.a.	n.a.	n.a.
1955	75.3	63.4	41	84.6	52
1956	69.7	73.5	34	67.7	65
1957	68.4	58.3	60	78.9	57
1958	75.7	74.0	50	76.5	98
1959	52.0	55.5	54	50.4	121
1960	65.1	65.0	43	65.1	86
Average	72.2				
Kennedy					
1961	81.5	83.1	65	80.6	124
1962	85.4	85.0	60	85.6	125
1963	87.1	83.1	71	89.6	115
Average	84.6				
Johnson					
1964	87.9	88.5	52	87.6	97
1965	93.1	93.8	112	92.6	162
1966	78.9	91.3	103	68.8	125
1967	78.8	75.6	127	81.2	165
1968	74.5	83.5	103	68.9	164
Average	82.6				
Nixon					
1969	74.8	72.3	47	76.4	72
1970	76.9	84.6	65	71.4	91
1971	74.8	82.5	57	69.5	82
1972	66.3	81.1	37	54.3	46
1973	50.6	48.0	125	52.4	185
1974	59.6	67.9	53	54.2	83
Average	67.2				
Ford					
1974	58.2	59.3	54	57.4	68
1975	61.0	50.6	89	71.0	93
1976	53.8	43.1	51	64.2	53
Average	57.6				
Carter					
1977	75.4	74.7	79	76.1	88
1978	78.3	69.6	112	84.8	151
1979	76.8	71.7	145	81.4	161
1980	75.1	76.9	117	73.3	116
Average	76.4				
Reagan					
1981	82.3	72.4	76	88.3	128
1982	72.4	55.8	77	83.2	119
1983	67.1	47.6	82	85.9	85
1984	65.8	52.2	113	85.7	77
1985	59.9	45.0	80	71.6	102
1986	56.5	34.1	88	81.2	80
1987	43.5	33.3	99	56.4	78
1988	47.4	32.7	104	64.8	88
Average	61.9				

President and year	House and Senate (%)	House (%)	No. of votes	Senate (%)	No. of votes
Bush					
1989	62.6	50.0	86	73.3	101
1990	46.8	32.4	108	63.4	93
1991	54.2	43.0	111	69.0	81
1992	43.0	37.0	105	53.0	60
Average	51.6				
Clinton					
1993	86.4	87.2	102	85.4	89
1994	86.4	87.2	78	85.5	62
1995	36.2	26.3	133	49.0	102
1996	55.1	53.2	79	57.6	59
1997	53.6	38.7	75	71.4	63
1998	50.6	36.6	82	67.0	72
Average	61.4				

Notes: n.a. = not available.

Percentages indicate the number of congressional votes supporting the president divided by the total number of votes on which the president had taken a position.

The findings for 1956, 1981, 1982, and 1983 differ slightly from previous editions owing to recalculation and corrections in the *Congressional Quarterly Almanac*. The *Congressional Quarterly Almanac* frequently rounds off House and Senate percentages of those votes, but figures in *Vital Statistics* are not rounded here.

Sources: Congressional Quarterly Almanac (Washington, D.C.: Congressional Quarterly, various years); *Congressional Quarterly Weekly Report,* January 2, 1982; December 31, 1983; October 27, 1984; January 11, 1986; October 25, 1986, 2690; January 16, 1988; November 19, 1988; December 30, 1989; January 6, 1990; December 22, 1990; December 28, 1991; December 19, 1992; December 18, 1993; December 31, 1994; January 27, 1996; December 21, 1996; January 3, 1998; January 9, 1999. Some percentages have been recalculated.

Table 8-2 Congressional Voting in Support of the President's Position, 1954–1998 (percent)

President and year	House			Senate		
	All Demo-crats	Southern Demo-crats	Repub-licans	All Demo-crats	Southern Demo-crats	Repub-licans
Eisenhower						
1954	54	n.a.	n.a.	45	n.a.	82
1955	58	n.a.	67	65	n.a.	85
1956	58	n.a.	79	44	n.a.	80
1957	54	n.a.	60	60	n.a.	80
1958	63	n.a.	65	51	n.a.	77
1959	44	n.a.	76	44	n.a.	80
1960	49	n.a.	63	52	n.a.	76
Kennedy						
1961	81	n.a.	41	73	n.a.	42
1962	83	71	47	76	63	48
1963	84	71	36	77	65	52
Johnson						
1964	84	70	42	73	63	52
1965	83	65	46	75	60	55
1966	81	64	45	71	59	53
1967	80	65	51	73	69	63
1968	77	63	59	64	50	57
Nixon						
1969	56	55	65	55	56	74
1970	64	64	79	56	62	74
1971	53	69	79	48	59	76
1972	56	59	74	52	71	77
1973	39	49	67	42	55	70
1974	52	64	71	44	60	65
Ford						
1974	48	52	59	45	55	67
1975	40	48	67	53	67	76
1976	36	52	70	47	61	73
Carter						
1977	69	58	46	77	71	58
1978	67	54	40	74	61	47
1979	70	58	37	75	66	51
1980	71	63	44	71	69	50
Reagan						
1981	46	60	72	52	63	84
1982	43	55	70	46	57	77
1983	30	45	74	45	46	77
1984	37	47	64	45	58	81
1985	31	43	69	36	46	80
1986	26	37	69	39	56	90
1987	26	36	64	38	42	67
1988	27	34	61	51	58	73

	House			Senate		
President and year	All Demo-crats	Southern Demo-crats	Repub-licans	All Demo-crats	Southern Demo-crats	Repub-licans
Bush						
1989	38	49	72	56	66	84
1990	26	35	65	39	49	72
1991	35	43	74	42	53	83
1992	27	38	75	33	41	75
Clinton						
1993	80	81	39	87	84	30
1994	78	68	49	88	88	44
1995	75	69	22	81	78	29
1996	74	70	38	83	75	37
1997	73	68	31	87	84	61
1998	78	72	27	86	84	42

Notes: n.a. = not available.

Percentages indicate the number of congressional votes supporting the president divided by the total number of votes on which the president had taken a position. The percentages are normalized to eliminate the effects of absences as follows: support = (support)/(support + opposition).

Sources: Congressional Quarterly Almanac, various years; *Congressional Quarterly Weekly Report,* January 2, 1982; October 27, 1984; January 11, 1986; October 25, 1986, 2690–93; January 16, 1988; November 19, 1988; December 30, 1989; January 6, 1990; December 22, 1990; December 28, 1991; December 19, 1992; December 18, 1993; December 31, 1994; January 27, 1996; December 21, 1996; January 3, 1998; January 9, 1999.

Figure 8-1 Presidential Victories on Votes in Congress, 1953–1998

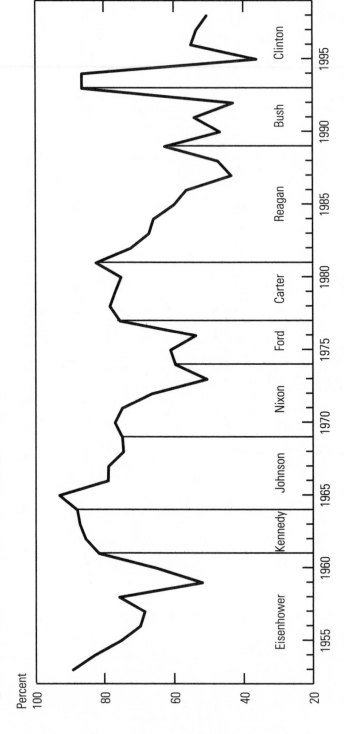

Note: Percentages indicate the number of congressional votes supporting the president divided by the total number of votes on which the president has taken a position.

Source: Table 8-1.

Table 8-3 Party Unity Votes in Congress, 1953–1998
(percentage of all votes)

Year	House	Senate	Year	House	Senate
1953	52	n.a.	1976	36	37
1954	38	47	1977	42	42
1955	41	30	1978	33	45
1956	44	53	1979	47	47
1957	59	36	1980	38	46
1958	40	44	1981	37	48
1959	55	48	1982	36	43
1960	53	37	1983	56	44
1961	50	62	1984	47	40
1962	46	41	1985	61	50
1963	49	47	1986	57	52
1964	55	36	1987	64	41
1965	52	42	1988	47	42
1966	41	50	1989	55	35
1967	36	35	1990	49	54
1968	35	32	1991	55	49
1969	31	36	1992	64	53
1970	27	35	1993	65	67
1971	38	42	1994	62	52
1972	27	36	1995	73	69
1973	42	40	1996	56	62
1974	29	44	1997	50	50
1975	48	48	1998	56	56

Notes: n.a. = not available.

Data indicate the percentage of all recorded votes on which a majority of voting Democrats opposed a majority of voting Republicans.

Sources: Congressional Quarterly Almanac, various years; *Congressional Quarterly Weekly Report,* January 9, 1982; January 15, 1983, 107; December 31, 1983, 2790; October 27, 1984, 2810; January 11, 1986, 87; November 15, 1986, 2902; January 16, 1988; November 19, 1988; December 30, 1989; December 22, 1990; December 28, 1991; December 19, 1992; December 18, 1993; December 31, 1994; January 27, 1996; December 21, 1996; January 3, 1998; January 9, 1999.

Table 8-4 Party Unity Scores in Congressional Voting, 1954–1998 (percent)

	House			Senate		
Year	All Democrats	Southern Democrats	Republicans	All Democrats	Southern Democrats	Republicans
1954	80	n.a.	84	77	n.a.	89
1955	84	68	78	82	78	82
1956	80	79	78	80	75	80
1957	79	71	75	79	81	81
1958	77	67	73	82	76	74
1959	85	77	85	76	63	80
1960	75	62	77	73	60	74
1961	n.a.	n.a.	n.a.	n.a.	n.a.	n.a.
1962	81	n.a.	80	80	n.a.	81
1963	85	n.a.	84	79	n.a.	79
1964	82	n.a.	81	73	n.a.	75
1965	80	55	81	75	55	78
1966	78	55	82	73	52	78
1967	77	53	82	75	59	73
1968	73	48	76	71	57	74
1969	71	47	71	74	53	72
1970	71	52	72	71	49	71
1971	72	48	76	74	56	75
1972	70	44	76	72	43	73
1973	75	55	74	79	52	74
1974	72	51	71	72	41	68
1975	75	53	78	76	48	71
1976	75	52	75	74	46	72

Year						
1977	74	55	77	72	48	75
1978	71	53	77	75	54	66
1979	75	60	79	76	62	73
1980	78	64	79	76	64	74
1981	75	57	80	77	64	85
1982	77	62	76	76	62	80
1983	82	67	80	76	70	79
1984	81	68	77	75	61	83
1985	86	76	80	79	68	81
1986	86	76	76	74	59	80
1987	88	78	79	85	80	78
1988	88	81	80	85	78	74
1989	86	77	76	79	69	79
1990	86	78	78	82	75	77
1991	86	78	81	83	73	83
1992	86	79	84	82	70	83
1993	89	83	87	87	78	86
1994	88	83	87	86	77	81
1995	84	75	93	84	76	91
1996	84	76	90	86	75	91
1997	85	79	91	86	76	88
1998	86	79	89	90	85	88

Notes: n.a. = not available.

Data show the percentage of members voting with a majority of their party on party unity votes. Party unity votes are those roll calls on which a majority of a party votes on one side of the issue and a majority of the other party votes on the other side. The percentages are normalized to eliminate the effects of absences as follows: party unity = (unity)/(unity + opposition).

Sources: Congressional Quarterly Almanac, various years; *Congressional Quarterly Weekly Report,* January 9, 1982; January 15, 1983, 108; October 27, 1984, 2804–5; January 11, 1986, 88; November 15, 1986, 2902–6; January 16, 1988; November 19, 1988; December 30, 1989; January 6, 1990; December 22, 1990; December 28, 1991, 3790–92; December 19, 1992, 3907–9, December 18, 1993, 3481–83; December 31, 1994, 3660–62; January 27, 1996; December 21, 1996; January 3, 1998; January 9, 1999.

Table 8-5 Conservative Coalition Votes and Victories in Congress, 1957–1998 (percent)

	House		Senate	
Year	Votes	Victories	Votes	Victories
1957	16	81	11	100
1958	15	64	19	86
1959	13	91	19	65
1960	20	35	22	67
1961	30	74	32	48
1962	13	44	15	71
1963	13	67	19	44
1964	11	67	17	47
1965	25	25	24	39
1966	19	32	30	51
1967	22	73	18	54
1968	22	63	25	80
1969	25	71	28	67
1970	17	70	26	64
1971	31	79	28	86
1972	25	79	29	63
1973	25	67	21	54
1974	22	67	30	54
1975	28	52	28	48
1976	17	59	26	58
1977	22	60	29	74
1978	20	57	23	46
1979	21	73	18	65
1980	16	67	20	75
1981	21	88	21	95
1982	16	78	20	90
1983	18	71	12	89
1984	14	75	17	94
1985	13	84	16	93
1986	11	78	20	93
1987	9	88	8	100
1988	8	82	10	97
1989	11	80	12	95
1990	10	74	11	95
1991	9	86	14	95
1992	10	88	14	87
1993	7	98	10	90
1994	7	92	10	72
1995	13	100	9	95
1996	11	100	12	97
1997	9	100	8	92
1998	8	95	3	100

Note: "Votes" is the percentage of all roll call votes on which a majority of voting southern Democrats and a majority of voting Republicans—the conservative coalition—opposed the stand taken by a majority of voting northern Democrats. "Victories" is the percentage of conservative coalition votes won by the coalition.

Sources: Congressional Quarterly Almanac, various years; *Congressional Quarterly Weekly Report,* January 9, 1982; January 15, 1983; December 31, 1983; October 27, 1984, 2821; January 11, 1986, 76–77, 81; November 15, 1986, 2908–9; January 16, 1988; November 19, 1988; December 30, 1989; January 6, 1990; December 22, 1990; December 28, 1991; December 19, 1992; December 18, 1993, 3485; December 31, 1994, 3663; January 27, 1996; December 21, 1996; January 3, 1998; January 9, 1999.

Table 8-6 Voting in Support of the Conservative Coalition, 1959–1998 (percent)

Year	House			Senate		
	Northern Democrats	Southern Democrats	Republicans	Northern Democrats	Southern Democrats	Republicans
1959	17	85	87	23	69	80
1960	8	66	77	21	77	74
1961	15	69	83	15	74	75
1962	14	65	75	29	77	79
1963	13	70	78	20	73	76
1964	13	72	76	20	78	72
1965	10	69	81	19	71	81
1966	13	69	82	17	75	80
1967	15	75	81	24	76	72
1968	16	77	75	31	77	74
1969	21	79	75	24	77	73
1970	19	79	78	21	74	72
1971	25	76	80	38	80	79
1972	24	75	79	20	78	74
1973	22	69	77	17	74	76
1974	24	72	69	19	79	69
1975	22	69	81	19	79	69
1976	25	72	80	21	73	76
1977	25	68	82	26	75	80
1978	26	68	79	24	70	69
1979	29	70	85	29	75	74
1980	27	69	81	26	72	74
1981	30	75	82	29	76	84

(table continues)

Table 8-6 *(continued)*

Year	House Northern Democrats	House Southern Democrats	House Republicans	Senate Northern Democrats	Senate Southern Democrats	Senate Republicans
1982	27	73	81	30	76	81
1983	22	68	81	30	69	81
1984	23	68	84	27	74	85
1985	23	67	84	30	72	82
1986	27	70	83	26	70	83
1987	27	71	87	30	70	79
1988	27	67	88	29	72	80
1989	27	68	87	31	69	84
1990	27	69	85	29	70	83
1991	30	69	90	33	71	84
1992	31	67	87	27	67	79
1993	31	63	87	31	70	84
1994	39	58	89	30	69	81
1995	28	57	90	24	68	87
1996	31	63	85	30	66	88
1997	34	65	90	32	73	88
1998	32	63	90	36	76	87

Note: Data indicate the percentage of conservative coalition votes on which members voted in agreement with the position of the conservative coalition. Conservative coalition votes are those on which a majority of northern Democrats voted against a majority of southern Democrats and Republicans—the conservative coalition. The percentages are normalized to eliminate the effects of not voting as follows: conservative coalition support = (support)/(support + opposition).

Sources: Congressional Quarterly Almanac, various years; *Congressional Quarterly Weekly Report,* January 9, 1982; January 15, 1983, 102; October 27, 1984, 2821; January 11, 1986, 76; November 15, 1986, 2908–12; January 16, 1988; November 19, 1988; December 30, 1989; January 6, 1990; December 22, 1990; December 28, 1991, 3795–97; December 19, 1992, 3902–4; December 18, 1993, 3486–88; December 31, 1994, 3665–67; January 27, 1996; December 21, 1996; January 3, 1998; January 9, 1999.

Table 8-7 House Committee Support of the Conservative Coalition, 1959–1997 (percent)

Committee	1959	1969	1977	1981	1983	1985	1987	1989	1991	1993	1995	1997
Agriculture												
All members	79	80	56	70	60	65	69	70	73	66	76	79
Democrats	69	72	44	58	48	52	56	58	62	51	53	67
Republicans	97	90	81	86	81	84	89	89	93	88	96	90
Appropriations												
All members	69	63	56	56	52	53	58	57	57	64	72	71
Democrats	55	54	42	42	37	36	41	39	39	47	42	43
Republicans	90	76	83	78	79	81	86	85	88	90	95	93
Armed Services												
All members	68	69	69	80	74	75	74	73	72	74	81	76
Democrats	55	63	59	71	65	67	63	62	59	61	62	56
Republicans	90	79	90	91	90	86	90	89	92	92	95	92
Banking and Financial Services												
All members	44	50	45	52	50	52	58	56	57	50	59	62
Democrats	26	37	33	34	34	34	39	35	39	26	23	37
Republicans	75	68	68	77	76	79	86	87	88	85	89	82
Budget												
All members	n.a.	n.a.	43	63	50	55	56	56	60	59	67	68
Democrats	n.a.	n.a.	26	47	32	34	33	34	43	45	38	44
Republicans	n.a.	n.a.	79	87	85	87	89	88	88	81	89	86
Commerce												
All members	65	60	48	58	50	56	57	60	60	59	66	67
Democrats	49	41	31	38	31	35	36	39	41	39	37	38
Republicans	92	84	81	85	84	87	87	93	94	86	94	92
District of Columbia												
All members	72	62	41	39	40	31	44	39	42	43	n.a.	n.a.
Democrats	65	54	37	17	15	15	17	7	6	14	n.a.	n.a.
Republicans	85	72	49	78	79	66	91	96	96	86	n.a.	n.a.
Education and the Workforce												
All members	39	40	42	44	39	42	49	44	46	48[a]	66	62
Democrats	16	17	26	25	25	21	28	19	23	26	24	34
Republicans	86	72	73	70	71	73	82	84	88	85[a]	90	84
Government Reform												
All members	55	37	47	54	53	54	57	50	53	50	67	58
Democrats	37	25	32	37	40	31	40	30	36	28	40	33
Republicans	81	55	78	77	78	86	85	83	85	83	88	84
House Administration												
All members	61	55	49	58	49	53	52	57	55	61	71	72
Democrats	52	37	32	41	30	32	38	35	31	42	42	31
Republicans	78	79	87	83	82	88	92	94	95	94	92	93
International Relations												
All members	48	42	41	51	42	45	50	45	47	50	63	66
Democrats	32	20	25	38	25	21	28	22	24	29	31	37
Republicans	78	68	73	70	74	79	81	80	81	80	89	86
Judiciary												
All members	58	43	45	51	47	50	52	49	52	52	62	66
Democrats	45	28	36	30	26	26	26	24	30	30	21	29
Republicans	83	63	62	79	85	87	90	87	88	86	93	91

(table continues)

Table 8-7 *(continued)*

Committee	1959	1969	1977	1981	1983	1985	1987	1989	1991	1993	1995	1997
Merchant Marine and Fisheries												
All members	54	52	49	63	53	61	61	65	66	61	n.a.	n.a.
Democrats	39	41	29	51	39	47	46	52	50	45	n.a.	n.a.
Republicans	82	67	71	79	76	83	84	85	91	88	n.a.	n.a.
Post Office and Civil Service												
All members	57	49	43	49	47	42	40	38	42	51	n.a.	n.a.
Democrats	40	28	24	23	21	14	17	17	21	31	n.a.	n.a.
Republicans	88	77	84	83	87	83	78	71	79	81	n.a.	n.a.
Resources												
All members	56	57	51	57	54	55	57	54	58	54	71	75
Democrats	36	36	33	34	33	30	36	31	37	32	35	48
Republicans	86	85	88	91	91	92	92	93	95	90	93	91
Rules												
All members	63	54	47	54	48	45	53	48	52	55	77	78
Democrats	44	39	26	36	28	25	35	32	32	38	35	41
Republicans	100	85	56	94	92	92	95	87	98	94	96	96
Science												
All members	52	58	56	58	55	60	64	62	69	67[a]	72	71
Democrats	34	46	47	49	43	47	52	52	58	56	52	52
Republicans	85	73	73	70	74	80	82	77	86	84[a]	89	86
Small Business												
All members	n.a.	n.a.	n.a.	59	55	60	63	61	61	59	66	73
Democrats	n.a.	n.a.	n.a.	44	47	43	48	46	43	39	38	38
Republicans	n.a.	n.a.	n.a.	79	71	84	88	85	91	89	91	87
Standards of Official Conduct												
All members	n.a.	n.a.	70	63	55	63	63	62	55	56	59	58
Democrats	n.a.	n.a.	67	57	29	37	38	38	22	31	25	26
Republicans	n.a.	n.a.	74	82	82	90	88	87	88	81	92	90
Transportation and Infrastructure												
All members	58	63	62	66	56	54	60	67	67	64	70	70
Democrats	45	45	53	51	39	34	42	49	53	50	46	51
Republicans	82	86	80	87	83	83	86	90	91	85	89	88
Veterans' Affairs												
All members	53	63	62	73	65	65	65	69	74	64	74	74
Democrats	46	54	53	65	53	51	52	56	62	47	50	44
Republicans	65	74	80	83	85	84	86	89	92	93	95	92
Ways and Means												
All members	62	56	54	60	54	53	55	55	55	54	65	65
Democrats	42	38	39	45	38	34	36	37	34	35	27	28
Republicans	95	83	86	87	85	87	87	86	91	86	91	90
Chamber average												
All members	59	56	51	61	55	56	60	56	60	60[a]	67	66
Democrats	44	42	38	45	39	36	41	37	42	42	38	42
Republicans	86	75	78	82	81	84	87	87	90	87[a]	91	88

Notes: n.a. = not available.

The data indicate the percentage of conservative coalition votes on which members voted in agreement with the position of the conservative coalition. Conservative coalition votes are those on which a majority of northern Democrats voted against a majority of southern Democrats and Republicans—the conservative coalition. The percentages are normalized to eliminate the effects of not voting as follows: conservative coalition support = (support)/(support + opposition).

In 1995 the new Republican majority abolished the District of Columbia, Merchant Marine and Fisheries, and Post Office and Civil Service Committees. Congressmen also renamed several committees. For the changes, please see chapter 4. The committee titles here reflect the current names.

a. A vacancy was left by the death of Rep. Paul B. Henry (R-Mich.) on July 31, 1993. Henry was eligible for eighteen conservative coalition votes in 1993. The support score adjusted for absences was zero percent.

Sources: Congressional Directory (Washington, D.C.: Government Printing Office, various years); *Congressional Quarterly Almanac,* various years; *Congressional Quarterly Weekly Report,* January 6, 1990; December 28, 1991; December 19, 1992; December 18, 1993, 3486–87; January 27, 1996; January 3, 1998.

Figure 8-2 House Committee Support of the Conservative Coalition, 1959, 1977, 1981, 1989, 1991, 1995, and 1997

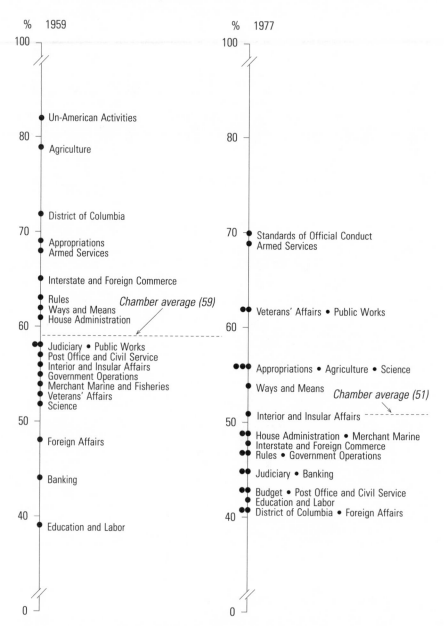

Note: The numbers show the percentage of conservative coalition votes on which members voted in agreement with the position of the conservative coalition. Conservative coalition votes are those on which a majority of northern Democrats voted against a majority of southern Democrats and Republicans—the conservative coalition.

Source: Table 8-7.

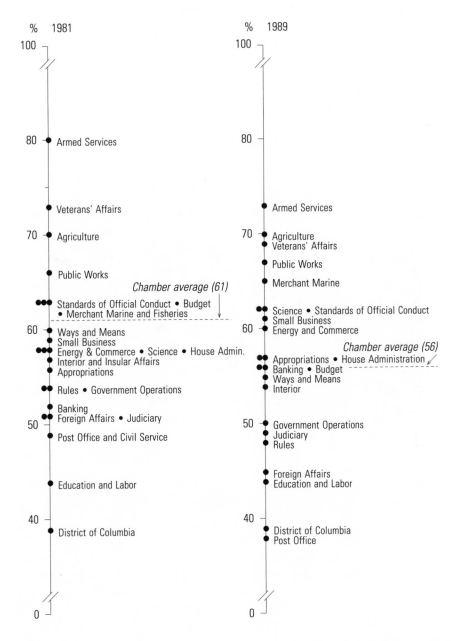

1981

% 1981

- 100
- 80 — Armed Services
- Veterans' Affairs
- 70 — Agriculture
- Public Works

Chamber average (61)

- Standards of Official Conduct • Budget
  • Merchant Marine and Fisheries
- 60 — Ways and Means
- Small Business
- Energy & Commerce • Science • House Admin.
- Interior and Insular Affairs
- Appropriations
- Rules • Government Operations
- Banking
- Foreign Affairs • Judiciary
- 50 — Post Office and Civil Service
- Education and Labor
- 40 —
- District of Columbia
- 0

1989

% 1989

- 100
- 80 —
- Armed Services
- 70 — Agriculture
- Veterans' Affairs
- Public Works
- Merchant Marine
- Science • Standards of Official Conduct
- Small Business
- 60 — Energy and Commerce

Chamber average (56)

- Appropriations • House Administration
- Banking • Budget
- Ways and Means
- Interior
- 50 — Government Operations
- Judiciary
- Rules
- Foreign Affairs
- Education and Labor
- 40 —
- District of Columbia
- Post Office
- 0

(figure continues)

Figure 8-2 *(continued)*

% 1991

100 ─

80 ─

● Veterans' Affairs
● Agriculture
● Armed Services
70 ─
● Science and Technology

● Public Works
● Merchant Marine

Chamber average (60)

● Small Business
60 ●● Budget ● Energy and Commerce ─────↓
● Interior
●● Appropriations ● Banking
●●● House Admin. ● Standards of Official Conduct
● ● Ways and Means
● Government Operations
●● Judiciary ● Rules
50 ─

● Foreign Affairs
● Education and Labor

●● District of Columbia ● Post Office
40 ─

0 ─

% 1995

100 ─

80 ─ ● Armed Services

● Rules
● Agriculture

● Veterans' Affairs

●● Appropriations ● Science and Technology
●● House Administration ● Natural Resources
70 ● Public Works

Chamber average (67)

●● Budget ● Government Operations ─────↙───
●●● Educ. & Labor ● Energy & Comm. ● Small Busin.
● Ways and Means

● Foreign Affairs
● Judiciary

60 ─
●● Banking ● Standards of Official Conduct

50 ─

40 ─

0 ─

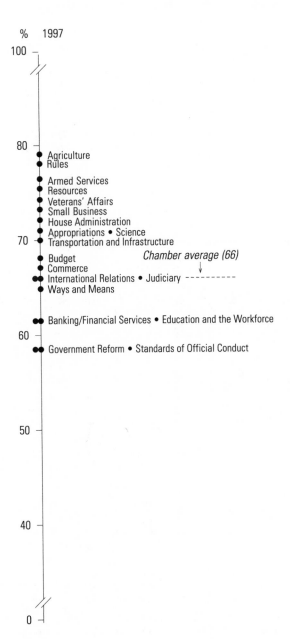

% 1997

100 —

80 —
● Agriculture
● Rules

● Armed Services
● Resources
● Veterans' Affairs
● Small Business
● House Administration
● Appropriations ● Science
70 — ● Transportation and Infrastructure

● Budget   *Chamber average (66)*
● Commerce   ↓
●● International Relations ● Judiciary ─ ─ ─ ─ ─ ─ ─ ─ ─
● Ways and Means

●● Banking/Financial Services ● Education and the Workforce
60 —

●● Government Reform ● Standards of Official Conduct

50 —

40 —

0 —

Table 8-8 Senate Committee Support of the Conservative Coalition, 1959–1997 (percent)

Committee	1959	1969	1977	1981	1983	1985	1987	1989	1991	1993	1995	1997
Agriculture, Nutrition, and Forestry												
All members	63	81	67	77	75	72	72	67	70	68	68	70
Democrats	51	78	51	62	61	53	54	46	52	48	40	42
Republicans	85	83	91	90	86	90	92	90	93	93	93	91
Appropriations												
All members	65	67	50	68	66	66	59	57	62	62	66	64
Democrats	55	58	47	53	49	49	44	38	45	42	41	34
Republicans	85	79	55	83	83	81	76	81	83	86	90	89
Armed Services												
All members	70	65	66	76	70	69	68	70	69	69	66	68
Democrats	68	55	47	58	46	47	56	55	54	53	41	41
Republicans	84	77	96	92	89	88	83	89	88	87	91	89
Banking, Housing, and Urban Affairs												
All members	49	49	46	55	59	60	58	58	60	59	60	65
Democrats	35	29	27	23	27	31	41	41	43	38	20	28
Republicans	76	57	74	83	84	85	80	82	85	89	95	91
Budget												
All members	n.a.	n.a.	53	69	63	65	67	64	64	60	62	60
Democrats	n.a.	n.a.	36	44	40	43	50	47	44	40	32	28
Republicans	n.a.	n.a.	82	89	81	83	87	86	89	87	89	86
Commerce, Science, and Transportation												
All members	55	52	58	72	58	70	61	73	72	70	71	72
Democrats	40	38	45	58	43	56	46	64	61	58	54	53
Republicans	83	72	80	84	71	83	78	84	85	85	89	88
Energy and Natural Resources												
All members	45	52	54	62	58	65	62	64	67	69	66	72
Democrats	23	29	34	37	38	44	48	43	52	56	39	45
Republicans	75	78	76	83	71	82	77	87	86	85	84	93
Environment and Public Works												
All members	40	53	51	63	60	58	51	61	51	52	64	66
Democrats	22	36	35	38	38	35	37	46	34	33	32	45
Republicans	75	78	76	85	77	78	68	80	73	79	92	88
Finance												
All members	67	63	51	67	63	67	55	59	59	58	65	78
Democrats	53	47	35	51	49	53	43	40	47	43	39	67
Republicans	94	90	74	80	74	78	70	81	76	76	89	87
Foreign Relations												
All members	44	45	36	55	52	54	50	56	55	51	58	60
Democrats	29	39	26	26	25	23	18	30	27	27	25	24
Republicans	71	55	51	78	76	82	86	85	89	84	87	90
Governmental Affairs												
All members	55	55	48	61	60	63	64	58	59	61	63	63
Democrats	39	43	41	47	44	51	52	42	47	48	38	35
Republicans	88	71	55	73	73	73	79	78	78	83	87	84
Health, Education, Labor, and Pensions												
All members	35	34	36	54	56	53	41	48	46	43	54	53
Democrats	12	14	18	14	23	18	16	18	23	22	16	15
Republicans	71	62	62	85	82	81	74	86	78	74	87	84

Committee	1959	1969	1977	1981	1983	1985	1987	1989	1991	1993	1995	1997
Judiciary												
All members	53	55	42	63	61	63	49	55	55	53	58	64
Democrats	43	36	35	36	38	38	28	30	32	29	27	35
Republicans	74	72	69	85	80	83	76	88	87	84	86	84
Rules and Administration												
All members	56	71	51	64	60	62	56	60	63	60	60	75
Democrats	43	65	39	38	36	41	33	41	45	40	40	46
Republicans	82	79	74	82	77	79	86	84	88	87	89	95
Veterans' Affairs												
All members	n.a.	n.a.	n.a.	63	59	66	48	61	53	55	65	61
Democrats	n.a.	n.a.	n.a.	34	38	40	31	42	34	40	34	28
Republicans	n.a.	n.a.	n.a.	84	74	84	68	85	78	76	82	84
Chamber average												
All members	54	55	51	65	62	63	60	61	61	60	64	65
Democrats	41	42	37	44	42	41	43	42	44	41	35	37
Republicans	80	73	73	84	79	82	79	84	84	84	87	88

Notes: n.a. = not available.

The data indicate the percentage of conservative coalition votes on which members voted in agreement with the position of the conservative coalition. Conservative coalition votes are those on which a majority of northern Democrats voted against a majority of southern Democrats and Republicans—the conservative coalition. The percentages are normalized to eliminate the effects of not voting as follows: conservative coalition support = (support)/(support + opposition).

Sources: Congressional Directory, various years; *Congressional Quarterly Almanac,* various years; *Congressional Quarterly Weekly Report,* January 6, 1990; December 28, 1991; December 19, 1992; December 18, 1993, 3488; January 27, 1996; January 3, 1998.

Figure 8-3 Senate Committee Support of the Conservative Coalition, 1959, 1977, 1981, 1989, 1991, 1995, and 1997

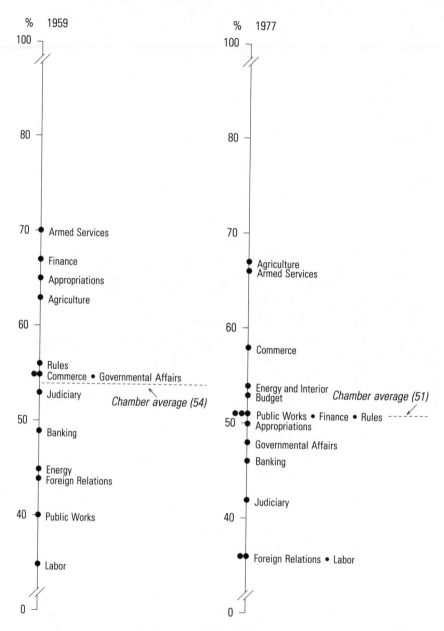

Note: The numbers show the percentage of conservative coalition votes on which members voted in agreement with the position of the conservative coalition. Conservative coalition votes are those on which a majority of northern Democrats voted against a majority of southern Democrats and Republicans—the conservative coalition.

Source: Table 8-8.

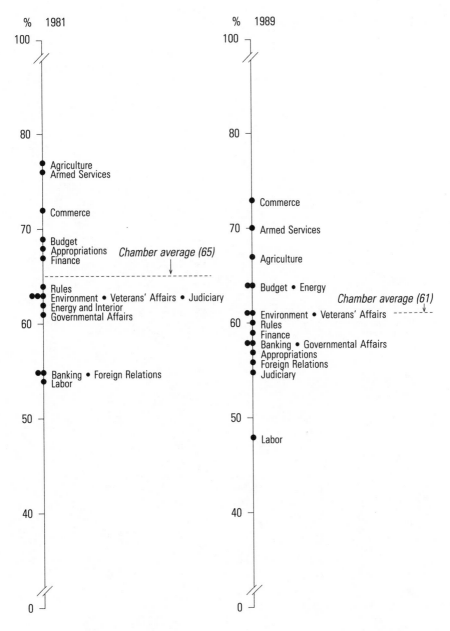

Figure 8-3 *(continued)*

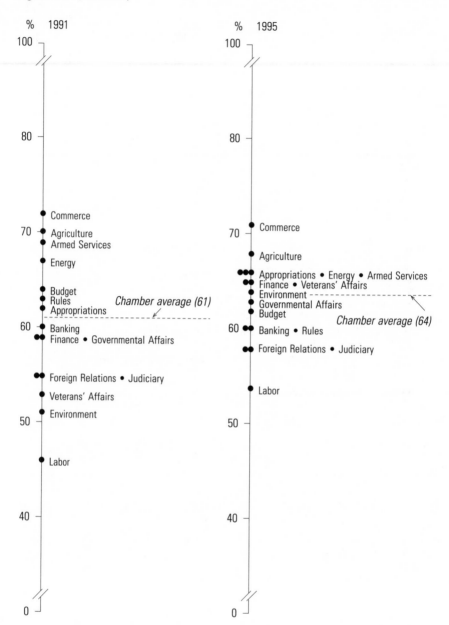

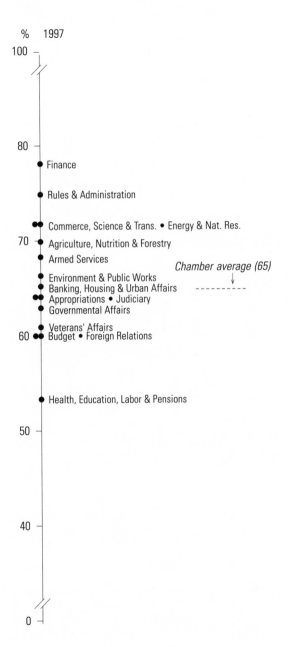

% 1997

100 —

80 —

● Finance

● Rules & Administration

●● Commerce, Science & Trans. ● Energy & Nat. Res.
70 ● Agriculture, Nutrition & Forestry
● Armed Services

Chamber average (65)

● Environment & Public Works
● Banking, Housing & Urban Affairs - - - - - - - - - -
●● Appropriations ● Judiciary
● Governmental Affairs

● Veterans' Affairs
60 ●● Budget ● Foreign Relations

● Health, Education, Labor & Pensions

50 —

40 —

0 —

Appendix

The appendix contains data on individual members of the 106th and 105th Congresses. Tables A-1 and A-3 show years of service, age, returns of the most recent election participated in (for House Members, 1998), and various voting ratings for each member of the 106th House (A-1) and Senate (A-3), all based on the year 1998. Tables A-2 and A-4 give comparable data on members of the 105th Congress, based on the year 1996. We use the following abbreviations throughout the tables in the appendix:

ACU	American Conservative Union
ADA	Americans for Democratic Action
AL	at large
CC	conservative coalition
conv.	nominated by convention
D	Democrat
I	Independent
PU	party unity
PS	presidential support
R	Republican
unopp.	unopposed

Note that we have recalculated the conservative coalition, party unity, and presidential support scores, all derived from Congressional Quarterly measures—to eliminate the effect of absences. We have not so altered scores for the Americans for Democratic Action and American Conservative Union.

Table A-1 House of Representatives, 106th Congress, 1999

State, district	Representative	Party	Years of service[a]	Age	% vote in 1998 Primary	% vote in 1998 General	1998 voting ratings CC	PU	PS	ADA	ACU	ACU (career)
Alabama												
1	Sonny Callahan	R	14	66	unopp.	unopp.	98	93	24	0	96	94
2	Terry Everett	R	6	61	unopp.	69	98	94	20	5	100	97
3	Bob Riley	R	2	54	unopp.	58	95	94	18	5	100	98
4	Robert B. Aderholt	R	2	33	unopp.	56	95	91	21	10	96	96
5	Robert E. Cramer	D	8	51	unopp.	70	98	60	54	65	44	45
6	Spencer Bachus	R	6	51	unopp.	72	88	89	20	5	84	94
7	Earl F. Hilliard	D	6	56	unopp.	unopp.	22	94	86	100	8	13
Alaska												
AL	Don Young	R	25	65	90	63	93	89	28	20	84	75
Arizona												
1	Matt Salmon	R	4	40	unopp.	64	93	94	26	5	96	98
2	Ed Pastor	D	7	55	unopp.	68	45	91	82	100	4	6
3	Bob Stump	R	22	71	unopp.	67	93	93	20	0	96	96
4	John Shadegg	R	4	49	unopp.	64	93	97	22	0	100	99
5	Jim Kolbe	R	14	56	77	52	83	81	40	15	72	78
6	Jay D. Hayworth	R	4	40	unopp.	52	88	94	23	0	100	99
Arkansas												
1	Marion Berry	D	2	56	unopp.	unopp.	83	70	63	70	28	36
2	Vic Snyder	D	2	51	unopp.	58	57	80	81	85	16	18
3	Asa Hutchinson	R	2	48	unopp.	81	87	90	26	5	92	90
4	Jay Dickey	R	6	59	unopp.	58	98	93	25	5	96	94
California												
1	Mike Thompson	D	0	47	51	62	—	—	23	—	—	—
2	Wally Herger	R	12	53	63	62	91	96	23	0	100	98

District	Name	Party										
3	Doug Ose	R	0	43	30	53	—	—	—	—	—	—
4	John T. Doolittle	R	8	48	65	62	46	94	17	5	100	99
5	Robert T. Matsui	D	20	57	71	72	31	92	82	85	4	7
6	Lynn C. Woolsey	D	6	61	65	68	17	95	85	100	8	2
7	George Miller	D	24	53	76	77	10	97	84	100	8	21
8	Nancy Pelosi	D	11	58	85	86	13	97	84	95	12	2
9	Barbara Lee	D	1	52	70	83	3	99	85	75	5	5
10	Ellen O. Tauscher	D	2	47	55	53	63	81	77	75	12	16
11	Richard W. Pombo	R	6	37	64	61	88	93	23	10	96	98
12	Tom Lantos	D	18	70	72	74	24	95	81	100	8	8
13	Pete Stark	D	26	67	69	71	5	98	87	90	8	5
14	Anna G. Eshoo	D	6	56	66	69	21	95	90	90	0	5
15	Tom Campbell	R	4	46	72	60	64	64	52	35	52	59
16	Zoe Lofgren	D	4	51	72	73	24	92	88	95	0	6
17	Sam Farr	D	6	57	60	64	22	95	87	100	0	3
18	Gary A. Condit	D	10	50	89	87	80	63	51	60	56	49
19	George P. Radanovich	R	4	43	82	80	88	96	20	0	100	98
20	Cal Dooley	D	8	44	44	61	62	80	80	85	4	10
21	William M. Thomas	R	20	57	79	79	95	89	23	0	92	80
22	Lois Capps	D	1	64	52	55	29	91	73	85	18	18
23	Elton Gallegly	R	12	54	63	60	90	90	21	15	76	89
24	Brad Sherman	D	2	44	54	58	38	83	72	95	20	26
25	Howard P. McKeon	R	6	59	79	75	98	95	24	5	96	95
26	Howard L. Berman	D	16	47	61	82	11	95	85	90	5	6
27	James E. Rogan	R	2	41	59	50	83	92	27	0	100	96
28	David Dreier	R	18	46	60	58	88	91	26	0	92	94
29	Henry A. Waxman	D	24	59	71	74	14	97	85	100	4	5
30	Xavier Becerra	D	6	40	80	82	8	99	88	90	0	2
31	Matthew G. Martinez	D	16	69	67	71	48	84	83	75	29	10
32	Julian C. Dixon	D	20	64	86	87	19	95	85	100	0	5
33	Lucille Roybal-Allard	D	6	57	86	87	5	99	86	100	0	3
34	Grace Napolitano	D	0	62	37	68	—	—	—	—	—	—
35	Maxine Waters	D	8	60	87	89	13	94	85	80	0	4

(table continues)

State, district	Representative	Party	Years of service[a]	Age	% vote in 1998 Primary	% vote in 1998 General	CC	PU	PS	ADA	ACU	ACU (career)
36	Steven Kuykendall	R	0	51	23	49	—	—	—	—	—	9
37	Juanita Millender-McDonald	D	2	60	61	85	16	96	84	95	4	9
38	Steven Horn	R	6	67	53	53	83	73	35	20	56	56
39	Ed Royce	R	6	47	67	63	73	90	21	5	100	99
40	Jerry Lewis	R	20	64	61	65	98	88	33	10	75	82
41	Gary Miller	R	0	50	32	53	—	—	—	—	—	—
42	George E. Brown, Jr.[b]	D	34	78	54	55	21	94	85	100	0	6
43	Ken Calvert	R	6	45	39	55	100	94	24	0	92	91
44	Mary Bono	R	1	37	58	60	95	92	23	0	95	95
45	Dana Rohrabacher	R	10	51	54	58	79	90	26	5	100	95
46	Loretta Sanchez	D	2	38	45	56	45	90	78	95	8	18
47	Christopher Cox	R	10	46	71	68	85	92	27	0	100	98
48	Ron Packard	R	16	67	71	77	100	94	21	5	96	93
49	Brian Bilbray	R	4	47	53	49	83	74	35	20	64	72
50	Bob Filner	D	6	56	unopp.	unopp.	7	97	85	100	4	5
51	Randy Cunningham	R	8	57	67	61	97	93	25	0	100	96
52	Duncan Hunter	R	18	50	78	76	90	93	20	5	100	95
Colorado												
1	Diana DeGette	D	2	41	unopp.	67	14	97	86	95	4	9
2	Mark Udall	D	0	48	44	52	—	—	—	—	—	—
3	Scott McInnis	R	6	45	unopp.	66	93	92	26	5	96	91
4	Bob Schaffer	R	2	36	unopp.	60	88	89	18	5	100	98
5	Joel Hefley	R	12	63	unopp.	73	88	92	21	0	100	96
6	Tom Tancredo	R	0	53	25	55	—	—	—	—	—	—
Connecticut												
1	John B. Larson	D	0	50	46	59	—	—	—	—	—	—
2	Sam Gejdenson	D	18	48	unopp.	61	20	94	83	100	9	5

District	Representative	Party										
3	Rosa DeLauro	D	8	55	unopp.	71	10	97	82	100	8	5
4	Christopher Shays	R	11	53	unopp.	69	50	58	57	45	40	43
5	Jim H. Maloney	D	2	50	unopp.	50	55	79	68	85	32	32
6	Nancy L. Johnson	R	16	63	unopp.	59	67	62	57	55	16	48
Delaware												
AL	Michael N. Castle	R	6	59	unopp.	66	76	63	51	30	42	59
Florida												
1	Joe Scarborough	R	4	35	unopp.	unopp.	83	91	26	10	96	98
2	Allen Boyd	D	2	53	unopp.	unopp.	86	69	62	65	32	38
3	Corrine Brown	D	6	52	unopp.	56	29	95	84	95	4	10
4	Tillie Fowler	R	6	56	unopp.	unopp.	95	91	27	5	88	87
5	Karen L. Thurman	D	6	47	unopp.	66	57	87	77	100	8	18
6	Cliff Stearns	R	10	57	unopp.	unopp.	93	92	18	5	96	95
7	John L. Mica	R	6	55	unopp.	unopp.	90	92	23	10	92	96
8	Bill McCollum	R	18	54	unopp.	66	88	92	26	5	84	90
9	Michael Bilirakis	R	16	68	unopp.	unopp.	93	91	20	5	92	85
10	C. W. Bill Young	R	28	68	unopp.	unopp.	100	92	24	0	90	84
11	Jim Davis	D	2	41	unopp.	65	69	81	74	85	16	16
12	Charles T. Canady	R	6	43	unopp.	unopp.	95	94	22	5	88	89
13	Dan Miller	R	6	56	unopp.	unopp.	88	90	32	10	88	87
14	Porter J. Goss	R	10	60	unopp.	unopp.	92	93	32	5	91	88
15	Dave Weldon	R	4	45	79	63	98	94	16	0	92	94
16	Mark Foley	R	4	44	unopp.	unopp.	90	84	38	20	80	84
17	Carrie P. Meek	D	6	72	unopp.	unopp.	29	93	87	95	4	9
18	Ileana Ros-Lehtinen	R	10	46	unopp.	unopp.	76	81	29	15	80	74
19	Robert Wexler	D	2	37	unopp.	unopp.	31	92	90	100	0	9
20	Peter Deutsch	D	6	41	unopp.	unopp.	52	88	82	95	4	18
21	Lincoln Diaz-Balart	R	6	43	unopp.	75	83	80	33	25	68	70
22	E. Clay Shaw, Jr.	R	18	59	unopp.	unopp.	90	88	34	10	72	84
23	Alcee L. Hastings	D	6	62	unopp.	unopp.	20	95	90	80	5	7

(table continues)

State, district	Representative	Party	Years of service[a]	Age	% vote in 1998 Primary	% vote in 1998 General	CC	PU	PS	ADA	ACU	ACU (career)
Georgia												
1	Jack Kingston	R	6	43	unopp.	unopp.	86	94	20	0	100	99
2	Sanford D. Bishop, Jr.	D	6	49	unopp.	57	83	71	58	70	44	26
3	Mac Collins	R	6	54	unopp.	unopp.	93	95	12	0	100	95
4	Cynthia McKinney	D	6	43	unopp.	61	10	92	87	100	8	6
5	John Lewis	D	12	58	unopp.	79	7	99	87	90	0	3
6	Johnny Isakson[c]	R	0	54	unopp.	65	—	—	—	—	—	—
7	Bob Barr	R	4	50	unopp.	55	90	93	20	5	100	97
8	Saxby Chambliss	R	4	55	unopp.	62	100	95	22	0	96	94
9	Nathan Deal	R	6	56	unopp.	unopp.	93	94	16	10	88	81
10	Charlie Norwood	R	4	57	unopp.	60	95	96	18	5	100	99
11	John Linder	R	6	56	unopp.	69	95	96	21	0	100	95
Hawaii												
1	Neil Abercrombie	D	8	60	91	62	24	92	82	95	12	5
2	Patsy T. Mink	D	21	71	90	69	14	95	85	95	8	4
Idaho												
1	Helen Chenoweth	R	4	60	71	55	86	89	29	20	92	94
2	Mike Simpson	R	0	50	40	53	—	—	—	—	—	—
Illinois												
1	Bobby L. Rush	D	6	52	89	86	5	95	84	95	8	3
2	Jesse Jackson, Jr.	D	4	33	unopp.	89	0	96	83	100	8	4
3	William O. Lipinski	D	16	61	unopp.	72	59	58	50	45	48	39
4	Luis V. Gutierrez	D	6	45	unopp.	82	2	93	83	90	16	9
5	Rod R. Blagojevich	D	2	41	unopp.	74	38	88	77	100	8	12
6	Henry J. Hyde	R	24	74	unopp.	67	88	92	20	0	92	86
7	Danny K. Davis	D	2	57	85	93	5	95	85	95	8	8

District	Name	Party										
8	Philip M. Crane	R	29	68	65	68	90	96	24	0	96	99
9	Jan Schakowsky	D	0	54	45	74	—	—	—	—	—	—
10	John E. Porter	R	19	63	unopp.	unopp.	79	69	41	15	46	62
11	Jerry Weller	R	4	41	unopp.	59	86	88	26	15	92	87
12	Jerry F. Costello	D	11	49	87	60	57	76	68	90	25	30
13	Judy Biggert	R	0	61	45	61	—	—	—	—	—	—
14	J. Dennis Hastert	R	12	56	unopp.	70	98	96	21	0	100	91
15	Thomas W. Ewing	R	8	63	unopp.	62	95	90	29	0	91	94
16	Donald Manzullo	R	6	54	unopp.	unopp.	93	95	21	0	92	98
17	Lane Evans	D	16	47	unopp.	52	19	92	83	90	16	6
18	Ray LaHood	R	4	53	unopp.	unopp.	86	83	28	20	60	68
19	David D. Phelps	D	0	51	83	58	—	—	—	—	—	—
20	John M. Shimkus	R	2	38	unopp.	61	98	93	25	10	88	88
Indiana												
1	Peter J. Visclosky	D	14	49	87	73	48	83	79	80	12	10
2	David McIntosh	R	4	40	unopp.	61	83	94	24	0	100	100
3	Tim Roemer	D	8	42	unopp.	58	71	66	61	65	44	20
4	Mark Souder	R	4	48	unopp.	63	85	90	25	15	83	95
5	Steve Buyer	R	6	40	unopp.	63	90	91	24	15	88	92
6	Dan Burton	R	16	60	84	72	95	93	21	5	96	97
7	Ed A. Pease	R	2	47	83	69	90	91	24	0	100	98
8	John N. Hostettler	R	4	37	unopp.	52	88	91	24	10	92	90
9	Baron Hill	D	0	45	70	51	—	—	—	—	—	—
10	Julia M. Carson	D	2	60	87	58	18	96	89	95	0	5
Iowa												
1	Jim Leach	R	22	56	unopp.	56	90	63	53	45	32	41
2	Jim Nussle	R	8	38	unopp.	55	98	89	27	10	84	84
3	Leonard L. Boswell	D	2	64	unopp.	57	93	65	65	65	36	32
4	Greg Ganske	R	4	49	unopp.	65	88	76	34	5	64	74
5	Tom Latham	R	4	50	unopp.	unopp.	98	94	24	0	92	85

(table continues)

Table A-1 *(continued)*

State, district	Representative	Party	Years of service[a]	Age	% vote in 1998 Primary	% vote in 1998 General	CC	PU	PS	ADA	ACU	ACU (career)
Kansas												
1	Jerry Moran	R	2	44	unopp.	81	98	90	29	10	92	94
2	Jim Ryun	R	2	51	78	61	93	96	21	0	100	67
3	Dennis Moore	D	0	53	74	52	—	—	—	—	—	—
4	Todd Tiahrt	R	4	47	unopp.	58	98	96	20	0	100	100
Kentucky												
1	Edward Whitfield	R	4	55	unopp.	55	88	90	24	5	96	93
2	Ron Lewis	R	5	52	unopp.	64	100	94	20	0	100	97
3	Anne M. Northup	R	2	50	unopp.	52	93	91	25	0	88	88
4	Ken Lucas	D	0	66	66	53	—	—	—	—	—	—
5	Harold Rogers	R	18	61	unopp.	78	100	92	23	5	92	84
6	Ernie Fletcher	R	0	47	76	53	—	—	—	—	—	—
Louisiana												
1	David Vitter[d]	R										
2	William J. Jefferson	D	8	51	unopp.	86	50	91	83	80	13	8
3	W. J. Tauzin	R	19	55	unopp.	unopp.	100	92	23	5	88	73
4	Jim McCrery	R	11	49	unopp.	unopp.	100	94	26	5	96	16
5	John Cooksey	R	2	57	unopp.	unopp.	98	95	25	0	96	94
6	Richard Baker	R	12	50	unopp.	51	100	94	20	0	100	93
7	Chris John	D	2	38	unopp.	unopp.	100	56	50	50	45	55
Maine												
1	Tom H. Allen	D	2	53	unopp.	60	19	93	84	100	4	8
2	John E. Baldacci	D	4	43	unopp.	76	33	92	80	95	4	10
Maryland												
1	Wayne T. Gilchrest	R	8	51	unopp.	69	80	71	38	35	44	64

District	Representative	Party										
2	Robert L. Ehrlich, Jr.	R	4	41	unopp.	69	85	87	25	5	92	81
3	Benjamin L. Cardin	D	12	55	90	78	36	91	78	95	8	7
4	Albert R. Wynn	D	6	47	87	86	40	93	83	100	4	4
5	Steny H. Hoyer	D	18	59	86	66	50	89	81	95	4	8
6	Roscoe G. Bartlett	R	6	72	unopp.	63	95	95	19	5	100	100
7	Elijah E. Cummings	D	3	47	91	86	26	95	83	100	4	4
8	Constance A. Morella	R	11	67	77	60	39	40	71	65	20	24
Massachusetts												
1	John W. Olver	D	8	62	unopp.	72	7	99	88	95	0	2
2	Richard E. Neal	D	10	49	unopp.	unopp.	21	95	80	95	12	11
3	Jim P. McGovern	D	2	48	unopp.	57	7	97	80	100	4	4
4	Barney Frank	D	18	58	unopp.	unopp.	20	94	81	100	4	4
5	Martin T. Meehan	D	6	42	87	71	10	97	88	100	4	13
6	John F. Tierney	D	2	47	unopp.	55	2	98	83	100	4	8
7	Edward J. Markey	D	22	52	23	71	11	95	82	90	4	4
8	Michael E. Capuano	D	0	47	unopp.	82	—	—	—	—	—	—
9	Joe J. Moakley	D	26	71	unopp.	unopp.	18	94	79	65	13	7
10	William D. Delahunt	D	2	57	unopp.	70	7	97	83	100	8	4
Michigan												
1	Bart Stupak	D	6	46	unopp.	59	41	83	75	90	20	21
2	Peter Hoekstra	R	6	45	unopp.	69	83	93	24	5	100	90
3	Vernon J. Ehlers	R	5	64	unopp.	82	74	78	33	25	56	71
4	Dave Camp	R	7	45	unopp.	91	93	92	27	10	96	88
5	James A. Barcia	D	6	46	unopp.	71	71	67	60	90	40	49
6	Fred Upton	R	12	45	unopp.	70	79	79	33	15	56	71
7	Nick Smith	R	6	64	unopp.	58	88	88	26	20	76	90
8	Debbie Stabenow	D	2	48	unopp.	57	49	87	78	100	9	11
9	Dale E. Kildee	D	22	69	unopp.	56	40	84	74	95	16	10
10	David E. Bonior	D	22	53	unopp.	52	7	95	84	95	16	5
11	Joe Knollenberg	R	6	65	unopp.	64	95	94	24	0	96	91
12	Sander M. Levin	D	16	67	unopp.	56	31	93	83	100	8	3

(table continues)

Table A-1 (continued)

State, district	Representative	Party	Years of service[a]	Age	% vote in 1998 Primary	General	CC	PU	PS	ADA	ACU	ACU (career)
13	Lynn Rivers	D	4	42	unopp.	57	19	90	76	100	12	12
14	John Conyers, Jr.	D	34	69	unopp.	87	8	95	90	80	0	5
15	Carolyn C. Kilpatrick	D	2	50	51	79	12	96	88	90	0	6
16	John D. Dingell	D	43	72	unopp.	67	44	89	82	85	8	9
Minnesota												
1	Gil Gutknecht	R	4	47	unopp.	55	90	92	24	5	92	94
2	David Minge	D	6	56	unopp.	57	69	81	72	85	24	22
3	Jim Ramstad	R	8	52	unopp.	72	79	68	43	20	60	68
4	Bruce F. Vento	D	22	58	unopp.	54	14	97	85	100	8	3
5	Martin O. Sabo	D	20	60	unopp.	67	36	90	89	90	0	3
6	Bill Luther	D	4	53	unopp.	50	41	89	75	90	4	15
7	Collin C. Peterson	D	8	54	unopp.	72	76	54	55	60	56	44
8	James L. Oberstar	D	24	64	unopp.	66	26	90	85	95	13	9
Mississippi												
1	Roger F. Wicker	R	4	47	unopp.	67	100	94	24	0	96	88
2	Bennie G. Thompson	D	6	50	unopp.	71	34	95	82	95	13	12
3	Charles W. Pickering, Jr.	R	2	35	unopp.	85	100	95	20	0	100	96
4	Ronnie Shows	D	0	52	57	53	—	—	—	—	—	—
5	Gene Taylor	D	10	43	unopp.	78	86	41	33	30	79	78
Missouri												
1	William L. Clay	D	30	67	unopp.	73	11	98	88	85	5	4
2	James M. Talent	R	6	42	90	70	95	93	20	5	96	97
3	Richard A. Gephardt	D	22	57	74	56	40	93	82	90	12	11
4	Ike Skelton	D	22	67	unopp.	70	93	64	58	65	36	51
5	Karen McCarthy	D	4	51	79	66	36	92	81	100	0	12
6	Pat Danner	D	6	64	unopp.	71	88	59	46	60	52	37

(table continues)

District	Name	Party										
7	Roy Blunt	R	2	48	unopp.	73	98	95	17	0	100	90
8	Jo Ann Emerson	R	2	48	unopp.	63	93	92	22	5	92	89
9	Kenny Hulshof	R	2	40	unopp.	62	88	89	25	15	88	90
Montana												
AL	Rick Hill	R	2	51	unopp.	52	98	92	28	10	79	86
Nebraska												
1	Doug Bereuter	R	20	59	unopp.	73	93	84	28	5	64	69
2	Lee Terry	R	0	37	40	66	—	—	—	—	—	—
3	Bill Barrett	R	8	69	unopp.	85	98	87	27	15	76	87
Nevada												
1	Shelley Berkley	D	0	48	81	49	—	—	—	—	—	—
2	Jim Gibbons	R	2	53	unopp.	81	86	93	22	20	92	92
New Hampshire												
1	John E. Sununu	R	2	34	unopp.	67	81	91	25	0	92	92
2	Charles F. Bass	R	4	46	83	53	81	78	33	10	63	78
New Jersey												
1	Robert E. Andrews	D	8	41	unopp.	73	41	86	77	95	12	25
2	Frank A. LoBiondo	R	4	52	unopp.	66	71	75	35	30	68	71
3	H. James Saxton	R	14	55	unopp.	62	83	80	32	25	63	77
4	Christopher H. Smith	R	18	45	53	62	71	79	27	25	72	56
5	Marge Roukema	R	18	69	unopp.	64	79	74	34	20	60	50
6	Frank Pallone, Jr.	D	10	47	unopp.	57	31	92	78	100	12	19
7	Bob Franks	R	6	47	unopp.	52	71	73	38	25	52	61
8	William J. Pascrell, Jr.	D	2	61	unopp.	62	46	86	70	95	16	26
9	Steven R. Rothman	D	2	46	unopp.	64	31	87	83	100	8	11
10	Donald M. Payne	D	10	64	92	83	3	97	89	90	9	5
11	Rodney Frelinghuysen	R	4	52	unopp.	68	83	77	37	10	52	58
12	Rush Holt	D	0	51	64	50	—	—	—	—	—	—
13	Robert Menendez	D	6	45	unopp.	80	29	90	78	95	12	10

State, district	Representative	Party	Years of service[a]	Age	% vote in 1998 Primary	% vote in 1998 General	CC	PU	PS	ADA	ACU	ACU (career)
New Mexico												
1	Heather Wilson	R	2	39	62	49	100	87	22	0	83	83
2	Joe Skeen	R	18	72	unopp.	58	93	89	27	10	84	84
3	Tom Udall	D	0	51	44	52	—	—	—	—	—	—
New York												
1	Michael P. Forbes[e]	R	4	48	unopp.	64	73	65	41	65	46	69
2	Rick A. Lazio	R	6	42	unopp.	66	83	73	37	40	52	65
3	Peter T. King	R	6	56	78	65	90	82	31	10	76	75
4	Carolyn McCarthy	D	2	56	79	66	36	82	68	90	24	20
5	Gary L. Ackerman	D	16	58	unopp.	65	15	97	86	100	0	4
6	Gregory W. Meeks	D	1	46	unopp.	unopp.	6	97	90	85	5	5
7	Joseph Crowley	D	0	37	unopp.	67	—	—	—	—	—	—
8	Jerrold Nadler	D	6	53	unopp.	86	10	96	79	100	8	5
9	Anthony Weiner	D	0	35	28	66	—	—	—	—	—	—
10	Edolphus Towns	D	16	66	52	95	20	93	85	95	9	4
11	Major R. Owens	D	16	64	unopp.	89	5	97	88	100	0	3
12	Nydia M. Velazquez	D	6	47	unopp.	82	8	96	81	95	8	4
13	Vito J. Fossella	R	1	34	unopp.	66	86	91	23	0	96	98
14	Carolyn B. Maloney	D	6	52	unopp.	50	23	93	82	100	8	4
15	Charles B. Rangel	D	28	68	unopp.	93	16	95	88	90	9	6
16	José E. Serrano	D	9	55	unopp.	95	13	95	85	90	0	3
17	Eliot L. Engel	D	10	51	80	88	11	97	82	95	4	6
18	Nita M. Lowey	D	10	61	unopp.	93	29	94	83	100	8	6
19	Sue Kelly	R	4	62	unopp.	63	74	66	41	45	48	61
20	Benjamin A. Gilman	R	26	76	unopp.	58	74	62	46	45	38	45
21	Michael R. McNulty	D	10	51	unopp.	74	32	89	76	75	21	26
22	John E. Sweeney	R	0	44	50	55	—	—	—	—	—	—
23	Sherwood L. Boehlert	R	16	62	unopp.	80	64	59	60	60	24	34

District	Name	Party										
24	John M. McHugh	R	6	50	unopp.	79	88	80	35	25	68	75
25	James T. Walsh	R	10	51	unopp.	69	88	73	36	30	44	66
26	Maurice D. Hinchey	D	6	60	unopp.	62	7	96	83	100	4	6
27	Thomas M. Reynolds	R	0	49	unopp.	58	—	—	—	—	—	—
28	Louise M. Slaughter	D	12	69	unopp.	64	23	96	82	100	8	7
29	John J. LaFalce	D	24	59	unopp.	57	37	90	83	85	8	14
30	Jack Quinn	R	6	47	unopp.	68	86	76	32	30	48	59
31	Amo Houghton	R	12	72	unopp.	68	79	66	49	30	29	54
North Carolina												
1	Eva Clayton	D	6	64	67	62	38	95	83	100	0	3
2	Bob Etheridge	D	2	57	unopp.	57	80	81	73	80	28	30
3	Walter B. Jones, Jr.	R	4	55	unopp.	62	88	92	21	5	100	99
4	David E. Price[f]	D	2	58	87	57	68	87	77	95	8	2
5	Richard Burr	R	4	42	unopp.	68	95	92	24	5	92	93
6	Howard Coble	R	14	67	unopp.	89	88	93	16	10	96	89
7	Mike McIntyre	D	2	42	94	91	93	61	52	60	52	56
8	Robin C. Hayes	R	0	54	unopp.	51	—	—	—	—	—	—
9	Sue Myrick	R	4	57	unopp.	69	98	94	19	5	88	96
10	Cass Ballenger	R	12	72	unopp.	86	98	94	22	5	91	89
11	Charles H. Taylor	R	8	57	unopp.	56	100	95	18	5	96	94
12	Melvin L. Watt	D	6	53	84	56	19	96	91	100	4	4
North Dakota												
AL	Earl Pomeroy	D	6	46	unopp.	56	79	80	75	90	21	23
Ohio												
1	Steve Chabot	R	4	45	unopp.	53	81	91	27	0	96	98
2	Rob Portman	R	6	43	unopp.	76	98	91	29	5	88	90
3	Tony P. Hall	D	20	56	unopp.	58	60	76	66	75	21	16
4	Michael G. Oxley	R	18	54	unopp.	64	100	91	25	5	96	88
5	Paul E. Gilmor	R	10	59	unopp.	67	95	87	29	5	68	80
6	Ted Strickland[g]	D	2	57	unopp.	57	50	85	66	85	32	24

(table continues)

Table A-1 *(continued)*

State, district	Representative	Party	Years of service[a]	Age	% vote in 1998 Primary	% vote in 1998 General	CC	PU	PS	ADA	ACU	ACU (career)
7	David L. Hobson	R	8	62	86	67	93	91	28	5	88	80
8	John A. Boehner	R	8	49	unopp.	71	100	96	25	0	96	95
9	Marcy Kaptur	D	16	52	unopp.	81	49	85	71	80	28	13
10	Dennis J. Kucinich	D	2	52	88	67	29	84	78	90	20	18
11	Stephanie T. Jones	D	0	50	51	79						
12	John R. Kasich	R	16	46	91	67	90	93	25	0	96	87
13	Sherrod Brown	D	6	46	unopp.	62	12	97	83	100	4	12
14	Tom C. Sawyer	D	12	53	unopp.	63	33	94	88	95	0	3
15	Deborah Pryce	R	6	47	unopp.	60	94	88	30	5	83	78
16	Ralph Regula	R	26	74	84	64	95	87	28	20	64	56
17	James A. Traficant, Jr.	D	14	57	unopp.	68	95	33	47	45	64	27
18	Bob Ney	R	4	44	unopp.	60	88	85	27	15	80	79
19	Steven LaTourette	R	4	44	unopp.	66	81	78	38	40	52	70
Oklahoma												
1	Steve Largent	R	4	43	unopp.	62	95	91	27	10	92	97
2	Tom Coburn	R	4	49	unopp.	58	98	94	16	5	100	96
3	Wes Watkins[h]	R	2	59	unopp.	62	98	94	24	5	92	96
4	J. C. Watts, Jr.	R	4	41	unopp.	62	95	92	21	10	84	95
5	Ernest J. Istook	R	6	48	unopp.	68	95	96	17	0	95	98
6	Frank D. Lucas	R	5	38	unopp.	65	98	95	26	0	100	96
Oregon												
1	David Wu	D	0	44	52	50						
2	Greg Walden	R	0	42	55	62						
3	Earl Blumenauer	D	2	50	unopp.	85	24	92	85	95	4	4
4	Peter A. DeFazio	D	12	52	unopp.	70	14	93	80	95	16	11
5	Darlene Hooley	D	2	59	unopp.	55	36	88	78	95	12	14

		Party											
Pennsylvania													
1	Robert A. Brady	D	1	54	64	81	10	97	88	50	0	0
2	Chaka Fattah	D	4	42	unopp.	86	7	96	88	95	0	1
3	Robert A. Borski	D	16	50	87	60	29	91	79	90	12	13
4	Ron Klink	D	6	47	unopp.	64	49	82	75	80	13	27
5	John E. Peterson	R	2	59	unopp.	85	95	95	24	0	96	96
6	Tim Holden	D	6	41	unopp.	61	67	73	61	70	24	43
7	Curt Weldon	R	12	51	67	72	80	81	28	25	60	67
8	James Greenwood	R	6	47	81	63	78	68	38	25	48	61
9	Bud Shuster	R	26	66	44	unopp.	97	95	26	10	96	93
10	Donald L. Sherwood	R	0	58	unopp.	49	—	—	—	—	—	—
11	Paul E. Kanjorski	D	14	61	unopp.	67	36	86	82	85	12	21
12	John P. Murtha	D	25	66	unopp.	68	70	73	73	75	21	35
13	Joseph M. Hoeffel	D	0	49	unopp.	52	—	—	—	—	—	—
14	William J. Coyne	D	18	62	27	60	21	95	83	100	4	3
15	Patrick Toomey	R	0	38	unopp.	55	—	—	—	—	—	—
16	Joseph R. Pitts	R	2	59	unopp.	71	90	96	21	0	96	96
17	George W. Gekas	R	16	68	65	unopp.	95	93	21	10	84	85
18	Mike Doyle	D	4	45	68	68	60	79	68	80	25	33
19	William F. Goodling	R	24	71	unopp.	68	85	94	19	5	92	76
20	Frank Mascara	D	4	68	unopp.	unopp.	62	80	73	85	20	31
21	Phil English	R	4	42	unopp.	63	81	81	36	35	68	75
Rhode Island												
1	Patrick J. Kennedy	D	4	32	unopp.	67	27	91	79	95	12	14
2	Robert A. Weygand	D	2	50	unopp.	72	45	87	73	90	20	23
South Carolina												
1	Mark Sanford	R	4	36	unopp.	91	74	76	33	20	72	86
2	Floyd Spence	R	28	68	unopp.	58	95	95	18	5	100	89
3	Lindsey Graham	R	4	41	unopp.	unopp.	95	92	22	15	88	93
4	John DeMint	R	0	48	53	58	—	—	—	—	—	—
5	John M. Spratt, Jr.	D	16	56	unopp.	58	83	81	73	85	17	23
6	James E. Clyburn	D	6	58	83	72	35	95	83	95	4	12

(table continues)

Table A-1 *(continued)*

State, district	Representative	Party	Years of service[a]	Age	% vote in 1998 Primary	% vote in 1998 General	CC	PU	PS	ADA	ACU	ACU (career)
South Dakota												
AL	John R. Thune	R	2	38	unopp.	75	98	95	23	5	92	90
Tennessee												
1	William L. Jenkins	R	2	61	unopp.	69	95	95	20	5	100	94
2	John J. Duncan, Jr.	R	10	51	unopp.	89	76	88	22	15	84	87
3	Zach Wamp	R	4	41	93	66	86	89	18	15	84	93
4	Van Hilleary	R	4	39	unopp.	60	90	93	20	5	96	98
5	Bob Clement	D	11	55	unopp.	83	86	76	65	85	24	27
6	Bart Gordon	D	13	49	unopp.	55	75	74	62	90	36	23
7	Ed Bryant	R	4	50	unopp.	unopp.	98	96	20	0	100	100
8	John Tanner	D	10	54	unopp.	unopp.	90	69	58	60	41	43
9	Harold E. Ford, Jr.	D	2	28	unopp.	79	47	91	75	80	14	11
Texas												
1	Max Sandlin	D	2	46	unopp.	59	88	72	63	80	40	38
2	Jim Turner	D	2	52	unopp.	58	95	58	53	65	48	48
3	Sam Johnson	R	8	68	unopp.	91	97	96	20	0	100	98
4	Ralph M. Hall	D	18	75	unopp.	58	95	23	30	15	96	81
5	Pete Sessions	R	2	43	unopp.	56	100	97	20	0	100	100
6	Joe Barton	R	14	45	73	73	95	94	20	5	100	94
7	Bill Archer	R	28	70	97	93	95	97	21	0	100	94
8	Kevin Brady[j]	R	2	43	89	91	100	94	20	0	92	96
9	Nick Lampson[j]	D	2	53	unopp.	64	63	86	81	90	16	20
10	Lloyd Doggett	D	4	52	unopp.	85	24	92	81	100	8	29
11	Chet Edwards	D	8	47	unopp.	82	69	84	81	90	8	88
12	Kay Granger	R	2	55	unopp.	62	100	91	28	5	84	98
13	William M. Thornberry	R	4	40	94	68	98	92	23	5	100	98
14	Ron Paul[k]	R	2	63	unopp.	55	56	76	31	20	88	84

District	Representative	Party										
15	Rubén Hinojosa	D	2	58	unopp.	59	59	91	79	95	16	23
16	Silvestre Reyes	D	2	53	unopp.	88	66	87	78	80	13	26
17	Charles W. Stenholm	D	20	60	unopp.	54	98	50	49	40	48	75
18	Sheila Jackson-Lee	D	4	48	unopp.	90	32	94	83	95	4	7
19	Larry Combest	R	14	53	unopp.	84	98	95	22	0	100	98
20	Charlie Gonzalez	D	0	54	62	63	—	—	—	—	—	—
21	Lamar Smith	R	12	51	unopp.	91	100	95	23	0	92	92
22	Tom DeLay	R	14	51	unopp.	65	100	95	20	0	96	96
23	Henry Bonilla	R	6	44	unopp.	64	88	85	30	10	92	92
24	Martin Frost	D	20	57	unopp.	58	80	84	73	95	8	18
25	Ken Bentsen	D	4	39	unopp.	58	67	85	78	95	4	9
26	Dick Armey	R	14	58	unopp.	88	98	97	22	0	100	97
27	Solomon P. Ortiz	D	16	61	unopp.	63	66	76	68	70	17	31
28	Ciro Rodriguez	D	1	53	76	91	51	92	81	100	4	15
29	Gene Green	D	6	51	unopp.	93	63	86	71	95	16	24
30	Eddie B. Johnson	D	6	63	unopp.	70	42	93	86	90	4	8
Utah												
1	James V. Hansen	R	18	66	unopp.	68	98	96	20	5	100	94
2	Merrill Cook	R	2	52	unopp.	53	95	90	19	15	84	86
3	Christopher B. Cannon	R	2	48	76	77	100	94	19	5	95	96
Vermont												
AL	Bernard Sanders	I	8	57	unopp.	63	17	95	85	100	0	6
Virginia												
1	Herbert H. Bateman	R	16	70	unopp.	77	97	92	27	5	86	79
2	Owen B. Pickett	D	12	68	unopp.	unopp.	90	60	60	55	16	39
3	Robert C. Scott	D	6	51	unopp.	77	43	91	89	95	20	11
4	Norman Sisisky	D	16	71	unopp.	unopp.	88	65	63	65	28	39
5	Virgil H. Goode, Jr.	D	2	52	unopp.	unopp.	90	28	26	30	83	84
6	Robert W. Goodlatte	R	6	46	unopp.	69	93	92	23	0	100	91
7	Thomas J. Bliley, Jr.	R	18	66	unopp.	74	93	94	23	0	100	91

(table continues)

Table A-1 *(continued)*

State, district	Representative	Party	Years of service[a]	Age	% vote in 1998 Primary	% vote in 1998 General	CC	PU	PS	ADA	ACU	ACU (career)
8	James P. Moran	D	8	53	unopp.	81	67	79	81	75	8	14
9	Rick Boucher	D	16	52	unopp.	61	70	81	79	95	4	12
10	Frank R. Wolf	R	18	59	unopp.	72	86	88	24	10	80	83
11	Thomas M. Davis III	R	4	49	unopp.	83	90	81	34	15	64	70
Washington												
1	Jay Inslee	D	0	48	44	51	—	—	—	—	—	
2	Jack Metcalf	R	4	71	51	55	81	86	21	20	80	89
3	Brian Baird	D	0	43	48	55						—
4	Richard Hastings	R	4	57	69	69	100	97	23	0	100	96
5	George R. Nethercutt	R	4	54	58	57	95	95	27	0	96	93
6	Norm D. Dicks	D	22	58	71	68	60	85	85	95	0	10
7	Jim McDermott	D	10	62	84	89	15	96	95	90	0	2
8	Jennifer Dunn	R	6	57	58	66	95	94	23	0	96	91
9	Adam Smith	D	2	33	58	65	55	83	80	100	0	10
West Virginia												
1	Alan B. Mollohan	D	16	55	87	85	67	74	69	70	32	31
2	Bob Wise	D	16	50	86	73	52	85	78	80	4	13
3	Nick Rahall II	D	22	49	82	87	52	78	77	85	24	17
Wisconsin												
1	Paul Ryan	R	0	29	57	81						—
2	Tammy Baldwin	D	0	37	37	53						—
3	Ron Kind	D	2	35	unopp.	72	57	86	77	85	20	8
4	Gerald D. Kleczka	D	15	55	89	57	50	85	75	90	20	11
5	Thomas M. Barrett	D	6	44	unopp.	85	26	93	89	95	4	10
6	Tom E. Petri	R	20	58	unopp.	93	71	86	31	15	88	76
7	David Obey	D	30	60	unopp.	61	31	92	89	95	16	8

(1998 voting ratings columns: CC, PU, PS, ADA, ACU)

8	Mark Green	R	0	39	80	55	—	—	—	—	—	—
9	F. James Sensenbrenner, Jr.	R	20	55	unopp.	91	69	86	22	5	92	86
Wyoming												
AL	Barbara Cubin	R	0	52	unopp.	58	95	96	21	5	100	99

Note: In compiling this table, we calculated the conservative coalition, party unity, and presidential support scores to eliminate the effects of absences as follows: support = support/(support + opposition).

a. Service beginning in or after November in a given year is not counted as a year of service.
b. Brown died on July 17, 1999.
c. In a February 23, 1999, special election, Isakson was elected to replace Newt Gingrich, who resigned.
d. Vitter was elected in a May 29, 1999, runoff election to replace Robert Livingston, who resigned.
e. Forbes changed his party affiliation to the Democratic Party.
f. Price was reelected to the U.S. House of Representatives after not serving from 1995–1997. Price had originally been elected to the House in 1986.
g. Strickland was reelected to the U.S. House of Representatives after not serving from 1995–1997. Strickland had originally been elected to the House in 1992.
h. Watkins was reelected to the U.S. House of Representatives after not serving from 1991–1997. Watkins had originally been elected to the House in 1976.
i. Brady was elected to the U.S. House of Representatives after winning a December 10, 1996, runoff election.
j. Lampson was elected to the U.S. House of Representatives after winning a December 10, 1996, runoff election.
k. Paul was reelected to the U.S. House of Representatives after not serving from 1977–1979, 1985–1987, and 1995–1997. Paul had originally been elected to the House in 1976.

Sources: Congressional Quarterly Almanac, various years; *Congressional Quarterly Weekly Report,* various years; American Conservative Union; Americans for Democratic Action.

Table A-2 House of Representatives, 105th Congress, 1997

State, district	Representative	Party	Years of service[a]	Age	% vote in 1996 Primary	% vote in 1996 General	CC	PU	PS	ADA	ACU	ACU (career)
Alabama												
1	Sonny Callahan	R	12	64	unopp.	64	100	94	38	0	100	94
2	Terry Everett	R	4	59	unopp.	63	100	95	34	5	100	97
3	Bob Riley	R	0	52	64	51	—	—	—	—	—	—
4	Robert B. Aderholt	R	0	31	49	50	—	—	—	—	—	—
5	Robert E. Cramer	D	6	49	unopp.	56	98	59	65	40	55	44
6	Spencer Bachus	R	4	49	unopp.	71	98	93	38	5	95	96
7	Earl F. Hilliard	D	4	54	unopp.	71	39	93	80	85	15	15
Alaska												
AL	Don Young	R	24	63	58	59	100	91	40	0	89	74
Arizona												
1	Matt Salmon	R	2	38	unopp.	60	92	92	33	10	100	96
2	Ed Pastor	D	6	53	unopp.	65	44	90	79	85	5	6
3	Bob Stump	R	20	69	unopp.	67	98	97	34	0	100	96
4	John Shadegg	R	2	47	74	67	90	96	30	5	100	96
5	Jim Kolbe	R	12	54	70	69	86	88	49	5	90	80
6	J. D. Hayworth	R	2	38	unopp.	48	94	96	37	0	100	100
Arkansas												
1	Marion Berry	D	0	54	52	53	—	—	—	—	—	—
2	Vic Snyder	D	0	49	51	52	—	—	—	—	—	—
3	Asa Hutchinson	R	0	46	—	56	—	—	—	—	—	—
4	Jay Dickey	R	4	57	unopp.	64	92	96	25	0	100	96

California	Name	Party										
1	Frank Riggs	R	2	46	unopp.	50	80	86	40	10	85	73
2	Wally Herger	R	10	51	84	61	94	96	33	0	100	98
3	Vic Fazio	D	18	54	82	54	57	89	84	80	0	6
4	John T. Doolittle	R	6	46	unopp.	60	100	95	28	5	100	100
5	Robert T. Matsui	D	18	55	unopp.	70	42	93	87	85	0	6
6	Lynn C. Woolsey	D	4	59	unopp.	62	4	98	84	95	0	2
7	George Miller	D	22	51	unopp.	72	4	96	81	90	0	22
8	Nancy Pelosi	D	9	56	unopp.	84	2	98	83	95	0	1
9	Ronald V. Dellums	D	26	61	85	77	2	97	76	100	0	6
10	Ellen O. Tauscher	D	0	45	75	49	—	—	—	—	—	—
11	Richard W. Pombo	R	4	35	unopp.	59	98	95	29	5	100	100
12	Tom Lantos	D	16	68	unopp.	72	15	97	87	95	0	8
13	Pete Stark	D	24	65	unopp.	65	0	95	74	80	0	5
14	Anna G. Eshoo	D	4	54	unopp.	65	12	92	83	85	0	5
15	Tom Campbell	R	2	44	unopp.	59	43	73	54	40	60	58
16	Zoe Lofgren	D	2	49	unopp.	66	16	91	77	85	5	7
17	Sam Farr	D	4	55	88	59	27	94	84	90	0	3
18	Gary A. Condit	D	8	48	unopp.	66	82	52	53	35	70	48
19	George P. Radanovich	R	2	41	unopp.	67	98	96	34	0	100	98
20	Cal Dooley	D	6	42	unopp.	57	67	74	81	55	15	11
21	William M. Thomas	R	18	55	79	66	100	90	42	5	90	79
22	Lois Capps	D	0	62	unopp.	48	—	—	—	—	—	—
23	Elton Gallegly	R	10	52	unopp.	60	94	95	38	0	100	91
24	Brad Sherman	D	0	42	54	50	—	—	—	—	—	—
25	Howard P. McKeon	R	4	57	85	62	96	95	33	0	100	96
26	Howard L. Berman	D	14	45	84	66	21	94	88	90	0	6
27	James E. Rogan	R	0	39	88	50	—	—	—	—	—	—
28	David Dreier	R	16	44	unopp.	61	98	98	33	0	100	94

(table continues)

Table A-2 *(continued)*

State, district	Representative	Party	Years of service[a]	Age	% vote in 1996 — Primary	% vote in 1996 — General	CC	PU	PS	ADA	ACU	ACU (career)
29	Henry A. Waxman	D	22	57	unopp.	68	6	97	83	90	0	5
30	Xavier Becerra	D	4	38	unopp.	72	9	98	84	85	0	3
31	Matthew G. Martinez	D	14	67	unopp.	67	57	78	79	80	10	8
32	Julian C. Dixon	D	18	62	unopp.	82	40	91	84	90	0	5
33	Lucille Roybal-Allard	D	4	55	unopp.	82	12	97	83	90	0	2
34	Esteban E. Torres	D	14	66	unopp.	68	27	95	84	90	0	3
35	Maxine Waters	D	6	58	unopp.	86	13	95	74	100	0	4
36	Jane Harman	D	4	51	unopp.	52	66	75	67	85	26	22
37	Juanita Millender-McDonald[b]	D	1	58	27	85	28	93	84	60	0	0
38	Steve Horn	R	4	65	unopp.	53	73	72	50	83	63	60
39	Ed Royce	R	4	45	unopp.	63	74	90	34	40	100	98
40	Jerry Lewis	R	18	62	77	65	100	88	46	15	83	84
41	Jay C. Kim	R	4	57	58	59	98	98	34	5	100	95
42	George E. Brown, Jr.	D	32	76	78	50	26	96	90	90	0	6
43	Ken Calvert	R	4	43	74	55	98	93	33	0	95	91
44	Sonny Bono	R	2	61	unopp.	58	98	94	37	0	95	96
45	Dana Rohrabacher	R	8	49	unopp.	61	78	92	28	15	100	95
46	Loretta Sanchez	D	0	36	35	47	—	—	—	—	—	—
47	Christopher Cox	R	8	44	unopp.	66	91	97	31	5	100	98
48	Ron Packard	R	14	65	unopp.	66	96	93	40	0	94	93
49	Brian Bilbray	R	2	45	unopp.	53	73	82	45	20	74	73
50	Bob Filner	D	4	54	55	62	12	97	86	90	0	6
51	Randy Cunningham	R	6	55	86	65	91	95	31	10	100	96
52	Duncan L. Hunter	R	16	48	unopp.	65	98	96	30	10	100	95

State/District	Representative	Party										
Colorado												
1	Diana DeGette	D	0	39	56	57						
2	David E. Skaggs	D	10	53	unopp.	57	33	93	85	90	0	7
3	Scott McInnis	R	4	43	unopp.	69	88	92	38	5	100	89
4	Bob Schaffer	R	0	34	40	56						
5	Joel Hefley	R	10	61	77	72	94	95	30	10	100	96
6	Dan Schaefer	R	14	60	unopp.	62	98	97	33	0	100	90
Connecticut												
1	Barbara B. Kennelly	D	15	60	unopp.	74	50	87	84	80	10	6
2	Sam Gejdenson	D	16	48	unopp.	52	33	92	83	90	0	4
3	Rosa DeLauro	D	6	53	unopp.	71	29	93	84	85	0	3
4	Christopher Shays	R	9	51	unopp.	60	33	69	53	30	60	42
5	Jim H. Maloney	D	0	48	unopp.	52						
6	Nancy L. Johnson	R	14	61	unopp.	50	78	74	58	20	55	51
Delaware												
AL	Michael N. Castle	R	4	57	unopp.	70	71	74	57	25	60	65
Florida												
1	Joe Scarborough	R	2	33	unopp.	73	79	89	31	10	95	96
2	Allen Boyd	D	0	51	64	59						
3	Corrine Brown	D	4	50	unopp.	61	59	90	84	90	0	10
4	Tillie Fowler	R	4	54	89	unopp.	96	92	36	10	95	87
5	Karen L. Thurman	D	4	45	unopp.	62	75	84	77	75	15	19
6	Cliff Stearns	R	8	55	unopp.	67	90	94	33	5	100	94
7	John L. Mica	R	4	53	unopp.	62	94	96	33	0	100	96
8	Bill McCollum	R	16	52	unopp.	67	96	94	33	0	95	91
9	Michael Bilirakis	R	14	66	80	69	90	91	33	5	90	85
10	C. W. Bill Young	R	26	66	unopp.	67	90	92	40	5	88	84

(table continues)

Table A-2 (continued)

State, district	Representative	Party	Years of service[a]	Age	% vote in 1996 Primary	% vote in 1996 General	CC	PU	PS	ADA	ACU	ACU (career)
11	Jim Davis	D	0	39	56	58	—	—	—	—	—	—
12	Charles T. Canady	R	4	42	unopp.	62	94	93	37	5	85	88
13	Dan Miller	R	4	54	unopp.	64	82	92	39	10	95	88
14	Porter J. Goss	R	8	58	unopp.	73	84	92	39	10	95	87
15	Dave Weldon	R	2	43	unopp.	51	94	93	38	5	100	98
16	Mark Foley	R	2	42	unopp.	64	78	84	43	10	90	87
17	Carrie Meek	D	4	70	unopp.	89	46	91	81	85	5	6
18	Ileana Ros-Lehtinen	R	8	44	unopp.	unopp.	76	77	48	30	60	73
19	Robert Wexler	D	0	35	65	66	—	—	—	—	—	—
20	Peter Deutsch	D	4	39	unopp.	65	46	87	84	70	18	20
21	Lincoln Diaz-Balart	R	4	42	unopp.	unopp.	90	77	51	30	60	70
22	E. Clay Shaw, Jr.	R	16	57	unopp.	62	92	90	40	10	95	85
23	Alcee L. Hastings	D	4	60	unopp.	73	47	93	86	95	0	4
Georgia												
1	Jack Kingston	R	4	41	unopp.	68	90	92	31	5	100	99
2	Sanford D. Bishop, Jr.	D	4	47	59	54	90	75	73	60	30	22
3	Mac Collins	R	4	52	unopp.	61	98	98	32	5	100	97
4	Cynthia McKinney	D	4	41	67	58	4	98	80	100	0	3
5	John Lewis	D	10	56	unopp.	unopp.	10	98	84	100	0	3
6	Newt Gingrich	R	18	53	unopp.	58	100	97	25	0	100	90
7	Bob Barr	R	2	48	unopp.	58	98	97	30	5	100	96
8	Saxby Chambliss	R	2	53	unopp.	53	100	96	35	0	100	98
9	Nathan Deal	R	4	54	unopp.	66	94	92	37	5	90	74

	Name	Party										
10	Charlie Norwood	R	2	55	unopp.	52	100	98	31	0	100	100
11	John Linder	R	4	54	unopp.	64	98	96	35	0	100	96
Hawaii												
1	Neil Abercrombie	D	6	58	72	50	47	90	78	90	0	2
2	Patsy T. Mink	D	19	69	60	60	25	95	78	95	5	3
Idaho												
1	Helen Chenoweth	R	2	58	68	50	92	92	28	10	95	93
2	Michael D. Crapo	R	4	45	86	69	96	95	36	0	95	91
Illinois												
1	Bobby L. Rush	D	4	50	89	86	10	96	84	95	0	2
2	Jesse Jackson, Jr.	D	2	31	unopp.	94	12	96	85	100	0	0
3	William O. Lipinski	D	14	59	unopp.	65	59	63	65	70	40	38
4	Luis V. Gutierrez	D	4	43	71	94	6	95	83	100	0	5
5	Rod R. Blagojevich	D	0	39	50	64	—	—	—	—	—	—
6	Henry J. Hyde	R	22	72	84	64	94	93	39	10	90	87
7	Danny K. Davis	D	0	55	33	82	—	—	—	—	—	—
8	Philip M. Crane	R	27	66	75	62	96	98	35	0	100	99
9	Sidney R. Yates	D	46	87	84	63	7	96	79	85	0	4
10	John E. Porter	R	17	61	68	69	58	81	42	25	80	64
11	Jerry Weller	R	2	39	unopp.	52	84	84	41	5	84	87
12	Jerry F. Costello	D	9	47	unopp.	72	60	75	67	70	30	31
13	Harris W. Fawell	R	12	67	unopp.	60	78	85	43	10	85	80
14	Dennis Hastert	R	10	54	unopp.	64	100	96	37	0	100	91
15	Thomas W. Ewing	R	6	61	unopp.	57	94	94	35	0	100	96
16	Donald Manzullo	R	4	52	unopp.	60	82	94	33	5	100	99
17	Lane Evans	D	14	45	unopp.	52	14	95	75	95	0	4
18	Ray LaHood	R	2	51	unopp.	59	76	84	39	10	80	76

Table A-2 *(continued)*

State, district	Representative	Party	Years of service[a]	Age	% vote in 1996 Primary	% vote in 1996 General	CC	PU	PS	ADA	ACU	ACU (career)
19	Glenn Poshard	D	8	51	unopp.	67	63	68	61	70	45	35
20	John M. Shimkus	R	0	38	51	50	—	—	—	—	—	—
Indiana												
1	Peter J. Visclosky	D	12	47	84	69	41	82	75	85	15	9
2	David McIntosh	R	2	38	86	58	96	95	36	0	100	100
3	Tim Roemer	D	6	40	unopp.	58	63	64	68	60	40	14
4	Mark Souder	R	2	46	82	58	92	92	37	10	95	98
5	Steve Buyer	R	4	38	unopp.	65	98	94	37	5	95	96
6	Dan Burton	R	14	58	unopp.	75	94	96	35	10	100	97
7	Ed A. Pease	R	0	45	30	62	—	—	—	—	—	—
8	John N. Hostettler	R	2	35	82	50	90	91	38	20	95	90
9	Lee H. Hamilton	D	32	65	86	56	88	56	63	45	45	23
10	Julia M. Carson	D	0	58	49	53	—	—	—	—	—	—
Iowa												
1	Jim Leach	R	20	54	unopp.	53	59	69	58	40	37	41
2	Jim Nussle	R	6	36	unopp.	53	90	96	33	5	95	83
3	Leonard L. Boswell	D	0	62	58	49	—	—	—	—	—	—
4	Greg Ganske	R	2	47	unopp.	52	61	84	45	20	83	78
5	Tom Latham	R	2	48	unopp.	65	94	96	32	0	95	90
Kansas												
1	Jerry Moran	R	0	42	76	73	—	—	—	—	—	—
2	Jim Ryun[c]	R	0	49	62	52	—	—	—	—	—	—

District	Name	Party										
3	Vince Snowbarger	R	0	47	44	50	—	—	—	—	—	—
4	Todd Tiahrt	R	2	45	unopp.	50	88	93	34	5	100	100
Kentucky												
1	Edward Whitfield	R	2	53	unopp.	54	98	89	38	5	85	89
2	Ron Lewis	R	3	50	unopp.	58	96	95	37	5	100	97
3	Anne M. Northup	R	0	48	unopp.	50	—	—	—	—	—	—
4	Jim Bunning	R	10	65	unopp.	68	98	96	33	5	100	96
5	Harold Rogers	R	16	59	unopp.	unopp.	100	91	39	10	95	84
6	Scotty Baesler	D	4	55	unopp.	56	76	70	73	60	25	31
Louisiana												
1	Bob Livingston	R	20	53	unopp.	—[d]	98	92	39	0	95	88
2	William J. Jefferson	D	6	49	unopp.	—[d]	54	90	79	85	5	6
3	W. J. Tauzin	R	17	53	unopp.	—[d]	98	93	35	0	90	71
4	Jim McCrery	R	9	47	71	—[d]	98	92	37	0	95	6
5	John Cooksey	R	0	55	34	58[d]	—	—	—	—	—	—
6	Richard Baker	R	10	48	69	53	100	94	34	0	95	92
7	Chris John	D	0	36	26							
Maine												
1	Tom H. Allen	D	0	51	52	55	—	—	—	—	—	—
2	John E. Baldacci	D	2	41	unopp.	72	47	89	86	80	10	15
Maryland												
1	Wayne T. Gilchrest	R	6	49	65	62	76	84	46	20	80	66
2	Robert L. Ehrlich, Jr.	R	2	39	83	62	96	94	33	10	100	82
3	Benjamin L. Cardin	D	10	53	90	67	38	87	83	75	11	6
4	Albert R. Wynn	D	4	45	85	85	37	91	86	90	0	4
5	Steny H. Hoyer	D	16	57	84	57	69	87	86	85	5	6
6	Roscoe G. Bartlett	R	4	70	85	57	96	95	30	0	100	100

(table continues)

Table A-2 *(continued)*

State, district	Representative	Party	Years of service[a]	Age	% vote in 1996 Primary	% vote in 1996 General	CC	PU	PS	ADA	ACU	ACU (career)
7	Elijah E. Cummings[e]	D	1	45	37	83	18	94	76	92	0	4
8	Constance A. Morella	R	10	65	65	61	38	56	73	50	30	25
Massachusetts												
1	John W. Olver	D	6	60	unopp.	53	6	98	85	95	0	2
2	Richard E. Neal	D	8	47	unopp.	72	18	93	81	75	11	9
3	Jim P. McGovern	D	0	46	unopp.	53	—	—	—	—	—	—
4	Barney Frank	D	16	56	unopp.	72	4	94	79	100	0	4
5	Martin T. Meehan	D	4	40	85	unopp.	8	93	87	85	0	16
6	John F. Tierney	D	0	45	86	48	—	—	—	—	—	—
7	Edward J. Markey	D	20	50	unopp.	70	0	97	81	95	0	4
8	Joseph P. Kennedy II	D	10	44	unopp.	84	4	95	84	95	0	5
9	Joe J. Moakley	D	24	69	unopp.	72	12	93	78	65	6	7
10	William D. Delahunt	D	0	55	37	54	—	—	—	—	—	—
Michigan												
1	Bart Stupak	D	4	44	unopp.	71	37	84	73	75	20	22
2	Peter Hoekstra	R	4	43	unopp.	65	66	91	34	10	95	88
3	Vernon J. Ehlers	R	3	62	unopp.	69	63	79	43	25	79	78
4	Dave Camp	R	5	43	unopp.	65	72	89	37	0	95	88
5	James A. Barcia	D	4	44	unopp.	97	75	69	71	45	47	46
6	Fred Upton	R	10	43	unopp.	52	55	82	39	10	85	72
7	Nick Smith	R	4	62	75	55	77	89	35	10	95	95
8	Debbie Stabenow	D	0	46	unopp.	54	—	—	—	—	—	—
9	Dale E. Kildee	D	20	67	unopp.	59	51	85	76	75	15	9

District	Representative	Party										
10	David E. Bonior	D	20	51	unopp.	54	19	95	79	95	5	4
11	Joe Knollenberg	R	4	63	unopp.	61	98	93	38	0	95	95
12	Sander M. Levin	D	14	65	unopp.	57	31	94	89	85	0	3
13	Lynn Rivers	D	2	40	unopp.	57	18	91	77	95	5	11
14	John Conyers, Jr.	D	32	67	unopp.	86	2	97	76	90	0	5
15	Carolyn C. Kilpatrick	D	0	51	51	88	—	—	—	—	—	—
16	John D. Dingell	D	41	70	unopp.	62	52	85	78	70	25	9
Minnesota												
1	Gil Gutknecht	R	2	45	unopp.	53	81	89	37	5	100	98
2	David Minge	D	4	54	unopp.	55	30	78	73	70	15	20
3	Jim Ramstad	R	6	50	unopp.	70	48	79	46	35	70	70
4	Bruce F. Vento	D	20	56	unopp.	57	6	97	89	95	0	3
5	Martin O. Sabo	D	18	58	unopp.	64	18	96	87	90	0	3
6	Bill Luther	D	2	51	unopp.	56	22	84	81	80	0	12
7	Collin C. Peterson	D	6	52	unopp.	68	63	61	61	55	53	41
8	James L. Oberstar	D	22	62	unopp.	67	22	88	76	80	20	8
Mississippi												
1	Roger F. Wicker	R	2	45	unopp.	68	100	96	35	0	100	90
2	Bennie G. Thompson	D	4	48	unopp.	60	64	91	81	90	5	10
3	Charles W. Pickering, Jr.	R	0	33	56	61	—	—	—	—	—	—
4	Mike Parker	R	8	47	unopp.	61	100	95	37	0	100	71
5	Gene Taylor	D	8	43	94	58	86	45	53	80	30	77
Missouri												
1	William L. Clay	D	28	65	78	70	12	96	76	80	6	4
2	James M. Talent	R	4	40	unopp.	61	90	93	32	10	100	97
3	Richard A. Gephardt	D	20	55	75	59	35	93	82	85	6	11
4	Ike Skelton	D	20	65	unopp.	64	100	58	66	40	50	52
5	Karen McCarthy	D	2	49	unopp.	67	22	87	84	80	5	15

(table continues)

Table A-2 (continued)

State, district	Representative	Party	Years of service[a]	Age	% vote in 1996 Primary	% vote in 1996 General	CC	PU	PS	ADA	ACU	ACU (career)
6	Pat Danner	D	4	62	77	69	63	67	63	55	45	27
7	Roy Blunt	R	0	46	56	65	—	—	—	—	—	—
8	Jo Ann Emerson[f]	R	0	46	—	50	—	—	—	—	—	—
9	Kenny Hulshof	R	0	38	50	49	—	—	—	—	—	—
Montana												
AL	Rick Hill	R	0	49	44	52	—	—	—	—	—	—
Nebraska												
1	Doug Bereuter	R	18	57	unopp.	70	82	82	51	50	60	69
2	Jon Christensen	R	2	33	97	57	90	94	35	5	100	96
3	Bill Barrett	R	6	67	unopp.	77	96	92	41	0	95	90
Nevada												
1	John Ensign	R	2	38	unopp.	50	68	80	40	5	85	91
2	Jim Gibbons	R	0	51	42	59	—	—	—	—	—	—
New Hampshire												
1	John E. Sununu	R	0	32	28	50	—	—	—	—	—	—
2	Charles F. Bass	R	2	44	66	50	80	91	34	0	100	86
New Jersey												
1	Robert E. Andrews	D	6	39	unopp.	76	43	83	77	65	25	27
2	Frank A. LoBiondo	R	2	50	unopp.	60	53	76	44	25	70	75
3	H. James Saxton	R	12	53	unopp.	64	83	85	40	15	84	79
4	Christopher H. Smith	R	16	43	unopp.	64	76	82	46	30	80	54

	Member	Party										
5	Marge Roukema	R	16	67	75	71	44	68	53	50	53	50
6	Frank Pallone, Jr.	D	8	45	unopp.	61	25	91	81	90	10	21
7	Bob Franks	R	4	45	unopp.	55	40	72	52	35	63	62
8	William J. Pascrell, Jr.	D	0	59	unopp.	51	—	—	—	—	—	—
9	Steven R. Rothman	D	0	44	79	56	—	—	—	—	—	—
10	Donald M. Payne	D	8	62	82	84	6	98	78	95	0	4
11	Rodney Frelinghuysen	R	2	50	unopp.	66	81	80	54	30	75	68
12	Michael Pappas	R	0	35	38	50	—	—	—	—	—	—
13	Robert Menendez	D	4	43	93	79	27	94	80	85	5	9
New Mexico												
1	Steven H. Schiff	R	8	49	unopp.	57	87	76	56	25	63	72
2	Joe Skeen	R	16	69	70	56	98	89	42	5	90	83
3	Bill Redmond[g]	D	14	49	unopp.	—	—	—	—	—	—	18
New York												
1	Michael P. Forbes	R	2	44	unopp.	55	91	76	43	15	84	82
2	Rick A. Lazio	R	4	38	unopp.	64	76	76	46	15	75	68
3	Peter T. King	R	4	52	88	55	85	83	49	20	79	79
4	Carolyn McCarthy	D	0	52	unopp.	57	—	—	—	—	—	—
5	Gary L. Ackerman	D	14	54	unopp.	64	33	96	89	85	0	4
6	Floyd H. Flake[h]	D	8	51	unopp.	85	26	94	86	80	6	2
7	Thomas J. Manton	D	12	64	82	71	66	80	75	65	26	14
8	Jerrold Nadler	D	4	49	unopp.	82	4	96	77	100	0	4
9	Charless E. Schumer	D	16	46	unopp.	75	24	91	83	90	5	4
10	Edolphus Towns	D	14	62	unopp.	91	9	97	79	85	0	3
11	Major R. Owens	D	14	60	unopp.	92	2	98	80	95	0	3
12	Nydia M. Velazquez	D	4	43	unopp.	85	2	96	79	100	0	3
13	Vito J. Fossella[i]	R	7	38	unopp.	62	81	84	41	20	88	72
14	Carolyn B. Maloney	D	4	48	unopp.	72	13	96	86	85	5	2

(table continues)

Table A-2 *(continued)*

State, district	Representative	Party	Years of service[a]	Age	% vote in 1996 Primary	% vote in 1996 General	CC	PU	PS	ADA	ACU	ACU (career)
15	Charles B. Rangel	D	26	66	unopp.	91	8	97	82	95	0	5
16	José E. Serrano	D	7	53	unopp.	96	12	96	82	95	0	2
17	Eliot L. Engel	D	8	49	77	85	22	95	84	95	0	6
18	Nita M. Lowey	D	8	59	unopp.	64	10	95	86	90	0	5
19	Sue Kelly	R	2	60	53	46	84	83	47	10	70	67
20	Benjamin A. Gilman	R	24	74	unopp.	57	78	63	61	35	45	45
21	Michael R. McNulty	D	8	49	57	66	39	83	72	60	22	26
22	Gerald B. H. Solomon	R	18	66	unopp.	60	98	96	37	5	95	89
23	Sherwood L. Boehlert	R	14	60	65	64	78	68	56	50	50	35
24	John M. McHugh	R	4	48	unopp.	71	88	85	42	10	79	82
25	James T. Walsh	R	8	49	unopp.	55	96	79	47	20	68	67
26	Maurice D. Hinchey	D	4	58	unopp.	55	20	93	78	95	5	6
27	Bill Paxon	R	8	42	unopp.	60	100	98	35	0	100	92
28	Louise M. Slaughter	D	10	67	unopp.	57	18	94	84	90	5	7
29	John J. LaFalce	D	22	57	unopp.	62	24	91	82	80	5	14
30	Jack Quinn	R	4	45	unopp.	55	80	70	58	35	58	63
31	Amo Houghton	R	10	70	unopp.	72	83	77	61	20	60	59
North Carolina												
1	Eva Clayton	D	4	62	unopp.	66	38	94	86	100	5	4
2	Bob Etheridge	D	0	55	unopp.	53	—	—	—	—	—	—
3	Walter B. Jones, Jr.	R	2	53	unopp.	63	94	93	30	5	100	98
4	David E. Price[j]	D	0	56	unopp.	54	—	—	—	—	—	—
5	Richard Burr	R	2	40	unopp.	62	96	96	32	5	100	94
6	Howard Coble	R	12	65	unopp.	73	88	95	30	15	90	88

7	Mike McIntyre	D	0	40	52	53	—	—	—	—	—	—
8	William G. Hefner	D	22	66	unopp.	55	94	76	71	55	30	30
9	Sue Myrick	R	2	55	unopp.	63	92	96	33	10	100	98
10	Cass Ballenger	R	10	70	unopp.	70	100	95	33	0	100	90
11	Charles H. Taylor	R	6	55	unopp.	58	100	95	33	5	100	94
12	Melvin L. Watt	D	4	51	unopp.	71	16	98	84	90	0	4
North Dakota												
AL	Earl Pomeroy	D	4	44	unopp.	55	67	80	81	80	11	18
Ohio												
1	Steve Chabot	R	2	43	unopp.	54	67	87	35	15	100	100
2	Rob Portman	R	4	41	unopp.	72	90	92	37	10	100	90
3	Tony P. Hall	D	18	54	unopp.	64	52	79	71	65	15	15
4	Michael G. Oxley	R	16	52	unopp.	65	98	93	37	5	100	89
5	Paul E. Gillmor	R	8	57	unopp.	61	73	91	40	15	84	81
6	Ted Strickland[k]	D	0	55	unopp.	51	—	—	—	—	—	—
7	David L. Hobson	R	6	60	86	68	94	90	38	0	90	78
8	John A. Boehner	R	6	47	unopp.	70	98	97	34	0	100	97
9	Marcy Kaptur	D	14	50	unopp.	77	31	84	75	75	15	11
10	Dennis J. Kucinich	D	0	50	77	49	—	—	—	—	—	—
11	Louis Stokes	D	28	71	unopp.	81	14	95	80	65	0	6
12	John R. Kasich	R	14	44	88	64	86	91	41	15	95	86
13	Sherrod Brown	D	4	44	unopp.	60	6	96	84	95	0	14
14	Tom C. Sawyer	D	10	51	80	54	37	93	88	90	0	3
15	Deborah Pryce	R	4	45	86	71	88	89	40	5	85	78
16	Ralph Regula	R	24	72	84	69	94	86	48	15	75	56
17	James A. Traficant, Jr.	D	12	55	unopp.	91	92	51	57	55	50	20
18	Bob Ney	R	2	42	unopp.	50	88	90	39	10	85	85

(table continues)

Table A-2 *(continued)*

State, district	Representative	Party	Years of service[a]	Age	% vote in 1996 Primary	% vote in 1996 General	CC	PU	PS	ADA	ACU	ACU (career)
19	Steven LaTourette	R	2	42	unopp.	55	90	85	45	15	80	80
Oklahoma												
1	Steve Largent	R	2	41	unopp.	68	92	96	30	10	100	100
2	Tom Coburn	R	2	47	unopp.	55	86	91	29	10	89	95
3	Wes Watkins[l]	R	0	57	79	51	—	—	—	—	100	98
4	J. C. Watts, Jr.	R	2	39	unopp.	58	98	93	32	0	100	98
5	Ernest J. Istook	R	4	46	unopp.	70	98	96	32	10	100	98
6	Frank D. Lucas	R	3	36	unopp.	64	100	96	34	0	100	96
Oregon												
1	Elizabeth Furse	D	4	60	unopp.	52	12	93	81	80	5	9
2	Robert F. Smith[m]	R	0	65	82	62	—	—	—	—	—	—
3	Earl Blumenauer	D	0	48	78	68	—	—	—	—	—	—
4	Peter A. DeFazio	D	10	49	unopp.	66	18	89	71	95	5	9
5	Darlene Hooley	D	0	57	51	51	—	—	—	—	—	—
Pennsylvania												
1	Thomas M. Foglietta	D	16	68	73	88	9	96	86	85	5	3
2	Chaka Fattah	D	2	40	unopp.	88	6	98	83	95	0	2
3	Robert A. Borski	D	14	48	91	69	37	86	82	80	10	13
4	Ron Klink	D	4	45	unopp.	64	62	75	63	65	30	29
5	John E. Peterson	R	0	57	38	60	—	—	—	—	—	64
6	Tim Holden	D	4	39	unopp.	59	78	62	61	45	47	44
7	Curt Weldon	R	10	49	83	67	88	85	45	15	84	68
8	James Greenwood	R	4	45	60	59	80	78	49	25	60	68

District	Name	Party										
9	Bud Shuster	R	24	64	unopp.	74	92	93	34	0	100	93
10	Joseph M. McDade	R	34	65	53	60	95	87	42	5	75	59
11	Paul E. Kanjorski	D	12	59	unopp.	68	55	78	68	65	30	22
12	John P. Murtha	D	23	64	unopp.	70	90	65	77	55	25	36
13	Jon D. Fox	R	2	49	unopp.	49	66	77	44	35	65	73
14	William J. Coyne	D	16	60	66	61	10	94	81	100	0	3
15	Paul McHale	D	4	46	unopp.	55	53	77	72	70	20	21
16	Joseph R. Pitts	R	0	57	45	59	—	—	—	—	—	—
17	George W. Gekas	R	14	66	unopp.	72	98	96	35	0	100	85
18	Mike Doyle	D	2	43	74	56	63	66	66	55	32	34
19	William F. Goodling	R	22	69	55	63	88	88	37	10	95	75
20	Frank Mascara	D	2	66	unopp.	54	76	70	70	60	35	38
21	Phil English	R	2	40	unopp.	51	83	81	46	10	74	79
Rhode Island												
1	Patrick J. Kennedy	D	2	29	unopp.	69	35	86	75	85	10	13
2	Robert A. Weygand	D	0	48	48	64	—	—	—	—	—	—
South Carolina												
1	Mark Sanford	R	2	36	unopp.	96	63	84	44	10	95	92
2	Floyd Spence	R	26	68	unopp.	90	100	96	35	5	100	89
3	Lindsey Graham	R	2	41	unopp.	60	98	96	35	0	100	98
4	Bob Inglis	R	4	37	unopp.	71	94	95	34	10	100	98
5	John M. Spratt, Jr.	D	14	54	unopp.	54	75	80	73	60	25	24
6	James E. Clyburn	D	4	56	88	69	65	91	84	95	5	13
South Dakota												
AL	John R. Thune	R	0	35	59	58	—	—	—	—	—	—
Tennessee												
1	William Jenkins	R	0	59	18	64	—	—	—	—	—	—

(table continues)

Table A-2 *(continued)*

State, district	Representative	Party	Years of service[a]	Age	% vote in 1996 Primary	% vote in 1996 General	CC	PU	PS	ADA	ACU	ACU (career)
2	John J. Duncan, Jr.	R	8	49	unopp.	71	60	82	32	30	85	87
3	Zach Wamp	R	2	39	unopp.	56	75	89	31	15	100	100
4	Van Hilleary	R	2	37	unopp.	58	86	93	32	0	95	98
5	Bob Clement	D	9	53	unopp.	72	86	69	73	60	30	27
6	Bart Gordon	D	12	47	89	54	80	66	63	45	50	21
7	Ed Bryant	R	2	48	unopp.	64	98	96	35	0	100	100
8	John Tanner	D	8	52	unopp.	67	100	63	67	45	47	44
9	Harold E. Ford, Jr.	D	0	26	60	61	—	—	—	—	—	—
Texas												
1	Max Sandlin	D	0	44	56	52	—	—	—	—	—	—
2	Jim Turner	D	0	50	59	52	—	—	—	—	—	—
3	Sam Johnson	R	6	66	unopp.	73	98	96	38	5	100	98
4	Ralph M. Hall	D	16	73	unopp.	64	92	29	44	15	90	79
5	Pete Sessions	R	0	41		53	—	—	—	—	—	10
6	Joe Barton	R	12	47	89	77	94	94	37	15	89	94
7	Bill Archer	R	26	68	unopp.	81	96	97	35	5	100	97
8	Kevin Brady[n]	R	0	41		59	—	—	—	—	—	96
9	Nick Lampson[o]	D	0	51		53	—	—	—	—	—	92
10	Lloyd Doggett	D	2	50	unopp.	56	29	90	90	80	0	4
11	Chet Edwards	D	6	45	unopp.	57	92	72	73	60	20	33
12	Kay Granger	R	0	53	69	58	—	—	—	—	—	66
13	William Thornberry	R	2	38	unopp.	67	100	97	35	0	100	98
14	Ron Paul[p]	R	0	61	54	51	—	—	—	—	—	63

District	Member	Party										
15	Rubén Hinojosa	D	0	56	52	62	—	—	—	—	—	41
16	Silvestre Reyes	D	0	51	51	71	—	—	—	—	—	16
17	Charles W. Stenholm	D	18	58	unopp.	52	90	50	53	50	65	77
18	Shelia Jackson-Lee	D	2	46	unopp.	77	43	93	88	90	5	3
19	Larry Combest	R	12	51	unopp.	80	100	96	35	0	95	98
20	Henry B. Gonzalez	D	35	80	unopp.	64	68	84	84	80	15	15
21	Lamar Smith	R	10	49	unopp.	76	98	95	35	10	100	92
22	Tom DeLay	R	12	42	unopp.	68	98	96	35	0	100	97
23	Henry Bonilla	R	4	55	unopp.	62	96	90	36	0	85	91
24	Martin Frost	D	18	37	64	56	90	79	83	65	10	18
25	Ken Bentsen	D	2	56	unopp.	57	82	78	81	75	10	9
26	Dick Armey	R	12	59	70	74	96	96	38	0	100	97
27	Solomon P. Ortiz	D	14	51	unopp.	65	94	70	67	60	37	32
28	Frank Tejeda[q]	D	4	49		72	—	—	—	—	37	36
29	Gene Green	D	4	49		68	70	82	78	60	28	20
30	Eddie B. Johnson	D	4	61	unopp.	55	55	91	87	80	0	7
Utah												
1	James V. Hansen	R	16	64	unopp.	68	98	94	41	0	100	94
2	Merrill Cook	R	0	50	52	55	—	—	—	—	—	—
3	Christopher B. Cannon	R	0	46	56	51	—	—	—	—	—	—
Vermont												
AL	Bernard Sanders	I	6	55	—	55	14	93	75	100	0	6
Virginia												
1	Herbert H. Bateman	R	14	68	80	unopp.	96	91	41	15	85	80
2	Owen B. Pickett	D	10	66	unopp.	65	92	57	68	45	50	44
3	Robert C. Scott	D	4	49	unopp.	82	59	90	85	90	0	9
4	Norman Sisisky	D	14	69	unopp.	79	100	52	61	35	55	41
5	Virgil H. Goode, Jr.	D	0	50	unopp.	60	—	—	—	—	—	41

Table A-2 (continued)

State, district	Representative	Party	Years of service[a]	Age	% vote in 1996 Primary	% vote in 1996 General	CC	PU	PS	ADA	ACU	ACU (career)
6	Robert W. Goodlatte	R	4	44	unopp.	67	88	93	30	5	95	92
7	Thomas J. Bliley, Jr.	R	16	64	unopp.	75	100	94	34	0	100	91
8	James P. Moran	D	6	51	unopp.	66	45	83	77	65	20	15
9	Rick Boucher	D	14	50	unopp.	65	72	78	73	65	15	13
10	Frank Wolf	R	16	57	unopp.	72	88	90	38	5	95	83
11	Thomas Davis	R	2	47	unopp.	64	84	78	52	15	79	70
Washington												
1	Rick White	R	2	43	50	54	88	92	44	0	95	84
2	Jack Metcalf	R	2	69	52	49	80	86	38	0	90	95
3	Linda Smith	R	2	46	52	50	90	90	36	5	84	90
4	Richard Hastings	R	2	55	55	53	98	97	33	0	100	96
5	George R. Nethercutt	R	2	52	51	56	98	94	33	0	95	92
6	Norm D. Dicks	D	20	56	67	66	59	84	88	65	0	10
7	Jim McDermott	D	8	60	79	81	8	97	82	95	0	2
8	Jennifer Dunn	R	4	55	65	65	92	94	38	0	100	90
9	Adam Smith	D	0	31	49	50	—	—	—	—	—	—
West Virginia												
1	Alan B. Mollohan	D	14	53	unopp.	unopp.	77	71	72	65	15	31
2	Bob Wise	D	14	48	86	69	64	82	85	70	10	12
3	Nick Rahall II	D	20	47	unopp.	unopp.	51	81	70	75	20	16
Wisconsin												
1	Mark W. Neumann	R	2	42	unopp.	51	51	85	43	15	95	98
2	Scott Klug	R	6	43	unopp.	57	51	75	46	40	75	60
3	Ron Kind	D	0	33	46	52	—	—	—	—	—	—

4	Gerald D. Kleczka	D	13	53	85	58	25	84	78	75	10	9
5	Thomas M. Barrett	D	4	42	unopp.	73	2	89	86	85	5	8
6	Tom E. Petri	R	18	56	unopp.	73	65	83	46	20	100	75
7	David Obey	D	28	58	unopp.	57	31	85	77	75	25	7
8	Jay Johnson	D	0	53	59	52						
9	F. James Sensenbrenner, Jr.	R	18	53	unopp.	74	61	85	37	20	100	6
Wyoming												
AL	Barbara Cubin	R	2	50	unopp.	55	98	96	31	0	100	95

Note: In compiling this table, we calculated the conservative coalition, party unity, and presidential support scores to eliminate the effects of absences as follows: support = support/(support + opposition).

a. Service beginning in or after November in a given year is not counted as a year of service.

b. Juanita Millender-McDonald was elected on March 26, 1996, to replace Walter Tucker III, who resigned in December 1995.

c. Jim Ryun began service on November 27, 1996, as a member of the 104th Congress after the early resignation of Sam Brownback from the U.S. House of Representatives.

d. Louisiana has a two-step election process in which candidates of all parties run against one another in a September primary. If no candidate wins 50 percent or more of the vote at that time, the top two candidates run against each other in November. If a clear winner emerges from the September primary, no candidates compete in the November election.

e. Cummings was elected on April 16, 1996, to replace Kweisi Mfume, who resigned in February 1996.

f. Emerson was elected on November 5, 1996, to fill the vacancy created when her husband, Bill Emerson, died of lung cancer. Emerson began service as a member of the 104th Congress on November 8, 1996.

g. Redmond won a special election with 43 percent of the vote on May 20, 1997.

h. Flake was replaced by Gregory W. Meeks in a 1998 special election.

i. Fossella won a special election with 61 percent of the vote on November 5, 1997.

j. Price was reelected to the U.S. House of Representatives after not serving from 1995–1997. Price had originally been elected to the House in 1986.

k. Strickland was reelected to the U.S. House of Representatives after not serving from 1995–1997. Strickland had originally been elected to the House in 1992.

l. Watkins was reelected to the U.S. House of Representatives after not serving from 1991–1997. Watkins had originally been elected to the House in 1976.

m. Smith was reelected to the U.S. House of Representatives after not serving from 1995–1997. Smith had originally been elected to the House in 1982.

n. Brady was elected to the U.S. House of Representatives after winning a December 10, 1996, runoff election.

o. Lampson was elected to the U.S. House of Representatives after winning a December 10, 1996, runoff election.

p. Paul was reelected to the U.S. House of Representatives after not serving from 1977–1979, 1985–1987, and 1995–1997. Paul had originally been elected to the House in 1976.

q. Tejeda died of cancer on January 30, 1997. A special election was held on March 15, 1997, to fill the remainder of Tejeda's term.

Sources: Congressional Quarterly Almanac, various years; *Congressional Quarterly Weekly Report*, various years; American Conservative Union; Americans for Democratic Action.

Table A-3   Senate, 106th Congress, 1999

State, senator	Party	Years of service[a]	Age	Previous Senate election			1998 voting ratings					
				Year	Primary (%)	General (%)	CC	PU	PS	ADA	ACU	ACU (career)
Alabama												
Richard C. Shelby	R	12	64	1998	unopp.	unopp.	100	91	34	5	92	71
Jeff Sessions	R	2	52	1996	59	52	100	98	28	0	100	100
Alaska												
Ted Stevens	R	30	75	1996	59	77	88	82	54	20	56	64
Frank H. Murkowski	R	18	65	1992	81	53	88	93	42	5	78	79
Arizona												
John McCain	R	12	62	1998	unopp.	68	75	84	49	20	68	86
Jon Kyl	R	4	56	1994	unopp.	54	88	96	33	0	96	96
Arkansas												
Tim Hutchinson	R	2	51	1996	unopp.	53	83	98	26	5	100	100
Blanche Lincoln	D	0	38	1998	62	55						
California												
Dianne Feinstein	D	6	63	1994	74	47	50	87	88	90	4	10
Barbara Boxer	D	6	58	1998	44	53	38	90	90	95	4	3
Colorado												
Ben Nighthorse Campbell	R	6	65	1998	71	62	100	82	47	25	76	40
Wayne Allard	R	2	54	1996	57	51	100	97	28	5	100	97
Connecticut												
Christopher J. Dodd	D	18	54	1998	unopp.	unopp.	38	91	93	95	4	9
Joseph I. Lieberman	D	10	56	1994	unopp.	67	38	80	83	80	16	20
Delaware												
William V. Roth, Jr.	R	28	77	1994	unopp.	56	100	79	64	15	65	69
Joseph R. Biden, Jr.	D	26	56	1996	unopp.	60	50	87	91	85	4	13

State / Senator	Party											
Florida												
Bob Graham	D	12	62	1998	unopp.	63	88	87	83	85	4	18
Connie Mack	R	10	58	1994	unopp.	70	100	85	50	0	80	94
Georgia												
Paul Coverdell	R	6	59	1998	unopp.	52	100	92	40	0	92	95
Max Cleland	D	6	49	1996	unopp.	49	88	87	87	85	0	4
Hawaii												
Daniel K. Inouye	D	36	74	1998	93	79	57	93	87	80	9	7
Daniel K. Akaka	D	9	74	1994	unopp.	72	50	96	91	85	10	2
Idaho												
Larry E. Craig	R	8	53	1996	unopp.	57	100	99	29	5	84	94
Michael Crapo	R	0	47	1998	87	69						
Illinois												
Richard J. Durbin	D	2	53	1996	65	56	13	95	90	95	8	1
Peter G. Fitzgerald	R	0	38	1998	52	51						
Indiana												
Richard G. Lugar	R	22	66	1994	unopp.	67	50	84	54	0	68	81
Evan Bayh	D	0	43	1998	unopp.	64						
Iowa												
Charles E. Grassley	R	18	65	1998	unopp.	68	75	86	39	5	80	80
Tom Harkin	D	14	59	1996	unopp.	52	13	98	88	95	5	9
Kansas												
Sam Brownback	R	2	42	1998	unopp.	65	88	96	37	0	92	97
Pat Roberts	R	0	62	1996	78	62	88	95	35	0	84	87
Kentucky												
Mitch McConnell	R	14	56	1996	89	55	100	95	39	0	92	89
Jim Bunning	R	0	67	1998	74	50						

(table continues)

Table A-3 *(continued)*

State, senator	Party	Years of service[a]	Age	Previous Senate election			1998 voting ratings					
				Year	Primary (%)	General (%)	CC	PU	PS	ADA	ACU	ACU (career)
Louisiana												
John B. Breaux	D	12	54	1998	unopp.	64	100	73	79	75	20	46
Mary L. Landrieu	D	2	42	1996	22	50	75	89	86	90	8	12
Maine												
Olympia J. Snowe	R	4	51	1994	unopp.	60	75	65	55	35	40	50
Susan M. Collins	R	2	45	1996	55	49	88	67	63	35	36	42
Maryland												
Paul S. Sarbanes	D	22	65	1994	79	59	25	99	92	95	4	6
Barbara A. Mikulski	D	12	62	1998	84	71	38	97	91	90	4	5
Massachusetts												
Edward M. Kennedy	D	36	66	1994	unopp.	58	0	100	96	95	0	3
John Kerry	D	14	55	1996	unopp.	57	38	95	94	75	4	5
Michigan												
Carl Levin	D	20	60	1996	unopp.	58	13	98	93	90	0	7
Spencer Abraham	R	4	46	1994	52	52	88	91	46	5	96	82
Minnesota												
Paul D. Wellstone	D	8	54	1996	86	50	0	97	87	100	4	4
Rod Grams	R	4	50	1994	58	49	75	99	39	0	88	97
Mississippi												
Thad Cochran	R	20	60	1996	96	71	88	86	33	0	76	81
Trent Lott	R	10	57	1994	95	69	100	96	39	0	92	93
Missouri												
Christopher S. Bond	R	12	59	1998	87	53	100	88	38	15	72	81
John Ashcroft	R	4	54	1994	83	60	95	98	24	5	100	99

Montana												
Max Baucus	D	20	57	1996	unopp.	50	50	94	81	80	5	11
Conrad Burns	R	10	63	1994	unopp.	62	100	84	38	0	84	89
Nebraska												
J. Robert Kerrey	D	10	55	1994	unopp.	55	75	81	90	95	0	8
Chuck Hagel	R	2	52	1996	62	56	88	89	42	0	72	76
Nevada												
Harry Reid	D	12	59	1998	unopp.	48	63	81	79	90	20	22
Richard H. Bryan	D	10	61	1994	unopp.	51	38	90	88	95	8	19
New Hampshire												
Robert C. Smith[b]	R	8	57	1996	unopp.	49	100	99	19	5	100	96
Judd Gregg	R	6	49	1998	86	68	88	91	43	5	76	80
New Jersey												
Frank R. Lautenberg	D	16	74	1994	81	50	25	17	90	95	4	6
Robert G. Torricelli	D	2	47	1996	unopp.	53	63	85	78	85	8	2
New Mexico												
Pete V. Domenici	R	26	66	1996	unopp.	65	88	83	57	5	70	69
Jeff Bingaman	D	16	55	1994	unopp.	54	57	87	87	85	0	11
New York												
Daniel Patrick Moynihan	D	22	71	1994	75	55	25	89	78	95	8	6
Charles Schumer	D	0	48	1998	51	54						
North Carolina												
Jesse Helms	R	26	77	1996	unopp.	53	100	97	32	0	100	99
John Edwards	D	0	45	1998	51	51						
North Dakota												
Kent Conrad	D	12	50	1994	unopp.	58	50	87	75	90	16	19
Byron L. Dorgan	D	6	56	1998	unopp.	63	50	87	76	90	12	18

(table continues)

Table A-3 (continued)

| State, senator | Party | Years of service[a] | Age | Previous Senate election | | | 1998 voting ratings | | | | | |
				Year	Primary (%)	General (%)	CC	PU	PS	ADA	ACU	ACU (career)
Ohio												
Mike DeWine	R	4	51	1994	52	53	88	82	51	10	64	83
George Voinovich	R	0	62	1998	72	56						
Oklahoma												
Don Nickles	R	18	50	1998	unopp.	59	100	96	23	0	96	95
James M. Inhofe	R	4	64	1996	75	57	100	97	14	5	100	98
Oregon												
Ron Wyden	D	3	49	1998	92	61	57	88	85	100	4	10
Gordon H. Smith	R	2	46	1996	78	50	75	85	55	5	72	72
Pennsylvania												
Arlen Specter	R	18	68	1998	67	61	40	49	60	45	33	37
Rick Santorum	R	4	40	1994	82	49	88	91	40	0	84	83
Rhode Island												
John H. Chafee	R	22	76	1994	69	65	50	57	77	45	32	30
Jack Reed	D	2	48	1996	86	63	25	98	90	95	0	0
South Carolina												
Strom Thurmond	R	44	96	1996	60	53	88	91	44	0	76	90
Ernest F. Hollings	D	32	76	1998	unopp.	53	67	81	74	55	33	41
South Dakota												
Tom Daschle	D	12	50	1998	unopp.	62	38	90	90	90	4	15
Tim Johnson	D	2	51	1996	unopp.	51	13	93	89	90	4	1
Tennessee												
Bill Frist	R	4	46	1994	44	56	100	94	45	10	84	85
Fred Thompson	R	4	56	1996	94	61	88	87	42	5	80	80

State / Senator	Party			Year	Election %							
Texas												
Phil Gramm	R	14	56	1996	85	55	88	99	33	0	96	93
Kay Bailey Hutchison	R	6	55	1994	84	61	88	92	37	0	88	93
Utah												
Orrin G. Hatch	R	22	66	1994	unopp.	69	100	87	48	5	80	90
Robert F. Bennett	R	6	65	1998	unopp.	64	100	84	53	10	95	91
Vermont												
Patrick J. Leahy	D	24	58	1998	97	72	13	87	83	90	12	6
James M. Jeffords	R	10	64	1996	unopp.	50	43	49	69	55	24	29
Virginia												
John W. Warner	R	20	71	1996	65	52	63	83	39	20	79	80
Charles S. Robb	D	10	68	1994	58	46	75	83	90	80	12	20
Washington												
Slade Gorton	R	16	68	1994	53	56	100	83	49	0	72	62
Patty Murray	D	6	48	1998	46	58	50	91	82	90	4	1
West Virginia												
Robert C. Byrd	D	40	80	1994	85	69	25	72	74	80	16	27
John D. Rockefeller IV	D	14	61	1996	88	77	50	88	94	90	0	10
Wisconsin												
Herb Kohl	D	10	63	1994	90	58	25	87	86	85	4	3
Russell D. Feingold	D	6	45	1998	unopp.	51	38	86	83	90	12	14
Wyoming												
Craig Thomas	R	4	65	1994	unopp.	59	75	94	39	0	84	86
Michael B. Enzi	R	2	54	1996	32	54	75	96	31	5	92	90

Note: In compiling this table, we calculated the conservative coalition, party unity, and presidential support scores to eliminate the effects of absences as follows: support = support/(support + opposition).

a. Service beginning in or after November in a given year is not counted as a year of service.

b. Smith changed his party affiliation to Independent on July 12, 1999.

Sources: Congressional Quarterly Almanac, various years; *Congressional Quarterly Weekly Report*, various years; American Conservative Union; Americans for Democratic Action.

Table A-4 Senate, 105th Congress, 1997

State, senator	Party	Years of service[a]	Age	Previous Senate election			1996 voting ratings					
				Year	Primary (%)	General (%)	CC	PU	PS	ADA	ACU	ACU (career)
Alabama												
Richard C. Shelby	R	10	62	1992	unopp.	65	92	94	33	5	90	69
Jeff Sessions	R	0	49	1996	59	52	—	—	—	—	—	—
Alaska												
Ted Stevens	R	28	73	1996	59	77	92	90	45	20	80	65
Frank H. Murkowski	R	16	63	1992	81	53	97	96	36	15	95	80
Arizona												
John McCain	R	10	60	1992	unopp.	56	89	95	32	0	95	88
Jon Kyl	R	2	54	1994	unopp.	54	97	98	23	5	100	96
Arkansas												
Dale Bumpers	D	22	71	1992	65	60	21	91	88	85	0	14
Tim Hutchinson	R	0	49	1996	unopp.	53	—	—	—	—	—	—
California												
Dianne Feinstein	D	4	63	1994	74	47	53	81	90	95	20	13
Barbara Boxer	D	4	56	1992	44	48	18	94	90	100	5	3
Colorado												
Ben Nighthorse Campbell	R[b]	4	63	1992	unopp.	52	86	82	48	45	78	33
Wayne Allard	R	0	52	1996	57	51	—	—	—	—	—	—
Connecticut												
Christopher J. Dodd	D	16	52	1992	unopp.	59	38	89	81	85	10	9
Joseph I. Lieberman	D	8	54	1994	unopp.	67	63	76	90	75	33	21

State / Senator	Party											
Delaware												
William V. Roth, Jr.	R	26	75	1994	unopp.	56	86	90	43	10	85	69
Joseph R. Biden, Jr.	D	24	54	1996	unopp.	60	42	79	92	80	20	13
Florida												
Bob Graham	D	10	60	1992	84	65	61	81	86	85	15	21
Connie Mack	R	8	56	1994	unopp.	70	100	93	34	0	100	95
Georgia												
Paul Coverdell	R	4	57	1992	50	51	97	98	34	5	100	97
Max Cleland	D	4	47	1996	unopp.	49	—	—	—	—	—	—
Hawaii												
Daniel K. Inouye	D	34	72	1992	76	57	51	87	86	85	11	7
Daniel K. Akaka	D	7	72	1994	unopp.	72	26	95	88	95	5	2
Idaho												
Larry E. Craig	R	6	51	1996	unopp.	57	97	98	32	0	95	95
Dirk Kempthorne	R	4	45	1992	57	57	97	98	32	0	95	98
Illinois												
Carol Moseley-Braun	D	4	49	1992	38	53	24	89	84	90	5	4
Richard J. Durbin	D	0	51	1996	65	56	—	—	—	—	—	—
Indiana												
Richard G. Lugar	R	20	64	1994	unopp.	67	92	90	31	5	95	83
Daniel R. Coats	R	8	53	1992	unopp.	57	89	96	30	10	100	91
Iowa												
Charles E. Grassley	R	16	63	1992	unopp.	70	82	92	32	15	90	80
Tom Harkin	D	12	57	1996	unopp.	52	18	91	85	80	10	9

(table continues)

Table A-4 *(continued)*

| State, senator | Party | Years of service[a] | Age | Previous Senate election | | | 1996 voting ratings | | | | | |
				Year	Primary (%)	General (%)	CC	PU	PS	ADA	ACU	ACU (career)
Kansas												
Sam Brownback	R	0	40	1996	55	54	—	—	—	—	—	—
Pat Roberts	R	0	60	1996	78	62	—	—	—	—	—	—
Kentucky												
Wendell H. Ford	D	22	72	1992	unopp.	63	74	79	83	70	40	27
Mitch McConnell	R	12	54	1996	89	55	95	95	39	10	95	89
Louisiana												
John B. Breaux	D	10	52	1992	73	unopp.	84	70	78	60	20	48
Mary L. Landrieu	D	0	40	1996	22	50	—	—	—	—	—	—
Maine												
Olympia J. Snowe	R	2	49	1994	unopp.	60	79	72	53	35	70	51
Susan M. Collins	R	0	43	1996	55	49	—	—	—	—	—	—
Maryland												
Paul S. Sarbanes	D	20	63	1994	79	59	18	94	90	95	0	6
Barbara A. Mikulski	D	10	60	1992	77	71	32	92	90	95	0	5
Massachusetts												
Edward M. Kennedy	D	34	64	1994	unopp.	58	8	94	88	90	0	3
John Kerry	D	12	53	1996	unopp.	52	18	92	92	95	25	5
Michigan												
Carl Levin	D	18	62	1996	unopp.	58	29	94	86	85	5	8
Spencer Abraham	R	2	44	1994	52	52	95	95	37	15	95	9

State / Senator	Party			Year								
Minnesota												
Paul D. Wellstone	D	6	52	1996	86	50	11	92	85	95	5	4
Rod Grams	R	2	48	1994	58	49	92	98	36	5	95	98
Mississippi												
Thad Cochran	R	18	58	1996	95	71	94	93	40	5	94	82
Trent Lott	R	8	55	1994	95	69	97	97	34	5	100	94
Missouri												
Christopher S. Bond	R	10	57	1992	83	52	100	95	37	10	90	82
John Ashcroft	R	2	54	1994	83	60	89	98	29	5	100	96
Montana												
Max Baucus	D	18	55	1996	unopp.	50	45	73	90	85	20	12
Conrad Burns	R	8	61	1994	unopp.	62	95	97	29	5	100	90
Nebraska												
Bob Kerrey	D	8	53	1994	unopp.	55	32	88	86	85	5	9
Chuck Hagel	R	0	50	1996	62	56	—	—	—	—	—	—
Nevada												
Harry Reid	D	10	57	1992	53	51	53	79	78	85	15	23
Richard H. Bryan	D	8	59	1994	unopp.	51	50	82	78	85	10	22
New Hampshire												
Robert C. Smith	R	6	55	1996	unopp.	49	92	96	29	5	100	96
Judd Gregg	R	4	49	1992	50	48	89	91	34	5	75	81
New Jersey												
Frank R. Lautenberg	D	14	72	1994	81	50	11	93	90	95	0	7
Robert G. Torricelli	D	0	45	1996	unopp.	53	—	—	—	—	—	—

(table continues)

Table A-4 *(continued)*

State, senator	Party	Years of service[a]	Age	Previous Senate election			1996 voting ratings					
				Year	Primary (%)	General (%)	CC	PU	PS	ADA	ACU	ACU (career)
New Mexico												
Pete V. Domenici	R	24	64	1996	unopp.	65	94	90	42	20	85	69
Jeff Bingaman	D	14	53	1994	unopp.	54	37	88	84	95	0	13
New York												
Daniel Patrick Moynihan	D	20	69	1994	75	55	19	90	81	90	10	6
Alfonse M. D'Amato	R	16	59	1992	unopp.	49	89	87	48	25	75	58
North Carolina												
Jesse Helms	R	24	75	1996	unopp.	53	97	97	25	5	100	99
Lauch Faircloth	R	4	68	1992	48	50	89	96	21	5	95	99
North Dakota												
Kent Conrad	D	10	48	1994	unopp.	58	39	87	83	85	15	20
Byron L. Dorgan	D	4	54	1992	unopp.	59	37	84	80	85	20	19
Ohio												
John Glenn	D	22	75	1992	unopp.	51	18	90	88	95	10	13
Mike DeWine	R	2	49	1994	52	53	92	88	41	15	85	87
Oklahoma												
Don Nickles	R	16	48	1992	unopp.	59	97	99	34	0	100	95
James M. Inhofe	R	2	62	1996	75	57	97	100	28	0	100	97
Oregon												
Ron Wyden	D	1	47	1996	80	48	24	92	95	95	15	10
Gordon H. Smith	R	0	45	1996	78	50	—	—	—	—	—	—

State / Senator	Party											
Pennsylvania												
Arlen Specter	R	16	66	1992	65	49	66	64	59	50	50	38
Rick Santorum	R	2	38	1994	82	49	92	93	40	15	95	83
Rhode Island												
John H. Chafee	R	20	74	1994	69	65	68	64	60	40	60	30
Jack Reed	D	0	46	1996	86	63	—	—	—	—	—	—
South Carolina												
Strom Thurmond	R	42	93	1996	60	53	95	97	39	5	95	90
Ernest F. Hollings	D	30	74	1992	unopp.	50	59	82	82	70	20	42
South Dakota												
Tom Daschle	D	10	48	1996	unopp.	51	24	94	93	90	0	16
Tim Johnson	D	0	50	1996	unopp.	51	—	—	—	—	—	—
Tennessee												
Fred Thompson	R	2	54	1996	94	61	92	96	36	0	85	84
Bill Frist	R	2	44	1994	44	56	97	96	40	0	95	89
Texas												
Phil Gramm	R	12	54	1996	85	55	97	99	25	0	100	93
Kay Bailey Hutchison	R	4	53	1994	84	61	95	98	34	5	100	94
Utah												
Orrin G. Hatch	R	20	64	1994	unopp.	69	97	94	32	5	100	92
Robert F. Bennett	R	4	63	1992	51	55	97	92	36	5	95	91
Vermont												
Patrick J. Leahy	D	22	56	1992	unopp.	54	33	88	75	90	5	5
James M. Jeffords	R	8	62	1996	unopp.	50	59	58	53	50	45	30

(table continues)

Table A-4 (continued)

State, senator	Party	Years of service[a]	Age	Previous Senate election			1996 voting ratings					
				Year	Primary (%)	General (%)	CC	PU	PS	ADA	ACU	ACU (career)
Virginia												
John W. Warner	R	18	69	1996	65	52	89	93	42	5	95	95
Charles S. Robb	D	8	66	1994	58	46	79	76	85	80	20	20
Washington												
Slade Gorton	R	14	66	1994	53	56	95	90	45	15	85	62
Patty Murray	D	4	46	1992	28	54	18	95	89	90	0	0
West Virginia												
Robert C. Byrd	D	38	78	1994	85	69	32	82	81	70	15	28
John D. Rockefeller IV	D	12	59	1996	88	77	30	93	93	85	16	1
Wisconsin												
Herb Kohl	D	8	61	1994	90	58	32	84	88	75	20	17
Russell D. Feingold	D	4	43	1992	70	53	16	87	86	95	10	10
Wyoming												
Craig Thomas	R	2	63	1994	unopp.	59	95	98	29	5	100	89
Michael B. Enzi	R	0	52	1996	32	54	—	—	—	—	—	—

Note: In compiling this table, we calculated the conservative coalition, party unity, and presidential support scores to eliminate the effects of absences as follows: support = support/(support + opposition).

a. Service beginning in or after November in a given year is not counted as a year of service.
b. Campbell switched from the Democratic Party to the Republican Party on March 3, 1995.

Sources: Congressional Quarterly Almanac, various years; *Congressional Quarterly Weekly Report*, various years; American Conservative Union; Americans for Democratic Action.

Index

Nixon, Richard, 2, 46, 47, 152, 192, 193

Occupations
    party differences in, 3–4
    of representatives, 3, 20–25
    of senators, 3, 26–31
Office of Technology Assessment, 126
Operating expenses of Congress, 127,
    144–47

Partisanship in Congress, 1–2, 4, 193–94
Party, *see* Political party
Political action committees, 75
    distributions to congressional candi-
        dates, 92, 102–6
    percentage of incumbents' campaign
        funds, 92
Political party
    change in seats (House), 49, 55
    change in seats (Senate), 56, 72
    contributions and coordinated expen-
        ditures for Congress, 107, 108–9
    differences in occupations, 3–4
    financial support for candidates,
        75–76, 107
    and House victories, 50
    net gains in general and special elec-
        tions, 52–53
    party-line voting, 47, 70–71, 193, 194
    president's, losses in midterm elec-
        tions, 44, 54
    of representatives and senators, 39–41
    splits, 193
    unity, 193–94, 201
    voting, party unity scores, 202–3
    See also Democratic party; Republi-
        can party
Presidential success rate, 191–92, 196–97,
    200

Reagan, Ronald, 44, 47, 127, 192, 193
    and budget, 152, 168, 171, 172
    and conservative coalition, 194
    and vetoes, 152
Redistricting, 74
Regional
    apportionment of House seats, 1, 5–7
    differences within parties, 2
    distribution of seats in House and
        Senate, 10–11, 14–15
    representation in House, 1
    strength of Democrats, 8–9, 12–13, 18

Religious affiliations
    patterns of, 4
    of representatives, 32–33
    of senators, 34–35
Representatives, *see* House of Representa-
    tives
Republican party and Republicans
    and budget resolutions, 168
    changes in committee, 113–14
    and committee chairmanships,
        114–15, 122, 123
    control of House, 43–44
    losses and gains in midterm elections,
        44
    and political action committees, 75
    representatives, occupations of, 24–25
    "Republican Revolution," 2
    seats in House by region, 10–11
    seats in Senate by region, 14–15
    senators, occupations of, 30–31
    in South, 1–2
    southern seats, 115
    support of Clinton, 193
    support of president, 198–99
Retirements, 45, 59

Senate
    allowances of senators, 127, 146–47
    campaign expenditures, 86–91
    campaign funding sources, 93–101
    Democratic seats in by region, 14–15
    Democratic party strength in, by
        region, 12–13
    elections, independent expenditures,
        107, 111
    elections won with 60% of major party
        vote, 65
    incumbents, 45–46, 58
    incumbents and challengers' campaign
        expenditures, 88–89
    incumbents, cost of election, 74
    incumbents, defeated, 62–63
    occupations of senators, 26–31
    105th Congress members' data,
        266–72
    106th Congress members' data,
        260–65
    open seats, campaign expenditures,
        90–91
    net party gains in elections, 52–53
    political party of senators, 39–41
    recorded votes, 158, 159

About the Authors

Norman J. Ornstein is a resident scholar at the American Enterprise Institute for Public Policy Research and cochair of the President's Advisory Committee on Public Interest Obligations of Digital Television Broadcasters. His books include *Renewing Congress* (with Thomas Mann, 1993), *Debt and Taxes* (with John Makin, 1994), and *Intensive Care: How Congress Shapes Health Policy* (with Thomas Mann, 1995).

Thomas E. Mann is director of governmental studies and the W. Averell Harriman Senior Fellow in American Governance at the Brookings Institution. With Norman J. Ornstein he codirected the AEI-Brookings Renewing Congress Project, which produced *Congress, the Press, and the Public* (1994) and *Intensive Care: How Congress Shapes Health Policy* (1995). His most recent book, *Campaign Finance Reform: A Sourcebook* (1997), was coedited with Anthony Corrado, Daniel Ortiz, Trevor Potter, and Frank Sorauf.

Michael J. Malbin is professor of political science at the State University of New York, Albany, and director of legislative studies at the Rockefeller Institute of Government, SUNY's institute for public policy research. His most recent book is *The Day after Reform: Sobering Campaign Finance Lessons from the American States* (with Thomas L. Gais, 1998).